Jane Austen

*A celebration
of her life
and work*

Lauren Nixon

WITH AN INTRODUCTION BY

Josephine Ross

AND CONTRIBUTIONS BY

John Wiltshire
Maggie Lane
Caroline Sanderson
Josephine Ross

WORTH
PRESS

Steventon Rectory, where Jane Austen lived from 1775 to 1801.

*The only confirmed true likeness of Jane, the portrait by her sister
Cassandra painted in around 1806 (opposite).*

Jane Austen

*A celebration
of her life
and work*

Lauren Nixon

Contents

Bath seen from Claverton Road in Widcombe from John Claude Nattes' Bath, *1806.*

Foreword

Josephine Ross

'There is a Mrs. Fletcher,' Jane Austen wrote to her sister Cassandra in 1813, 'who is all curiosity to know about me – what I am like, & so forth.' She seemed amused, but alarmed, by the thought that a complete stranger, having enjoyed *Pride and Prejudice*, should now be eager to learn more about her, her character and life. With evident relief, she added, 'I am not known to her by *name*, however.'

Keeping her name concealed from the public was a matter of the highest importance to Jane Austen. She published all her novels anonymously, and was dismayed when her brother Henry – 'in the warmth of his Brotherly vanity & Love' – betrayed 'the Secret' to some aristocratic acquaintances. 'A Thing once set going in that way; – one knows how it spreads!' she remonstrated. Though (like most authors) she relished praise, and longed for what her schoolboy nephew, in his Regency slang, called 'Pewter' to result from her labours, Jane Austen shrank from the thought of achieving fame, and becoming, as she put it, 'A wild Beast', to be pointed at and talked about like one of the caged animals in the Exeter Exchange menagerie.

'Emma hung about him affectionately' from *Emma* (Hugh Thomson).

In the wake of '*P&P*'s modest success (and Henry's immodest revelations), she did, fleetingly, toy with giving up all attempts at anonymity and trying to make rather 'all the Money than all the Mystery I can' out of her next novel, *Mansfield Park*. Typically, she started a joke about one day being a celebrity: 'I do not despair of having my picture in the Exhibition at last,' she wrote to Cassandra, 'all white & red, with my Head on one Side.' But her innate discretion and reserve (that 'delicacy' she so prized in her heroines) prevailed; and it was not until July 1817, when her few brief obituary notices appeared in the press, that 'the Secret' was finally revealed to the public at large. That now, 200 years after her death, the name 'Jane Austen' should be famous throughout the world is one of history's most poignant ironies.

Today, to most of us, it is virtually impossible to read Jane Austen's novels without being 'all curiosity' to find out more about their author, her work and her world. Her appeal is, of course, timeless. Her characters, from spirited Lizzy Bennet in *Pride and Prejudice* and shy Fanny Price in *Mansfield Park* to querulous, food-faddish old Mr Woodhouse in *Emma* and sexist oaf John Thorpe in *Northanger Abbey*, are as familiar now as when they were created. Her wit is as fresh: lines such as 'Through some unaccountable bias in favour of beauty, he was the husband of a very silly woman' have lost nothing in two centuries. Her observations on human nature are as wise – so that the opening sentence of *Pride and Prejudice*, 'It is a truth universally acknowledged...', has taken its rightful place in everyday usage, as well as every *Dictionary of Quotations*. And many an author of modern 'chicklit' fiction can only envy her evocations of the pleasures (and hazards) of shopping, flirting and dancing.

Yet her works, first published between 1811 and 1817, are the product of another age; and to appreciate and enjoy them to the full it is necessary to understand their historical context. Every nuance of Jane Austen's art is exquisitely crafted; every detail has a significance which would have been recognised by her original readers. How her characters apply the rules of 'calling'; how they dress; which authors they admire; what expressions they use: all are vital to the narrative, and pointers to the outcome. Her men and women may think and feel just as we do, but they are constantly obliged by the rules of Regency society to behave very differently, and her plots often hinge on these dramatic constraints. In *Sense and Sensibility* the hero, Edward Ferrars, cannot, in honour, break off his engagement to a woman he has ceased to care for; in *Persuasion* the heroine, Anne Elliot, has to watch helplessly while the man she loves courts another, since she must not admit that she regrets their parting. It is a tribute to Jane Austen's powers that, in the twenty-first century, we feel utterly drawn into these moral dilemmas and emotional trials, which nowadays could be simply resolved in some brief dialogue. She certainly enables us to identify completely with one of her original readers – no less than Lord Byron's wife Annabella Milbanke, who wrote of *Pride and Prejudice*: 'The interest is very strong, especially for Mr Darcy.'

'Fanny was obliged to introduce him to Mr Crawford', from Mansfield Park *(Hugh Thomson).*

In the two centuries since Mrs Fletcher made her enquiries about the unknown 'authoress' of *Pride and Prejudice,* and Henry disclosed her identity to his friends, Jane Austen has become not only known, but revered, by millions. Visitors of all nationalities flock to see the cottage where she lived at Chawton, the places she wrote of in Bath, Portsmouth and Lyme, and her marble tombstone in Winchester Cathedral. The 'Pewter' earned by her books – and their film and television dramatisations – is incalculable; her sketchy portrait by Cassandra (looking distinctly red and white, with her head turned quizzically to one side) is a best-selling image in gallery and exhibition gift-shops. Apart from Shakespeare, few English writers are more celebrated than Jane Austen.

Much has been written about her – but much remains to be said. There are reinterpretations of her fiction to be made, and also misinterpretations to be cleared up, about her life and writing: from the occasional ignorant

The Pump Rooms at Bath.

accusation that she wrote lightweight, 'heaving bosom' fiction, to the ludicrous assumption that *Mansfield Park* contains an obscene joke. (Mary Crawford's improper pun about 'Rears and Vices' refers, of course, to the Regency fashion for whipping, not 'an unnatural vice', then punishable by the death penalty.)

There is so much to discuss, discover and enjoy about Jane Austen and her times: the fashions, the politics, the literature, the social background, all repay endless study and research. For those who share Mrs Fletcher's curiosity, this book is indispensable.

The Great House and Park at Chawton, c.1780 painted by Adam Callander (fl.1780–1811).

Introduction

It is a truth universally acknowledged that Jane Austen is one of the greatest novelists ever to have been published. When she started writing novels in earnest in 1809 there is no doubt she had publication in mind. After years of writing and two failed attempts at getting published, 1811 would finally see Austen's work in print. *Sense and Sensibility* appeared anonymously in that year, and gained such considerable praise that by 1816 it had been followed by *Pride and Prejudice*, *Mansfield Park* and *Emma*.

Could Jane ever have imagined that two centuries later her name would be internationally known and adored? Since the late nineteenth century Austen's novels have been unfalteringly popular, dominating the classics sections of bookstores worldwide. Modern novels continue to be indebted to her characters and storylines, and Hollywood remains enamoured with her charms.

For a writer so uninterested in fame, Jane Austen's staying power is remarkable. She may have shrunk from 'notoriety' as her brother Henry claimed, but that has not stopped generation after generation of admirers, and an unbounded interest in her life as well as in her work.

Like many great writers, Austen's own lifetime offers a key to unlocking the brilliance of her work. Her father's love of novels, her mother's wit, and the atmosphere of her childhood all shaped her style as a writer. The loves and lives of her friends and siblings provided her with keen insight and an understanding of her society that would allow her to create timeless characters. Austen's brilliance is inescapably connected with her life; to celebrate her work is to celebrate the life that shaped it.

The younger daughter of a country clergyman, Jane Austen is a permanent fixture in the literary firmament. Why is it that two hundred years since her print debut, readers continue to be enamoured with Miss Austen? In 2001, *Bridget Jones's Diary* showed that even in the twenty-first century we are still

An adaption of a portrait of Jane Austen commissioned by her nephew James Edward Leigh from an original painting by Jane's sister Cassandra (above).

The famous watercolour study of Jane sitting on a grassy bank, painted by Cassandra in 1804 (opposite).

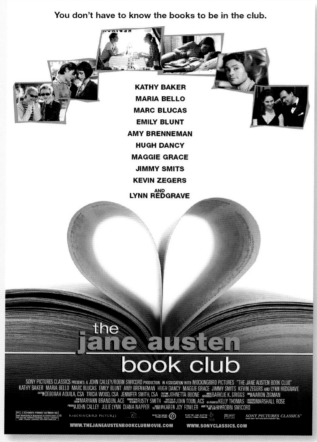

making the same misjudgements as Elizabeth Bennet did, and Mr Darcy is still able to win our hearts. The 2007 film *The Jane Austen Book Club* proved that even the most modern of dilemmas cause us to stop and ask, 'What would Jane do?'

And this is the true brilliance of Austen's work. Her characters are complex, deep and brilliantly observed. In many ways they are more like studies of human behaviour than fictional characters. This is why their relevance never wanes. We do not need to understand the details of what Bath was like in 1816 to enjoy *Northanger Abbey*; we are amused by Catherine's naivety and Isabella's shallowness because of the strength of their characters.

But of course Austen is not only a master of character; she understands the connection between a person and their society, and the differences between those that move within it. We may not reside in grand country houses like Hartfield or Pemberley, but it is still easy to relate to Emma's failed attempts at matchmaking as well as her blindness to her own feelings.

Publicity poster for The Jane Austen Book Club, *a popular 2007 film (above).*

'Lady Catherine, said she …', a Thomson illustration from Pride and Prejudice *(right).*

Sitting under the trees with Fanny, a Thomson illustration from Mansfield Park *(above).*

Colin Firth, every Janeite's favourite Darcy (left).

Similarly, it is not their wealth and status that attracts us to Mr Darcy or Mr Knightley. The goodness of their characters and the honesty of their affections may make them appear close to male perfection, but their flaws and intricacies keep them human.

At the heart of Jane Austen's work is a natural realism, which is what makes her work timeless. Her novels are undoubtedly a product of the Regency — the period's social conventions, its values and even its fashions are all part of Austen's charm. But at the same time Austen captures the truth of her society so brilliantly that it never ages. We will always be able to laugh at the pompousness of Lady Catherine de Bourgh or Sir Walter Elliot, and we will always be drawn to the strong-willed, quick-minded Elizabeth Bennet.

What would Jane have thought had she known how her work would withstand the test of time? With museums, festivals and websites dedicated to the memory of her life and the brilliance of her writing, Jane Austen is an indisputable part of modern culture. Two hundred years after her first publication, this book is a celebration of the woman and the work. Jane's books have become important to many people, just as they were to the members of the Jane Austen Book Club, not just as good literature but as a source of sound advice and a familiar place to escape to.`

Early Work and Fragments

For Jane Austen writing was a lifelong passion. From an early age she was influenced by her father's love of reading, an interest that came to be shared by the whole family. Not only did the Austens take pleasure in reading aloud: from when Jane was only around seven or eight years old they also performed plays with their friends and cousins. Growing up in a house so fond of literature, it's no wonder that Austen began writing so early.

Preserved in three volumes of notebooks, Austen's early work is now known as the *Juvenilia*. These early works, painstakingly copied in Austen's clear, elegant hand, give an insight into the way in which Austen developed as a writer. Like her father's novels, these short stories were written to be read aloud for her family's amusement. By 1790 Austen had written five short stories, including *Love and Freindship* (Austen's own misspelling) which criticised the cult of sensibility, mocking young women who faint and swoon. Even in her early work we see Austen's unique wit and keen observation. The themes explored in *Love and Freindship* would be revived in both *Sense and Sensibility* and *Northanger Abbey*; clearly even in her early teens Austen was beginning to look at the world in a way that would shape the style and tone of her later work. By 1794, the nineteen-year-old Austen was a well-practised writer.

The epistolary form of her novella *Lady Susan* is a nod towards contemporary writers such as Fanny Burney, but the genius is all Austen's. Clever, quick and engagingly amusing, *Lady Susan* shows that even by her early twenties Austen was a skilled and adept writer when she began the early drafts of *Sense and Sensibility*, *Pride and Prejudice* and *Northanger Abbey*. Though her work did not appear in print until she was 35, apart from the period between 1801 and 1809 Austen was almost always constantly writing and redrafting her work. By the time of her

Madame Frances D'Arblay (Fanny Burney), painted by Edward Francisco Burne.

first publication in 1811 she was already a fine writer, and after so many years of putting pen to paper it is no wonder that her novels are so polished and refined.

Just as her *Juvenilia* give a glimpse of Jane's development from a talented child writer to a powerfully skilled authoress, her unfinished fragments provide an intriguing glimpse of what was occupying her mind at the time of their creation. *The Watsons*, written in 1804 or 1805, is the only work Jane penned during her five-year stay in Bath. Austen had a notoriously difficult relationship

Lyme Regis in the early nineteenth century.

with the city, and despite Bath being the setting for both *Northanger Abbey* and *Persuasion* her creativity almost ceased while she was living there. *The Watsons* focuses on the daughters of a poor and ailing clergyman, and it is likely that Jane could not bear to continue with the work after the death of her own beloved father. The fragment deals with fears about the fates of the daughters, and the subject matter was probably too close to home. The heroine, Emma Watson, is an outsider in the society she finds herself unwillingly thrown into, dismayed by her sisters' husband-hunting. Unlike her sisters, she fails to find Mr Tom Musgrave amiable, and is unimpressed by the majority of their acquaintances. Considering Jane's own situation at the time of writing and her dislike for the Bath lifestyle, *The Watsons* offers a fascinating gateway into Jane's mindset during this elusive period of her life.

Austen's other major fragment of work would also be her last, as the first eleven chapters of *Sanditon* were written during her final illness. *Sanditon*, originally called *The Brothers*, was left by Austen with the intention of completing the novel after her health had recovered. Focusing upon the fictional seaside town of Sanditon, the fragment deals with society's preoccupation with health and appearance, but also with the way that towns like Brighton or Lyme Regis slipped in and out of popularity. Some critics have speculated that if Austen had completed the novel, it may have been her best work. Certainly *Sanditon* shows Austen at the height of her powers; it displays not only her keen appreciation of character but the nature of Regency society. When she began the work, Austen would be in the final six years of her life — could her satirical treatment of the hypochondriac sisters also have been her defiance of her own illness?

Lady Susan

Written sometime between 1793 and 1794, *Lady Susan* marks Jane Austen's shift from juvenile storyteller to mature authoress. Produced towards the end of her teenage years, the novella lacks the maturity of her later novels, but is distinctly a more skilful work than *Love and Freindship* or *Lesley Castle*. Though Jane would never again write a novel quite like *Lady Susan*, it signifies her decision to move away from the burlesque satires of her youth towards the more intricately constructed plots of her adulthood. Like much of her *Juvenilia*, the novella is epistolary, a fashionable form at the time thanks to writers such as Fanny Burney, but one that Jane soon chose to abandon for a third-person narrative. *Lady Susan* is essentially Austen's final teenage experiment, an exercise in how far she could take the epistolary form and also a test of her own skills and preferences as an author. Though she would pick up some of the piece's themes again, the

A MEMOIR
OF
JANE AUSTEN

BY HER NEPHEW
J. E. AUSTEN LEIGH

SECOND EDITION
TO WHICH IS ADDED
LADY SUSAN
AND FRAGMENTS OF
TWO OTHER UNFINISHED TALES BY MISS AUSTEN

LONDON
RICHARD BENTLEY AND SON
NEW BURLINGTON STREET
Publishers in Ordinary to Her Majesty
1871

The 1871 Bentley edition of Austen Leigh's Memoir of Jane Austen, *which included* Lady Susan *(above).*

Samuel Richardson, painted by Joseph Highmore (right).

novella is an entirely different entity to her earlier novels. It is not simply its style and tone that separates it, but its cast of characters and the focus it takes.

The novella chronicles the schemes of its main character, Lady Susan Vernon, a wealthy widow whose considerable beauty conceals her ruthless, manipulating mind. Lady Susan is no typical Austen heroine; she would sit far more comfortably with Mary Crawford or Isabella Thorpe than Elinor Dashwood or Anne Elliot. The novella's plot follows Lady Susan to her downfall, as she attempts to bully and coerce her daughter Frederica into a marriage with a man she cannot love for status and money. Shockingly for Austen, sexuality in *Lady Susan* is not a veiled matter. Lady Susan herself is a powerfully sexual character, an adulteress who is aware and unashamed of her influence over men. Her daughter Frederica, however, is pure to the point of meekness, unable to act for herself as we would expect an Austen heroine to do. Indeed *Lady Susan* is far more a Georgian text than the novels that followed it; the story betrays the influence of Samuel Richardson and Henry Fielding, whereas her novels are clearly products of the Regency and the changes it brought about. Her final and most substantial adolescent work, *Lady Susan* seems to have been Austen's final experiment. Her later writing would become unique, powerful and timeless.

The 'Rice Portrait', painted by Ozias Humphry c.1790, *which some claim to be a portrait of Jane Austen at the age of fourteen. Even if it is not of Jane, it portrays a young woman of the period who looks very much like the young Jane would have appeared.*

Fame and Influence

Princess Charlotte Augusta of Wales with King Leopold I, c.1811.

In October 1811, an anonymous novel in three volumes named *Sense and Sensibility* was published by Thomas Egerton. The novel became unexpectedly popular, attracting readers from all levels of society – even the young Princess Charlotte adored the novel, and identified strongly with Marianne Dashwood. By 1813 the first edition had entirely sold out, and Egerton had no hesitations in publishing a second edition as well as another novel by its anonymous author.

After years of writing, Jane Austen finally saw her work published. By 1816 *Pride and Prejudice*, *Mansfield Park* and *Emma* had followed *Sense and Sensibility* into print, and brought Jane further success. The four novels made Austen around £700, which would have been a considerable sum to a single woman reliant on her male relations for income. Independence wasn't something generally achievable for women in the Regency period, at least not for a woman of Austen's social standing.

Despite the books' authorship being hidden behind the title page's description 'By a Lady', by the time *Mansfield Park* appeared the knowledge of her identity had 'spread so far as to be scarcely the shadow of a secret'. The publication of *Emma* shows just how much popularity Austen's novels enjoyed amongst contemporary society. Princess Charlotte was not the only admirer Jane found within the royal family, and her status as a writer was cemented when *Emma* was dedicated to the Prince Regent, later George IV. Though the dedication is proof of her success, it was done begrudgingly. The request for the dedication occurred by chance, when Henry Austen became ill during Jane's visit to him in London. The physician treating him quickly deduced that the sister of his patient was the elusive novelist and revealed that he was in fact physician to the Prince, who is said to have kept a copy of each of her novels in every one of his lodgings.

The result of this chance encounter was an invitation for Jane to take a tour of Carlton House, given by the Prince's Librarian, James Stanier Clarke. Clarke himself may have been a little enamoured with Austen, and the visit would result not only in a friendship between the two, but also in the royal

request for a dedication. Though the Prince may have admired Austen, the feeling was hardly mutual. Austen had little respect for the extravagant Regent, and it shows. The dedication in *Emma* – 'This work is, by his royal highness's permission, most respectfully dedicated, by his royal highness's dutiful and obedient humble servant' – is hardly warm, indeed sneakily sarcastic in its tone. But then what more would we expect of Jane?

By her death in 1817, Austen had finally achieved the success her father must have believed she was capable of when he encouraged her earlier writing. Yet Henry Austen's biographical notice to the posthumously published *Northanger Abbey* and *Persuasion* suggests that the Austens never imagined the full extent of Jane's popularity. Austen's work has remained in print ever since the first printing of *Sense and Sensibility* in 1811, an incredible feat spanning two full centuries.

The three volumes of the first edition of Emma, *which was dedicated by Jane to the Prince Regent.*

How did an early nineteenth-century writer become one of the greatest writers in English literature? And how has she avoided the 'curse of the classic', and remained one of the most widely-read authors of all time?

At the heart of her popularity, of course, is Austen's brilliant and unique style. Her closely-observed and realistically-portrayed society launched her work at the beginning of the nineteenth century, marking a distinct move away from the popular Gothic novels of the later eighteenth century. As Catherine Morland discovers in *Northanger Abbey*, the works of writers like Ann Radcliffe offered little insight into contemporary society, filled instead with tales of far-off castles, helpless maidens and villainous uncles. But Austen's natural style and keen insight is not the only reason for her contemporary success – it is her witty observations, sharp understanding and command of character that have fuelled her continuing fame.

However well-received her work was when it was first published, the early Victorian period saw a decline in her popularity. Though the novels never went out of print, they lost much of the acclaim that they had enjoyed. This all changed in 1869 when James Austen's son, James Edward Austen Leigh, decided to publish a memoir of his aunt with the help of his sisters Anna and Caroline. Concerned that 'the generation who knew her is passing away', the memoir was a chance to make sure Austen's life and legacy were not forgotten. The publication of *A Memoir of Jane Austen* saw an instant revival

of Austen's work, despite the biography itself being very much a Victorian work. Suddenly Jane Austen was once again a celebrated talent, and her novels were quickly reissued as public demand grew. Illustrated editions of her work appeared, along with collectors' sets and lavish printings, signalling the start of what has now become a following of global proportions. As popular as Austen was in her own time, it is nothing in comparison to the adoration of her work that began in the 1880s and has hardly lost any momentum in the twenty-first century.

Leslie Stephen, Virginia Woolf's father, called the frenzy around Austen's work 'Austenolatry', though the term coined by readers who considered themselves true Austen fans is the one that has lasted – 'Janeite'. The cult of Jane Austen had begun, and more than a century later it shows no sign of stopping. As the twentieth century dawned, so did a new age of Jane Austen. A new burst of criticism and biographical work emerged as insatiable readers demanded more than the six novels. Austen became the beloved 'Aunt Jane', revered by her readers. Through the war period she became a symbol of Englishness, a source of patriotic pride and comfort. By the 1940s the status of her work had become unquestionable, thanks to respected literary figures such as F.R. Leavis, who asserted that Austen was one of the greatest English writers.

With such an extensive following it is no wonder that the details of Austen's life have become public property, something the rather private Austen would have found amusing and rather embarrassing. Facts about her private life were in demand, and artefacts relating to her life, as well as early editions of the novels, have become keenly sought-after collectors' items. The Jane Austen Society was founded in 1940 to raise money to restore Austen's beloved home in Chawton, now the Jane Austen's House Museum. Readers pored over her letters in order to know their favourite author better, and to uncover new and exciting details about her quiet life. The thirst for an understanding of Austen's private life has hardly wavered; year after year articles and books appear making new claims about Austen's personal – and, most importantly, romantic – life.

Chawton, home of the Jane Austen Society and the Jane Austen's House Museum (top).

A poster for the 1940 film version of Pride and Prejudice *(above).*

The technological revolution has served to escalate Austen's popularity to dizzying heights. Since the first film adaptation of *Pride and Prejudice* in 1940, Austen's novels have been adapted for film and television on numerous occasions. The BBC's 1995 adaptation of *Pride and Prejudice*, with Colin Firth as the archetypal Darcy, is arguably the one that has had the most impact.

'*A gentleman politely drew back*', *a Thomson illustration from* Persuasion *(left)*.

Sense and Sensibility and Sea Monsters, *published by Quirk Books in 2009, a clever parody by Ben Winters in Regency style in which an event known as 'The Alteration' has turned the creatures of the sea against humankind.*

Stage versions, as well as the occasional musical, have also been created, together with a Facebook version of *Pride and Prejudice*, told through status updates. As well as straight adaptations of Jane's novels, films like *Clueless* and *Bridget Jones's Diary* take elements of Austen's work and rework them into a modern setting and storyline. And it's not just on screen that Austen's work has been tweaked and twisted – there are countless takes on her own life and work. Today you can read everything from racy imaginings of life at Pemberley to Gothic tales of an undead Darcy, not to mention the likes of *Sense and Sensibility and Sea Monsters* and *Pride and Prejudice and Zombies*.

Though Charlotte Brontë may have snubbed her work and Mark Twain famously wrote that 'every time I read *Pride and Prejudice* I want to dig her up and hit her over the skull with her own shin-bone', it is undeniable that Austen's novels have had a massive influence. Her witty style and keen eye for characters gave inspiration to an entire movement of literature, and her eternally engaging prose appeals to generation after generation.

You do not need a history lesson to enjoy an Austen novel. As much as her work is clearly of its period, Austen's method of observing society and understanding intimately the lives of others, with all their flaws and foibles, creates something very special in her work. Her subtle use of language allows the most modern of readers to laugh along with her at the Caroline Bingleys and Mr Collinses of our own acquaintance.

SENSE AND SENSIBILITY AND SEA MONSTERS

BY JANE AUSTEN AND BEN H. WINTERS

Austen and Place

Steventon

From her birth in 1775 to her father's retirement in 1801, Steventon Rectory was Jane's home. Presented as a living to her father in 1761 by his distant cousin, Thomas Knight, and set in the heart of the Hampshire countryside, not far from Basingstoke, the Rectory was perfect for the Austens, with plenty of rooms and enough land for small-scale farming. Here Jane enjoyed a childhood similar to that of Catherine Morland, free to enjoy the benefits of a country upbringing. Apart from a few years' formal schooling in Oxford, and later Reading, much of Jane's childhood was spent at home, where her father's intelligence and mother's sharp mind encouraged her to grow into the writer she would later become.

The boarding school her parents ran within their home also had a great influence on Jane's education. Though Mr Austen had a comfortable income as a clergyman, the school provided extra money for luxuries such as holidays to Lyme Regis or Mr Austen's collection of books. Not only did the school provide classmates for the elder boys, it allowed Jane

A drawing of Steventon Rectory in the 1820s by Anna Austen Lefroy.

and Cassandra a wider education than was granted to most girls of the period. In the late eighteenth century girls of the Austens' position would have received little more than basic arithmetic in addition to what were considered acceptable female accomplishments, such as French, music, needlework and drawing. To be constantly surrounded by an atmosphere of education and to be part of such thoughtful society must have had an effect on the young Jane – certainly Steventon became a house devoted to literature. Reading novels became a family pastime, with chapters read aloud to one another as evening entertainment, and the house often played host to amateur theatricals organised by Jane's eldest brother James.

Steventon shaped Jane as both a person and a writer. Her love of the countryside and the lifestyle it offered influenced her feelings towards fashionable cities such as London or Bath, as well as the position and characters of her heroines. *Pride and Prejudice*, *Emma* and *Persuasion* all champion the country way of life and Jane certainly was never short of society. The family enjoyed a close friendship with many of their neighbours, particularly the Lefroys of Ashe Rectory and the Lloyds during their time at Deane Parsonage. Mary Lloyd would later go on to be James Austen's second wife, but it was Martha who Jane and Cassandra considered to be almost a sister. The Lefroys were the Austen's closest neighbours and, despite their age difference, Jane became close friends with Madam Anne Lefroy, the cultured and poetic wife of the Reverend Lefroy. Madam Lefroy shared her young friend's love of literature and Jane spent much of her time at Ashe where, much to her delight, she was allowed to use the library.

It was through her friendship with the family at Ashe that Jane began her now infamous flirtation with her 'Irish friend', Tom Lefroy. In a letter dated 9 January 1796, Jane wrote to her absent sister with the news from Steventon, including her flirtation with the Lefroys' visiting nephew. An aspiring lawyer, Jane wrote that he was a 'very gentlemanlike, good-looking, pleasant young man' and made no secret of her preference for him – though she did think 'that his morning coat is a great deal too light!' Apart from dancing together three times at neighbouring Manydown House, it seems the two also discussed literature. Jane muses that Tom's dress sense must be inspired by Henry Fielding's *Tom Jones*, which she knows him to be a great admirer of. Yet the relationship was to be little more than a flirtation; neither Jane nor Tom was rich and marriage would never have been a sensible option. A week later Jane wrote again to her sister that 'the day is come on which I am to flirt my last with Tom Lefroy ... My tears flow as I write, at the melancholy idea.'

Anne Lefroy (above).

Thomas Langlois Lefroy (1776–1869) (left).

Bath

The new century marked a significant change for the Austen family, when George Austen made the decision to retire and hand over the living to his eldest son, James. In need of a new residence and with their sons now settled into careers, George and Cassandra decided to move their downsized family to the city of Bath. Jane, then aged twenty-five, would have to leave the only home she had ever known. Indeed, the news came as such a shock that she reportedly fainted on hearing it. Though her loss of composure may seem a little out of character, it is understandable that Jane found the news upsetting. Though she had enjoyed short visits to the city, observing the city with the amused eyes of the narrator of *Northanger Abbey*, it was not a place she wanted to call home. Certainly, their leaving Steventon became quite an upheaval as furniture, artwork and even Mr Austen's beloved book collection were sold in preparation for the move. For Jane, it could not have been easy to see all she had ever known slip away from her.

For her parents, however, Bath was not such a surprising choice. Favoured for its good air and supposedly healing spa waters, Bath was an ideal city to retire to, as Mrs Austen's own parents had. Additionally, it was in Bath that George had courted and married Cassandra, so the city probably held some fond memories; perhaps Mrs Austen saw the move as a chance to settle her two unmarried daughters. Throughout the eighteenth century Bath had been a centre of fashion and culture as well as home to some of the period's finest architecture, including the lavish Royal Crescent, the Circus and the Grand Pump Room. Though its popularity was waning by 1800, it still remained a key part of fashionable Regency society; it was an opportunity to flaunt wealth, fashion, friends and even one's own children. Though Jane may have enjoyed satirising the follies and nonsense of Bath in *Northanger Abbey*, it was a city that would have a severe effect on her creativity.

Bath: Pulteney Street and Laura Place. An 1806 engraving by John Claude Nattes.

The Austens moved to Bath in 1801, staying initially with Mrs Austen's brother, the wealthy Mr James Leigh Perrot, and his wife in the Paragon. Though Mrs Austen had desired a house on Laura Place, it was nearby Sydney Place that was to be their first home in Bath. Number four, Sydney Place sat in a pleasant part of the city and even Jane was pleased with the house, despite her dismay at the move. However, Jane still took any opportunity to escape the city. The family took a number of holidays to the coast, including a trip to Lyme Regis in 1803 where Jane was able to swap the bustle of the city streets for the calm of the coastal town. The sisters also visited their brother Edward in Kent and often spent time at Manydown House, the home of their Steventon friends Althea and Catherine Bigg. It was in fact at Manydown that Jane had danced with Tom Lefroy, and in December 1802 it became host to another event in Jane's romantic life when she received a marriage proposal from her host's younger brother. Just twenty years old, Harris Bigg-Wither had grown from the shy, stammering boy Jane had once known into a young man of considerable fortune. At twenty-seven, Jane's chances of marrying so well were unlikely and Harris, with his sizeable income, would have been more than a sensible match in marriage. Not only would he provide her with a life of comfort but she would also be part of a family she was great friends with; Jane accepted his proposal. However the marriage was never to be, and the next morning she announced her change of mind; perhaps Jane, like so many of her heroines, could not bring herself to marry a man she did not love.

The years at Bath may have begun promisingly, but by 1803 things had begun to take a turn for the worse. Jane had come to Bath a bright, talented woman in possession of three completed manuscripts and at the start of the year things were looking up. Henry had helped her to sell *Susan*, later to become *Northanger Abbey*, for the sum of £10 and it seemed that Jane would finally have a career. But as the lease on Sydney Place came to an end, the Austens realised that their income was not large enough for the Bath lifestyle and they left their pleasant home for a smaller residence at Green Park Buildings. Jane waited anxiously for *Susan*'s publication and began work on another novel, *The Watsons*. But the novel never appeared in print, and as the year wore on into the next, her father's health began to deteriorate. On 21 January 1805, after a short and sudden illness, Jane's father passed away, leaving his widow and unmarried daughters in emotional and financial turmoil. Jane and Cassandra had not only lost their beloved father, but their source of income – the Church offered no benefits for the widows and orphans of clergymen. It was up to Jane's brothers to come to their

4 Sydney Place, Bath. The Austens' home from 1801 to 1804.

Bath: Royal Crescent, by John Claude Nattes.

aid, each pledging what they could to support their mother and sisters. However, with families to care for, not even the adopted Edward could afford to give a large sum of money. Francis's brothers forced him to halve the amount he proposed to give and Henry chose to ignore Charles's plea to offer money altogether, knowing his naval brother was in no position to give up any part of his income.

The family were forced to reduce their household and move again, this time to a set of rooms at 25 Gay Street. These considerably smaller lodgings must have felt claustrophobic to Jane, who was used to the space and freedom of the countryside. Disillusioned after *Susan* and devastated by the death of her father, the pen that had been so active since childhood fell silent. *The Watsons* was abandoned, never to be completed, and Jane began to despair with life in Bath. After six months the women were forced to move again, from the respectable Gay Street to an unknown address on Trim Street, dangerously close to the more undesirable areas of the city. With such a small income, Bath life was becoming almost impossible for the Austen women and though very few letters survive from the period, there is no doubt that Jane was uncomfortable and uninspired. It must have been a relief when, at the end of 1806, Francis offered his mother and sisters a home with his young family at Southampton. Years later, Jane would remember her departure from Bath as being one marked by 'feelings of happy escape'.

Chawton

Chawton House in the late eighteenth century.

On 10 October 1808, just days after the birth of her eleventh child, Edward Austen's beloved wife Elizabeth passed away. Cassandra had been at Godmersham, as she had been for the birth of most of Edward's children, helping to run the house while Elizabeth was confined to her bed. The Austens had been at Southampton with Francis for nearly two years and Edward, perhaps in a bid to have his mother and sisters closer to hand, decided to offer them a house of their own on one of his estates. Of the houses offered, the cottage at Chawton suited their tastes best. Tucked away in the picturesque village, with a good-sized garden and tranquil atmosphere, it would be a more than welcome change. So on 7 July 1809 Jane finally returned to her beloved Hampshire.

With a house of their own once again, joined by their long-time friend Martha Lloyd, the Austen women quickly settled back into the country lifestyle. Though Jane and Cassandra continued to share a bedroom as they had at Steventon, Chawton offered Jane the space and privacy that Bath and Southampton had not. Matured by her experiences in Bath, but also sharpened by the people she had met and their behaviour, Jane began to revise *Sense and Sensibility*. Within a few months the novel was finished and, despite the failure of *Susan*, Henry set out once again to seek publication for his sister, this time with John Murray. Renewed by life at Chawton, Jane took up *Pride and Prejudice*, bringing it up to date and sharpening it as she had done with *Sensibility*.

Chawton Church and House, c. 1809.

Sense and Sensibility appeared in print in October 1811 and Jane remained remarkably productive, penning *Mansfield Park, Emma* and *Persuasion* in quick succession. It seems that much of Austen's creativity stemmed from her situation: she could not write if she was not comfortable. At Chawton she was again the person she had been at Steventon, but it is clear that her five years in Bath had a lasting effect. Polished and refined, her novels show an Austen who has seen enough of the world she speaks of to pick out the intricacies and flaws in people from various backgrounds. Though she may not have been able to abide the follies and nonsense of Bath society, the observations she made allowed her to bring to life characters such as Caroline Bingley and Sir Walter Elliot. Yet during this period in Bath she also matured; her father's death, the disappointment of *Susan,* her brush with poverty and even Harris's proposal transformed her into a woman who could write not only with clever observation and honesty, but with wisdom.

Jane Austen's desk at Chawton.

Though they did not enter into the rich social life they had once had at Steventon, Chawton was never short of visitors. Being close to Steventon, to former friends and with a branch of Henry's bank close by, there was plenty of company, particularly when James's eldest daughter Anna became a permanent resident rather than a frequent visitor. James's first wife had passed away in 1795, just two years after Anna was born, and his eldest daughter never took to her stepmother, Mary Lloyd. Clever and passionate, it seems that Anna valued her Austen aunts more than her stepmother and she was a particular favourite with Jane. Perhaps her adoration of her witty aunt prevented her from connecting with her stepmother. The teenaged Anna certainly caused plenty of trouble for James and Mary. Feisty and impulsive, by fifteen years old Anna was quite a free spirit, cutting off her own hair and developing a passion for literature. By sixteen she had engaged herself to a young man, only to change her mind later, much to her father's despair. At a loss, James and Mary sent Anna to her aunts at Chawton. Considering her connection with Jane and love of Cassandra and Mrs Austen, it was hardly a punishment. For Jane she must have been a welcome companion, someone to discuss literature with and a great appreciator of her own work.

It was not until her illness in 1817 that Jane left Chawton for more than a few months. Concerned by her deteriorating condition, Henry and Cassandra decided it was best to move her to Winchester to be treated by a doctor there. Accompanied by Cassandra Jane spent the end of her life at 8 College Street, visited often by relatives. It was there, on 18 July 1817, that Jane passed away of unknown causes in the company of Cassandra and their sister-in-law, Mary.

Godmersham

Edward Austen's estates came to him in an odd line of inheritance. The properties in Hampshire and in Kent had once been separate estates, brought together by Thomas Brodnax May Knight, a distant descendant to the families of both estates. It was Thomas's son who would become Edward Austen's adoptive father and, as Edward Knight, Jane's brother would be a man of great inheritance. After the second Thomas Knight's death, Godmersham Park became Edward's permanent home. Set in the isolation of the splendid Kent countryside, Godmersham was surely in mind when Jane wrote of Mansfield Park or Pemberley. Built in 1732 and extended in the 1770s, the house was tastefully fashionable and suitably grand for a man of Edward's fortune. Its sprawling gardens were perfect for walking, with walled gardens, an orchard and even a Greek-inspired temple set into the hills.

The church lay within walking distance of the house, a route that included the lime avenue that Jane particularly adored. At Godmersham Jane would have experienced a way of life poles apart from the one she knew in Hampshire. Like Darcy or Knightley, Edward was a landed gentleman and a member of the upper classes. Responsible for acres of land and the tenants who occupied it, he was required to adhere to certain social conventions. The family had a separate entrance to the nearby church, as well as their own pew, which faced out to the congregation. Though Cassandra was often at Godmersham without her, Jane still paid many visits to her brother's family, including a long visit in 1813. Through Edward and life at Godmersham Jane came to understand the intricacies of a gentleman's life and the pressures felt by a man in his position. As with Anna, Jane enjoyed a close relationship with Edward's eldest daughter Fanny, who often sought her aunt's advice on matters of the heart. Jane's letters are filled with the sentiments expressed in her novels and Fanny, mistress of the house at just sixteen years old, probably gave Jane the insight she needed to create a character like Emma Woodhouse.

Godmersham Park, c. *1800.*

Godmersham provided Jane with the background to create novels, such as *Pride and Prejudice* and *Mansfield Park*, which showed an understanding of the complexities of two different levels of society. Through her experiences and observations of the Austen Knights, Jane was seeing society not only through the eyes of Lizzie Bennet and Fanny Price, but also Mr Darcy and Edmund Bertram. Without such experiences, would she have so skilfully crafted the tensions and misunderstandings between Lizzie and Darcy or so keenly felt Fanny Price's dual feelings towards life at Mansfield Park?

Lyme Regis

Lyme Regis, c. *1810.*

The Austens first visited Lyme Regis, a Dorset coastal town, in 1803 and they returned in 1804. For Jane, the visits were a much needed respite from the claustrophobia of life in Bath, and Lyme's natural beauty captured her heart. Lyme hosts the pivotal moment in *Persuasion*, when Louisa Musgrove falls from The Cobb and the reader breathlessly realises Captain Wentworth has never stopped loving Anne. The scene is one of Austen's most powerful and The Cobb is remembered by many for it – supposedly, when Alfred Lord Tennyson visited Lyme, his first demand was to be shown 'the exact spot where Louisa Musgrove fell!' Jane describes Lyme Regis as possessing a 'retired bay, backed by dark cliffs, where fragments of low rock among the sands' provided 'the happiest spot for watching the flow of the tide, for sitting in unwearied contemplation.' Like Anne Elliot, Austen marvelled at the wild naturalness of Lyme and clearly felt more at home in its simple beauty than the carefully constructed rigidity of Bath.

Austen and Fashion

Both men's and women's fashions became much simpler after the French Revolution.

Though her novels may imply a time of peace and stability, Austen's lifetime was a period of momentous change. Born in the year that the American War of Independence (1775–1783) began, Jane would have felt, and seen, the effects of the French Revolution and the subsequent Napoleonic wars. Not only did she have three brothers in service, but the Comtesse Eliza de Feuillide, a cousin and later Henry's wife, lost her first husband to the guillotine. As the French monarchy fell, so did the splendour and excess of its fashions. In the aftermath of the Revolution, nobody in France wished to appear an aristocrat. The excessive brocades, powdered wigs and large hooped skirts that had defined pre-revolutionary France and, in turn, Georgian England fell suddenly from fashion. With its steadily growing middle class, ideas in England had also begun to change, inspired somewhat by the revolutionary sentiments of France and America and, as trade with France became difficult, English fashions experienced a radical shift.

Men's Fashion

The Regency period was inspired by classical ideals which had an effect on fashion for men as well as women. Previously gentlemen's attire had consisted of lavish suits of silk or satin, often intricately embroidered, with flared coats, ruffled lace shirts and knee-length breeches, as well as silk stockings and high-heeled shoes. Complemented with powdered hair worn long, or even wigs for formal occasions, these over-the-top fashions did not suit the sentiments of a post-revolutionary society. The turn to the simple, neutral suit that defined the Regency gentleman was almost entirely inspired by just one man: Beau Brummell. Friend to the Prince Regent, Brummell implemented the simple yet elegant fashion of the era – a cut-away riding coat, tight pantaloons and tall hat. Inspired partially by the military, the understated, tailored silhouette Brummell introduced was greatly influenced by statues of classical figures – tall, lean and heroic. The elegant, close-fitting cut gave the impression of masculinity and strength, as did the pale-coloured, tight-fitting pantaloons and long boots. As powder became increasingly hard to acquire, men opted for shorter hairstyles that complemented their new fashions.

Women's Fashion

For women, the Regency era was a period of liberation. The tight corsets and hooped skirts of the Georgian period were abandoned to create a more natural, classical silhouette, and the heavily embroidered brocade was replaced by simple materials such as cotton and muslin. Gowns were cut on an empire line to emulate those of Ancient Greece and Rome. This style was considerably more comfortable than the rigid shape of previous fashions. However, society still dictated certain etiquettes and women's costume was separated into three categories – undress, half dress and full dress. 'Undress' referred to simple gowns of sturdier materials, or 'morning dress', that were worn for breakfast and morning pursuits such as writing letters or sewing. 'Half dress' was a more formal attire to be worn for afternoon promenades, shopping or visiting relatives. 'Full dress' was the most formal, with ornate dresses and hairstyles intended for balls. Often lace or a high-necked undershirt would be worn beneath dresses used in the daytime, yet the fashion was for evening gowns to be low cut with short, puffed sleeves. Though gossamer white muslin dresses were considered the height of fashion, pastel colours such as pink or green were also popular, particularly for 'half dress'. Often dresses were enlivened by bold-coloured ribbons tied beneath the breast or jewellery such as cameo brooches or necklaces made from topaz or amethyst.

An example of gentlemen's dress in the style of Beau Brummel.

Underwear

Though the Regency period released women from the confinement of corsets, underwear still remained somewhat restrictive. However, the desire for a more natural shape meant that women were no longer

31

A Spencer.

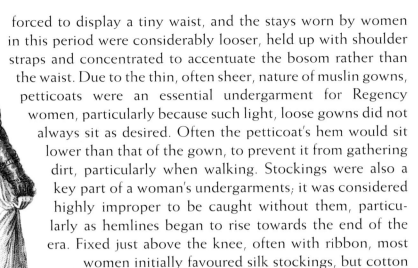

forced to display a tiny waist, and the stays worn by women in this period were considerably looser, held up with shoulder straps and concentrated to accentuate the bosom rather than the waist. Due to the thin, often sheer, nature of muslin gowns, petticoats were an essential undergarment for Regency women, particularly because such light, loose gowns did not always sit as desired. Often the petticoat's hem would sit lower than that of the gown, to prevent it from gathering dirt, particularly when walking. Stockings were also a key part of a woman's undergarments; it was considered highly improper to be caught without them, particularly as hemlines began to rise towards the end of the era. Fixed just above the knee, often with ribbon, most women initially favoured silk stockings, but cotton became increasingly popular as production quality increased.

The Spencer

Cut just beneath the bust to match the line of a gown, the 1790s saw the Spencer jacket become a popular method of keeping warm while remaining stylish. Supposedly created when Lord Spencer stood too close to an open fire and singed his coat tails, the Spencer was usually cut along the bodice, with long fitted sleeves and a high neckline. Typically they were made of a woollen cloth or silk or velvet, usually in a strong colour to complement and contrast with the pastel or, most often, white dress underneath.

The Pelisse

Like the Spencer, the pelisse was designed to accentuate the line of the gown it was worn over. Originally taking its name from a fur-trimmed jacket worn by the Prussian Hussars, the pelisse, worn with a long skirt over the scant muslin gowns worn by many women, provided warmth. Often made of heavier materials such as velvet or wool, the pelisse became an item equally as fashionable as the gown it covered. Particularly in the warmer months, pelisses were made of silk and trimmed to show off the taste of the wearer, thereby becoming an important part of women's fashion. Fanny Price is looked down on by her Bertram cousins because 'she neither played pianoforte nor wore fine pelisses'.

With light muslin dresses, a pelisse would have been essential in the winter months.

Bonnets, Hairstyles and Accessories

As the large, piled hairstyles of the Georgian period fell from fashion, the bonnet became an essential part of a woman's outfit. Since hair was now worn in short cropped curls at the front, with long hair at the back twisted and piled neatly on top of the head, women had more freedom with the shape and style of their bonnets. Tall, military bonnets became extremely fashionable, inspired again by military hats, whereas wide-brimmed straw bonnets were popular for informal visits or country walks. Though many women could not make their own bonnets, as they did often with shoes, many women chose to trim bonnets themselves to match a favourite Spencer or pelisse. For the evening, hairstyles remained simple, usually worn with ostrich feathers for decoration, though many younger women opted for a bandeau or tiara.

Bonnets became important fashion accessories, and would be elaborately trimmed and decorated.

Typical ladies' half dress, worn for afternoon promenading or visits.

Due to the slim, simple cut of Regency gowns, there was no place for pockets and reticules became a popular accessory for holding belongings. Though sold by milliners, creating a reticule became a popular pastime for many young ladies, allowing them to display their accomplishments. Fans remained a popular accessory, and women still wore gloves. The parasol became a must-have accessory, because although walking had become fashionable for women, tanned skin certainly hadn't!

Jane and Fashion

Though only her most foolish characters speak openly of fashion, Jane Austen took a great interest in fashion. Letters to Cassandra reveal that the sisters often discussed clothes and relied on one another to relay the latest fashions of Bath or London. In a letter written in October 1798 '... I bought some Japan Ink likewise, & next week shall begin my operations on my hat, on which [Y]ou know my principal hopes of happiness depend'. Clearly, Jane was a person who both understood and took pleasure from the changing fashions of her day, but in her novels we see her bestow little regard for people who constantly speak of clothes; a person with true taste, it seems, never

An example of morning dress (right), which would be worn for breakfast and early chores or activities.

speaks too much of fashions. However, Austen uses fashion very cleverly and carefully in her novels, as a method of demonstrating character. She was a great observer, with a keen understanding of her own society; she understood the importance of fashion within society and uses clothes as a way of indicating what a character is like. We are aware that Darcy, sensible and understated in his dress, is a gentleman and that Caroline Bingley, quick to criticise others and extravagant in her tastes, is shallow. Silly characters like Mrs Allen betray themselves by their obsessions with clothes, whereas we warm to Anne Elliot for her simplicity in contrast to her extravagant father and sister. Though there may be little discussion of fashion in Austen's stories, it is what is unsaid that counts.

Simpler fashions followed the French Revolution. The dress here still has the wide Georgian skirt, but shows the shift to Regency classical simplicity.

Austen Abroad

The first translations of Austen's work appeared during her own lifetime. However, it is possible that Jane never heard of these early translations, and she certainly didn't profit from them. French translations published at this time were unofficial, and pirated texts began to appear in America. The French translations in particular were often substantially different from Austen's own text: scenes were cut, characters added and dialogue changed. However, their popularity was somewhat short-lived and it wasn't until the end of the nineteenth century that Austen became a real presence abroad, particularly in France.

In 1898 the first true French translation of an Austen novel appeared. This careful translation showed painstaking attention to detail and even punctuation. Oddly, it was *Northanger Abbey* that sparked this new French interest but even odder is the story behind its appearance. The translator was a man named Félix Fénéon, an art critic and anarchist, who came across Austen while in prison as a suspect for the bombing of a Parisian café. *Northanger Abbey* was one of the few novels available to the inmates and Fénéon seems to have been captivated by Austen's social satire. Jane's keen insights and subtle mockery of fashionable society in Regency Bath must have appealed to Fénéon's anarchistic sensibilities because he became devoted to the novel. After his release from prison, he began working on his translation, which appeared as a serial in *La Revue Blanche* as *Catherine Morland*. The translation caught the attention of French intellectual circles and once again launched Austen's popularity abroad.

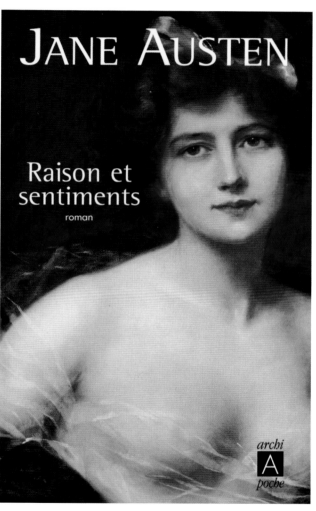

Sense and Sensibility *in French translation, with a very French cover illustration!*

The First and Second World Wars also had a significant part to play in the growth of Austen's global popularity, particularly in the United States. Jane Austen became synonymous with Englishness, the heart of the country its soldiers were fighting to protect. Certainly, as Austen gained more critical attention and study in the mid-twentieth century, so did her worldwide readership. The Jane Austen Society of North America was founded in 1979 and now boasts around four thousand members in over sixty groups across the States, publishing their own journals and hosting conferences, Austen events and tours of Jane's England. The Jane Austen Society of Australia, founded in 1989, is also a very popular organisation and countries such as Canada, Japan and the Netherlands now have their own Austen societies.

Austen in Film and Television

Pride and Prejudice

Colin Firth as Darcy and Jennifer Ehle as Elizabeth in the 1995 BBC adaptation of Pride and Prejudice.

Generally considered to be the finest of Austen's works, it is no surprise that *Pride and Prejudice* has been so often and successfully adapted for the screen. The first adaptation in 1940, directed by Robert Z. Leonard, starred Greer Garson and Laurence Olivier as the first on-screen incarnations of Elizabeth Bennet and Mr Darcy. The film won over Hollywood and was hugely popular with audiences, though some were disappointed with its deviations from the novel; Lady Catherine de Bourgh's character was significantly altered and many felt that the decision to use flamboyant 1830s costume distracted from the satire that permeates the novel. However, the film's success sparked the beginning of an on-screen infatuation with Austen, with a number of small adaptations for television over the next few decades. In 1980 the BBC produced a five-part serialisation starring David Rintoul and Elizabeth Garvie, which enjoyed a considerable success. Though Rintoul's portrayal of Darcy was well received and thought to be extremely faithful to the novel, it was almost entirely overshadowed some years later by the BBC's next adaptation in 1995. Written by Andrew Davies, the six-part series won a number of awards, and a new generation's adoration for Austen.

Jennifer Ehle captivated audiences as Elizabeth and, though he initially turned the role down, Colin Firth's turn as Darcy proved to be an unforgettable one – so much so that for a modern reader it is almost impossible to read *Pride and Prejudice* without picturing him. Capturing the vivacity and humour of *Pride and Prejudice*, the adaptation received a number of BAFTA nominations and a lasting popularity. The now iconic scene where Firth appears wet-shirted from the river was named 'one of the most unforgettable moments in British TV history' by *The Guardian* and women worldwide simultaneously swooned for his Mr Darcy. The most recent adaptation appeared in 2005, starring Matthew Macfadyen and Keira Knightley, and was another Hollywood success for Miss Austen. With a beautiful soundtrack and breathtaking cinematography, the film was considered a success despite the fact that much of the novel had to be cut due to time limitations. *Pride and Prejudice* is almost an obsession for many fans – Elizabeth's wit and spirit endears her to generation after generation of women and Darcy, with his brooding presence, is the ideal screen hero. The engaging plot and the amusing characters of Mrs Bennet and Mr Collins have given *Pride and Prejudice* the fame that Jane could never have envisaged.

Sense and Sensibility

Like *Pride and Prejudice*, *Sense and Sensibility* was serialised for television by the BBC in the early 1980s. However, it was Emma Thompson's 1995 adaptation that bought big screen success for Austen's first published novel. Directed by Ang Lee, the film featured Thompson herself as Elinor Dashwood and Kate Winslet as the fiery Marianne. Sensitive to the emotions at the heart of the novel, the film won over cinema audiences and critics alike with its faithful and engaging script. The film, with its all-star cast, including Hugh Grant as Edward Ferrars and Alan Rickman as Colonel Brandon, remains the most acclaimed adaptation of an Austen novel. It received a number of Academy Award Nominations, three BAFTAs and two Golden Globes, including an Oscar for Emma Thompson for Best Adapted Screen Play. Interestingly, though Thompson received a BAFTA for her performance, she had never originally intended to play the role. Director Ang Lee insisted she make Elinor twenty-seven, rather than nineteen, so that she could play the role. Indeed, with its faithful script, beautiful costumes and superb acting, Andrew Davies's 2008 television adaptation had a lot to live up to. Starring relative unknowns Hettie Morahan and Charity Makepeace as the Dashwood girls, Davies's script

Elinor Dashwood played by Emma Thompson in the 1995 adaptation of Sense and Sensibility.

played upon the novel's darker, more scandalous undertones. Though Davies received some criticism for his more sexualised version, it allowed new audiences to understand the severity of Willoughby's shocking past.

Mansfield Park

Mansfield Park is often viewed as somewhat an outsider; it has neither the sparkle and wit of *Northanger Abbey* or *Pride and Prejudice* nor the charm and tenderness of *Persuasion*. Though it has been adapted once for film, and twice for television, *Mansfield Park* doesn't take to the screen as well as *Sense and Sensibility* or *Emma*. Without the lively nature that attracts us to Elizabeth Bennet and Emma Woodhouse, Fanny's innocence and morality does not transfer well from page to film. A 1983 BBC series attempted a faithful adaptation, but failed to inspire audiences as other Austen series had. Lacking the pace and light-hearted nature of her other novels, critics found *Mansfield Park* to be too languid and Fanny too nervous to be compelling as a heroine. Patricia Rozema's 1999 film adaptation may have made Fanny a more engaging heroine, but it sacrificed her character; instead, elements of Austen's own personality were used to create a more wilful, outspoken Fanny. ITV's 2007 adaptation starred Billie Piper as a more faithful Fanny, yet certain major parts of the novel, such as Fanny's time in Portsmouth, were cut from the adaptation, much to the disappointment of fans. Though all the adaptations have their merits, including some fantastic performances and sharp portrayals of the Crawford siblings, *Mansfield Park* remains elusive.

Sylvestra Le Touzel and Nicholas Farrell in the 1983 BBC adaptation of Mansfield Park.

Doran Godwin and John Carson in the 1972 BBC version of Emma.

Emma

Though Austen may have feared upon writing her that no one but she would like her Miss Woodhouse, *Emma* has proven perfect for adaptation. Despite its lack of any major action, *Emma*'s charm as a novel passes easily onto the screen, partly thanks to the heroine, but also because of its setting. The stately home, the country village and the beautiful English countryside allow a visual setting that enhances the story. A BBC adaptation in 1972, starring Doran Godwin as Emma and John Carson as Mr

Knightley, was praised for its witty script and faithful portrayals. But Emma's real screen success came in 1996, in Douglas McGrath's film adaptation. With rising stars Gwyneth Paltrow and Ewan McGregor as Emma Woodhouse and Frank Churchill, as well as great comic performances from Alan Cumming and Juliet Stevenson as Mr and Mrs Elton, the film became a global success. Remaining faithful to Austen's novel, the film played with *Emma*'s class ideals, its countryside setting and emphasised Austen's use of period etiquette in the construction of comedy. A television adaptation also appeared in the same year, adapted by Andrew Davies and starring Kate Beckinsale in the titular role. Beckinsale's

Gwyneth Paltrow as Emma in 1996.

performance was well received by critics, though the adaptation was somewhat overshadowed by Paltrow's film. In 2009 the BBC adapted the novel again for television, in a four-part series with Romola Garai as the matchmaking Miss Woodhouse and Johnny Lee Miller as Mr Knightley. Despite its stunning visuals and a fantastic performance from Michael Gambon as the hypochondriac Mr Woodhouse, it received mixed reviews from critics.

Persuasion

Persuasion, Austen's most mature novel, is by far her most powerful love story. Though it lacks the light-hearted wit of its predecessors, *Persuasion* has made the transition to the screen far more successfully than the moral *Mansfield Park*. Television adaptations have made use of Austen's careful choice of contrasting locations – the stunning, natural beauty of Lyme Regis and the intricately designed splendour of Regency Bath. The BBC adapted the novel for a mini-series first in 1960 and again in 1971, before making a television movie in 1995 starring Amanda Root and Ciarán Hinds. With careful attention to Austen's plot, characters,

The 1995 adaptation of Persuasion *with Amanda Root as Anne Elliot.*

setting and themes the adaptation won over general audiences and critics and claimed six BAFTA awards. ITV adapted the novel again in 2007 as a teleplay with Sally Hawkins and Rupert Penry-Jones, and Anthony Head as Sir Walter Elliot. Though not as successful as the 1995 film, Sally Hawkins' performance received considerable praise, as did the film's cinematography.

Felicity Jones and J.J. Field in the 2007 adaptation of Northanger Abbey.

Northanger Abbey

Of all Austen's novels, *Northanger Abbey* has been somewhat overlooked when it comes to adaptations. A satirical take on the hugely popular Gothic novels of the late eighteenth century, *Northanger Abbey* was first adapted by the BBC in 1986. Despite its lavish costumes and location, the adaptation failed to make an impression. Katherine Schlesinger as Catherine, wide-eyed and innocent, may have suited Austen's youngest heroine but critics argued that Peter Firth, despite a strong performance, was far too old for the part of the young clergyman Henry Tilney. Many felt that it focused too heavily on the very Gothic aspects that Austen had mocked in the novel; to put it simply, the adaptation seemed to miss the joke. For years *Northanger Abbey* was neglected until ITV decided to adapt it in 2007 for their *Jane Austen Season*. With a screenplay by respected Austen adapter Andrew Davies, and starring Felicity Jones and J.J. Field, it finally brought *Northanger Abbey* alive on screen. Unlike the 1986 adaptation, it captured the splendid ridiculousness of the eighteenth-century Gothic, using voiceovers and lurid dream sequences to convey the humour to a modern audience. Jones and Field look every inch Catherine and Mr Tilney, their innocence and awkwardness as uncomfortable as Austen had intended, yet they are still likeable and endearing. Though, like his *Sense and Sensibility*, Davies's adaptation takes a somewhat darker turn; its understanding of the sexual threats prevalent in the Gothic novel, but also in early nineteenth-century Bath, open *Northanger Abbey*'s intricacies up for the modern viewer. Not only was it very well received, its two lead stars enjoyed great praise and a career boost, as did Carey Mulligan for her turn as the fantastically shallow Isabella Thorpe.

Jane, Bridget and Bollywood

Jane's on-screen power doesn't end with the adaptation of her own novels, however. It's not just that the misunderstandings of the love stories of Darcy and Lizzie or Knightley and Emma continually inspire Hollywood; they seem to be perfect for modern

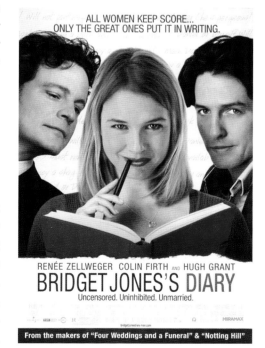

*Bridget Jones, Bollywood and Zombies all owe a
great debt to Jane Austen's enduring popularity.*

re-interpretations. The 1995 version of *Clueless* set the tribulations of Miss
Emma Woodhouse in a Beverley Hills High School, while in 2001 the
hugely popular *Bridget Jones's Diary* brought *Pride and Prejudice* to modern-
century London, with Colin Firth once again playing a Mr
Darcy. In 2008 ITV's *Lost in Austen* revealed that even in the
twenty-first century we still dream of our own Mr Darcy,
as Jemima Rooper's Amanda Price found herself switching
lives with Elizabeth Bennet, and in 2007 *The Jane Austen
Book Club* had women worldwide asking 'What would Jane
do?' Yet it's not only the American and British screens that
continue to adore Austen. In 2004 the Bollywood-style
musical *Bride and Prejudice* opened, and in 2010 *Aisha* put
Emma in modern-day Delhi. Even popular teenage films
such as the 2007 revamp of *St Trinians* made a number of
references to *Pride and Prejudice*, with Colin Firth striding
about in a wet shirt yet again.

With stage plays and even musicals, it seems the infatuation with Austen adaptations is far from over. *Becoming
Jane* (2007), despite its inaccuracies and fictional construc-
tions, proved that audiences still hunger for more Austen.
Even genre mash-up *Pride and Prejudice and Zombies* is
currently being considered for a big-budget Hollywood
production. Considering that Jane could never have
dreamt of such a fate for her novels, their lasting power in
film and television is more than remarkable.

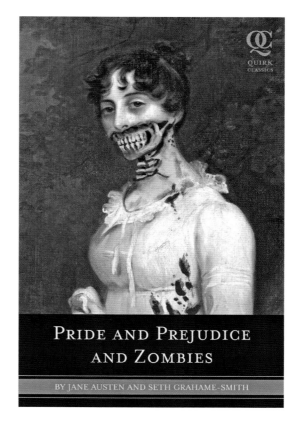

Modernity and Memorabilia

It is a truth universally acknowledged that any twenty-first century Austen fan must be in want of an 'I Love Mr Darcy' bag. In an age of statement bumper stickers and slogan T-shirts, Austen's words and characters have become a fashion accessory. In the early twentieth century, at the beginning of the Janeite craze, her letters, possessions and other family memorabilia became collectors' items, and rare and early editions of her novels are still sought after – in 2008 an 1816 first edition of *Emma* sold at auction for £180,000. In 1940 Dorothy Darnell founded the Jane Austen Society in a bid to restore Chawton Cottage to the home Austen had lived in, and to return as much memorabilia as possible. Fortunately many collectors chose to donate items to the Society, including a lock of Jane's hair and two amber crosses, presents from Charles Austen to Jane and Cassandra, all of which are housed at Chawton, now the Jane Austen's House Museum.

Indeed, for the modern Janeite, Austen is infinitely accessible; there are numerous internet communities, blogs and fan sites dedicated to her life and work. In addition, fans can follow Austen's footsteps with companies now running tours of Austen's England as well as the adaptation locations. After a visit to the Jane Austen's House Museum, it's easy to understand why Jane felt so inspired after moving to Chawton. Containing a selection of Jane's own personal belongings, family pictures and other artefacts, Chawton is a dream come true for any Austen fan. In addition to the museum at Chawton Cottage, Chawton House is also available for visits by request. Just a short walk from the cottage, Jane would have visited the house often when Edward was staying at his Hampshire estates. Restoration to the house began in 1997, and in 2003 it reopened as Chawton House Library. Tours of the house cover its long and rich history, as well as its connection to Jane, and include a tour of the large library dedicated specifically to early women writers.

In Bath, the Jane Austen Centre welcomes thousands of visitors every year. Due to the Austens' short stay in the city and constant change of address, few artefacts survive from their time here, and their lodgings at Green Park Buildings and Trim Street no longer exist. Stationed at number 40 Gay Street, the Centre is a few doors down from the Austens' third home in Bath and is an almost identical building. The permanent exhibition is dedicated to the Austens' five-year residence in the city, to the society and

The excellent and much-visited Jane Austen Centre in Gay Street, Bath, which offers visitors an idea of Jane's Bath experience.

the lifestyle that Jane would have enjoyed, or endured, as the case may be. Devoted to a period that is otherwise often overlooked or forgotten, the Centre offers visitors a taste of life in Regency Bath as well as an insight into the inspiration behind *Northanger Abbey* and *Persuasion*. The Centre is also responsible for the annual Jane Austen Festival, which has taken place every September since 2000 with great success. In 2009 the Festival's Grand Promenade broke the Guinness World Record for the largest gathering of people in Regency costume, and year after year attracts Janeites from across the globe. With dances, dinners, soirees and even a Grand Ball, the Festival is a chance for fans to experience Bath as Catherine Morland might have done, to follow the paths of Anne Elliot and Captain Wentworth and, of course, retrace the steps of Jane herself.

As well as Lyme Regis, Winchester and Kent have also become popular places on Austen pilgrimages. A plaque commemorating Jane's stay at College Street is now a much-visited site, as is her grave inside Winchester Cathedral. The Cathedral itself is brimming with history and has housed a number of Austen exhibitions, as well as displaying rare editions of her work. Kent, of course, is the location of Edward's stately home, Godmersham Park. Though the house itself is now a college, the Godmersham Park Heritage Centre was set up in 2007 to preserve the history of the house and its surrounding villages. The Heritage Centre houses a vast collection of photographs, artefacts and papers, including copies of Fanny Austen Knight's letters to her Aunt Jane, silhouettes and records of the Knight family. The nearby church can also be visited, where both Edward and his wife Elizabeth are buried and remembered by a monument within the church. The vast gardens that Jane so adored are still maintained and can be visited, as with the church and the Heritage Centre, by request.

Austen family heraldic arms.

Jane Austen's Family

As the seventh of eight children, it is no surprise that Jane Austen's family had great impact on her, both personally and professionally. Though Jane's own life may have been a relatively quiet one, her family would provide her with a wealth of experience to draw upon in her work. The Austens were members of that middle class gentry which all readers of Austen understand – after all, it is the same social space occupied by Elizabeth Bennet and Catherine Morland. Like both of these heroines, Austen's family were not particularly rich, but Jane's father's income was enough to live comfortably at the family home of Steventon in Hampshire.

The Reverend George and Mrs Cassandra Austen had a great impact on their daughter's life and work, their lives and attitudes shaping Jane's unique outlook on society. Orphaned when he was young, George was fortunate enough to fall under the patronage of his uncle, Francis Austen, a wealthy lawyer who recognised the young man's intellect and secured him a good education. Clever and good-natured, George went on to St John's College, Oxford, where he would eventually take his orders.

His fine looks earned him the nickname of 'the handsome proctor', and it is no wonder that he won the attention of one Miss Cassandra Leigh. An attractive woman of twenty-four, Cassandra could probably have used her family's aristocratic connections to make a more profitable match than a country clergyman, but Cassandra, quick-minded and witty, made a perfect match for the intelligent George. Accounts by the family show that the pair were more than happily married. Jane was very fortunate in her choice of parents, who bestowed on her not only their own clever natures and quick minds, but also a first-hand understanding of what it was to marry for love.

Jane's father, Rev George Austen (1731–1805) (above).

Jane's mother, Cassandra Austen née Leigh (right). She was very proud of her prominent nose – a sign of good breeding.

With George Austen's love of books – by 1801 he had a collection of almost five hundred volumes – and his wife's talent for comic verse, it is clear that Jane not only inherited some of her talent from her parents, but was encouraged by their pursuits to develop her own. She was fortunate to have a family that were so supportive of her work, her greatest admirer being her father. Rather than telling his youngest daughter to swap her pen for her needle and concentrate on finding a husband, he fully encouraged the idea of Jane's writing career. He even sought a publisher for an early draft of *Pride and Prejudice*, though the manuscript was returned unread.

As well as support from her father, Jane received constant encouragement from her sister Cassandra. Of all her relationships, it seems to be the one with Cassandra that Austen valued most. As children it seems that where Cassandra led, her sister would follow. Their mother once joked that 'if Cassandra's head had been going to be cut off, Jane would have hers cut off too'. As a young woman Jane regularly looked to her sister for guidance and advice, as her letters to Cassandra demonstrate. Though Cassandra's wise advice was not always followed, Jane clearly highly valued her sister's opinion.

Austen's closeness with her sister lasted throughout the two women's lives. Neither of the Austen girls married. For Jane this appears to have been out of stubbornness, born maybe from her experience of her parents' union and her determination only to marry for love. Cassandra's story is far more tragic. At twenty she became engaged to Thomas Fowle, a former pupil of the boarding school run by her father at Steventon. Tom's lack of income meant that the pair could not marry immediately, leading him to take a chaplaincy aboard a ship to the Caribbean, where he died from yellow fever. Cassandra, twenty-six by this time, was left heartbroken. The sisters became one another's constant companions and Cassandra's influence on Jane's writing is evident, particularly in characters such as Elinor Dashwood and Jane Bennet.

However close Jane was to her sister Cassandra, the importance of her brothers on both her writing and her personal life cannot be overlooked. As single women with no fortune, the lives of both Austen sisters would probably have been very different had it not been for their brothers. It was their lifestyles and careers which allowed Jane to live comfortably and to continue writing after their father's death in 1805. As well as material support, Jane's brothers also provided unique inspiration for much of her work. Arguably one of Austen's greatest achievements, and certainly one that keeps readers returning to her work, is her male characters. The Mr Darcys and Captain Wentworths of Austen's novels are some of the most adored in English literature, and it was Austen's brothers who allowed her such insight into the lives of her male characters.

James, the eldest of the Austen boys, shared his sister's passion for literature and talent for writing, and may have been instrumental in spurring Jane's desire to pick up her pen. After university, James took his orders, and would later inherit his father's parishes. As sister, daughter and friend to a clergyman, it is little wonder that Jane had such an understanding of the

Jane's sister, Cassandra (1773–1845), by John Meirs.

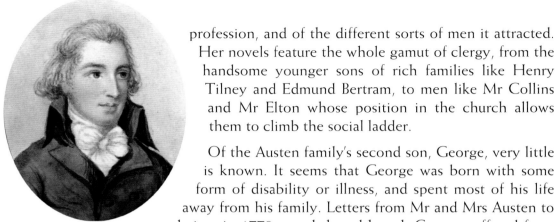

James Austen (1765–1819) (above).

Edward Austen (1767–1852) (below).

profession, and of the different sorts of men it attracted. Her novels feature the whole gamut of clergy, from the handsome younger sons of rich families like Henry Tilney and Edmund Bertram, to men like Mr Collins and Mr Elton whose position in the church allows them to climb the social ladder.

Of the Austen family's second son, George, very little is known. It seems that George was born with some form of disability or illness, and spent most of his life away from his family. Letters from Mr and Mrs Austen to relatives in 1770 reveal that although George suffered from fits, they hoped for his recovery. However, George was sent out to live with a family in Monk Sherborne, which was already caring for Mrs Austen's brother, Thomas Leigh, who may have suffered a similar condition.

The next Austen brother, Edward, was to enjoy a lifestyle that would rival that of the most affluent characters his sister ever created. At around sixteen years old, Edward was adopted by the Austens' distant cousins and landlords, Mr and Mrs Thomas Knight of Godmersham Park in Kent. Edward had been a favourite with the Knights for some time, and was their natural choice of heir when their marriage produced no children. As Mr Knight, Edward would have an annual income even greater than Mr Darcy's much-talked-of £10,000 a year. Not only did Edward provide for Jane after her father's death, his situation as part of the landed gentry gave her in-depth observation of another facet of society, and allowed her to create characters such as Emma Woodhouse, or the Bertrams of Mansfield Park.

Though Jane had a good relationship with all of her brothers, it was fourth-born Henry who appears to have been her favourite. Henry shared much of Jane's sharpness and sense of humour, as well as inheriting his father's handsome looks. It seems that they did not see eye to eye, however, particularly after Henry chose to join the militia rather than the church. Considering that Austen's military characters are by far her most badly behaved, it seems that she did not approve of her brother's choice of profession. Could it be that handsome, charming Henry inspired the likes of Captain Tilney and Mr Wickham? Possibly so. Henry certainly seems to have been on the flirtatious side, making and breaking a hasty engagement to a Miss Pearson, only to marry his elder and long-adored cousin, the widowed Comtesse Eliza de Feuillide, née Hancock.

On the other hand, Jane bestows her younger brother's name on the far more respectable Henry Tilney, and without brother Henry's help she may never have been published. After giving up his military career, Henry chose to settle in London as a banker. It was Henry who acted as Jane's literary agent, using his connections and money to secure anonymous publication for *Sense and Sensibility* in 1811.

Francis and Charles, the two youngest Austen brothers, would not have had the same opportunities as the elders. Unlike James and Henry they were not scholarly, and there were no more rich relatives to offer adoption. At twelve years old the boys entered the Royal Naval Academy at Portsmouth to begin a career which was both dangerous and demanding. Entering active naval service at just fourteen years old, the brothers could be away for anything from six months to almost a decade. Charles found himself in the West Indies for so long that he was married with two daughters before he returned home. In the early years of their careers they worked hard to prove their worth, much like William Price in *Mansfield Park*.

Yet despite the dangers they faced, the two youngest Austens benefited from their career choice. The Napoleonic Wars meant that there were plenty of opportunities for officers to prove themselves suitable for promotion. Francis seems to have been perfect for a naval life, deemed 'an excellent young man' by Lord Nelson himself, and though both brothers would achieve the rank of Admiral, Francis was also honoured with a knighthood. Jane may not have lived to see her brothers reach their greatest achievements, but her respect for the navy in *Persuasion* is clearly a result of her pride in Francis and Charles.

Henry Austen (1771–1850).

Jane Austen's Family Tree

William Austen ——— Rebecca Walter
(1701–1737)   (*née Hampson*)

Tysoe Saul Hancock ——— Philadelphia   Rev George ——— Cassandra Leigh   Leonora
(d. 1775)   (1730–1792)   (1731–1805)   (1739–1827)   (1732–1783)

Jean Capot de Feuillide ——— Eliza ——— *Henry Austen*   Rev James   George   Edward   Henry
(guillotined 1794)   (Elizabeth)   (1765–1819)   (1766–1838)   (1767–1852)   (1771–1850)
      (1761–1813)

Cassandra   Francis   **Jane**   Charles
(1773–1845)   (1774–1865)   **(1775–1817)**   (1779–1852)

Francis Austen (1774–1865) (above).
Charles Austen (1779–1852) (left).

Jane Austen's Letters

The edited versions of Jane Austen's letters reproduced in this section are taken from the standard edition edited by R.W. Chapman (The Clarendon Press, 1932).

A painting by Cassandra Austen of Fanny Knight, Jane's niece and friend, painting at her desk (above). Being a constant and enjoyable correspondent was an important trait in a Regency lady.

One of Jane Austen's few surviving letters (opposite), written to her niece Anna in September 1815.

Like most middle-class women of her day, Jane Austen was a keen letter writer. The art of letter-writing was something highly valued by Georgian and Regency society – the way in which a person wrote a letter was a clear indication of their character. The letters of Jane Fairfax and Frank Churchill in *Emma* are much admired by their society, and the style of Frank's letter-writing leads the reader to make assumptions about his character before he has even been introduced.

The letter was a vitally important aspect of Regency life, and Jane Austen reflects this in her work. The letters of Mr Darcy and Captain Wentworth are important plot devices; they reveal feelings and truths that might not be uttered in person. For Jane herself letters were an important part of her life, especially when family members spent time abroad. Though Cassandra destroyed a great bulk of her sister's correspondence, what survives provides an invaluable insight into Jane's personal life.

Jane Austen is a notably private writer; she would surely have approved of Cassandra's destruction of her private letters, especially if she could have had any suspicion of the fame that her writing would bring her. In the years since they were published, Jane Austen's letters have become almost as often-quoted as her novels. Though the majority of what survives is addressed to her elder sister, letters to her brothers and also to her two eldest nieces, Anna and Fanny, and her nephew James Edward also survive. This collection of correspondence, though not complete, provides us with an intimate portrait not only of Jane Austen the writer, but also of Jane Austen the sister, aunt, and friend.

In her letters Jane is amusing and satirical, and in this personal form of expression less subtle and reserved than the writer of a novel like *Mansfield Park*. The early letters to Cassandra reveal a Jane who is flirtatious and even daring as she reports her brief flirtation with Tom Lefroy. From these letters it is not hard to see how Austen created such a passionate character as Marianne Dashwood, and her observations often echo the comments made by Elizabeth Bennet. But her letters also display Jane's attachment to her family. The tenderness of her letter to her brother Francis on her father's death is very moving, and her letters to Fanny Knight hint at her enjoyment in her position as aunt.

The following letters have been selected to give an idea of the person behind the writer, of the way in which her mind worked, and how her ideas were shaped.

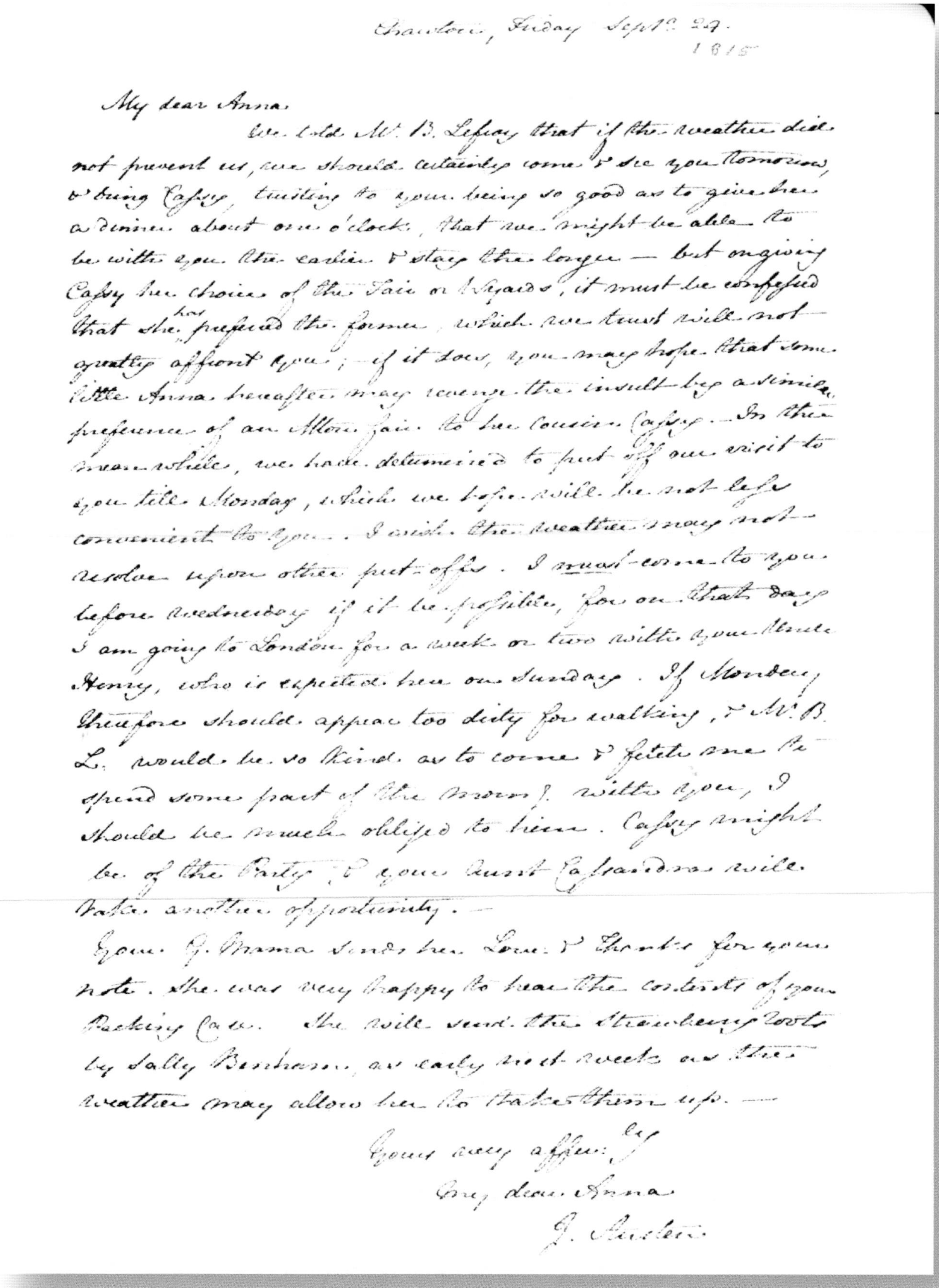

Chawton, Friday Sept.r 29.
1815

My dear Anna,

We told M.r B. Lefroy that if the weather did not prevent us, we should certainly come & see you tomorrow, & bring Cassy, trusting to your being so good as to give her a dinner about one o'clock, that we might be able to be with you the earlier & stay the longer — but on giving Cassy her choice of the Fair or Wyards, it must be confessed that she has preferred the former, which we trust will not greatly affront you; — if it does, you may hope that some little Anna hereafter may revenge the insult by a similar preference of an Alton fair to her cousin Cassy. In the mean while, we have determined to put off our visit to you till Monday, which we hope will be not less convenient to you. I wish the weather may not resolve upon other put-offs. I must come to you before Wednesday if it be possible, for on that day I am going to London for a week or two with your Uncle Henry, who is expected here on Sunday. If Monday therefore should appear too dirty for walking, & M.r B. L. would be so kind as to come & fetch me to spend some part of the morn.g with you, I should be much obliged to him. Cassy might be of the Party; & your Aunt Cassandra will take another opportunity. —

Your G. Mama sends her Love & Thanks for your note. She was very happy to hear the contents of your Packing Case. She will send the Strawberry roots by Sally Benham, as early next week as the weather may allow her to take them up. —

Yours very affec.ly

my dear Anna

J. Austen.

A twenty-year-old Jane writes to her absent sister Cassandra to keep her informed of events at home, including her now infamous flirtation with Mr Tom L:efroy.

To Cassandra Austen
Saturday 9 January 1796

In the first place I hope you will live twenty-three years longer. Mr. Tom Lefroy's birthday was yesterday, so that you are very near of an age.

After this necessary preamble I shall proceed to inform you that we had an exceeding good ball last night, and that I was very much disappointed at not seeing Charles Fowle of the party, as I had previously heard of his being invited. In addition to our set at the Harwoods' ball, we had the Grants, St. Johns, Lady Rivers, her three daughters and a son, Mr. and Miss Heathcote, Mrs. Lefevre, two Mr. Watkins, Mr. J. Portal, Miss Deanes, two Miss Ledgers, and a tall clergyman who came with them, whose name Mary would never have guessed.

We were so terrible good as to take James in our carriage, though there were three of us before; but indeed he deserves encouragement for the very great improvement which has lately taken place in his dancing. Miss Heathcote is pretty, but not near so handsome as I expected. Mr. H. began with Elizabeth, and afterwards danced with her again; but *they* do not know how *to be particular*. I flatter myself, however, that they will profit by the three successive lessons which I have given them.

You scold me so much in the nice long letter which I have this moment received from you, that I am almost afraid to tell you how my Irish friend and I behaved. Imagine to yourself everything most profligate and shocking in the way of dancing and sitting down together. I *can* expose myself, however, only *once more*, because he leaves the country soon after next Friday, on which day we *are* to have a dance at Ashe after all. He is a very gentlemanlike, good-looking, pleasant young man, I assure you. But as to our having ever met, except at the three last balls, I cannot say much; for he is so excessively laughed at about me at Ashe, that he is ashamed of coming to Steventon, and ran away when we called on Mrs. Lefroy a few days ago.

We left Warren at Dean Gate, in our way home last night, and he is now on his road to town. He left his love, &c., to you, and I will deliver it when we meet. Henry goes to Harden to-day in his way to his Master's degree. We shall feel the loss of these two most agreeable young men exceedingly, and shall have nothing to console us till the arrival of the Coopers on Tuesday. As they will stay here till the Monday following, perhaps Caroline will go to the Ashe ball with me, though I dare say she will not.

I danced twice with Warren last night, and once with Mr. Charles Watkins, and, to my inexpressible astonishment, I entirely escaped John Lyford. I was forced to fight hard for it, however. We had a very good supper, and the greenhouse was illuminated in a very elegant manner.

We had a visit yesterday morning from Mr. Benjamin Portal, whose eyes are as handsome as ever. Everybody is extremely anxious for your return, but as you cannot come home by the Ashe ball, I am glad that I have not fed them with false hopes. James danced with Alethea, and cut up the turkey last night with great perseverance. You say nothing of the silk stockings; I flatter myself, therefore, that Charles has not purchased any, as I cannot very well afford to pay for them; all my money is spent in buying white gloves and pink persian. I wish Charles had been at Manydown, because he would have given you some description of my friend, and I think you must be impatient to hear something about him.

Henry is still hankering after the Regulars, and as his project of purchasing the adjutancy of the Oxfordshire is now over, he has got a scheme in his head about getting a lieutenancy and adjutancy in the 86th, a new-raised regiment, which he fancies will be ordered to the Cape of Good Hope. I heartily hope that he will, as usual, be disappointed in this scheme. We have trimmed up and given away all the old paper hats of Mamma's manufacture; I hope you will not regret the loss of yours.

After I had written the above, we received a visit from Mr. Tom Lefroy and his cousin George. The latter is really very well-behaved now; and as for the other, he has but *one* fault, which time will, I trust, entirely remove – it is that his morning coat is a great deal too light. He is a very great admirer of Tom Jones, and therefore wears the same coloured clothes, I imagine, which he did when he was wounded.

Sunday   By not returning till the 19th, you will exactly contrive to miss seeing the Coopers, which I suppose it is your wish to do. We have heard nothing from Charles for some time. One would suppose they must have sailed by this time, as the wind is so favourable. What a funny name Tom has got for his vessel! But he has no taste in names, as we well know, and I dare say he christened it himself. I am sorry for the Beaches' loss of their little girl, especially as it is the one so much like me.

I condole with Miss M. on her losses and with Eliza on her gains, and am ever yours,

J. A.

Again to the still-absent Cassandra, who was visiting the family of her fiancé Mr Tom Fowle, Jane speaks again of Tom Lefroy, to tell her sister that he has left Steventon.

To Cassandra Austen
Thursday 14 January 1796

I have just received yours and Mary's letter, and I thank you both, though their contents might have been more agreeable. I do not at all expect to see you on Tuesday, since matters have fallen out so unpleasantly; and if you are not able to return till after that day, it will hardly be possible for us to send for you before Saturday, though for my own part I care so little about the ball that it would be no sacrifice to me to give it up for the sake of seeing you two days earlier. We are extremely sorry for poor Eliza's illness. I trust, however, that she has continued to recover since you wrote, and that you will none of you be the worse for your attendance on her. What a good-for-nothing fellow Charles is to bespeak the stockings! I hope he will be too hot all the rest of his life for it!

I sent you a letter yesterday to Ibthorp, which I suppose you will not receive at Kintbury. It was not very long or very witty, and therefore if you never receive it, it does not much signify. I wrote principally to tell you that the Coopers were arrived and in good health. The little boy is very like Dr. Cooper, and the little girl is to resemble Jane, they say.

Our party to Ashe to-morrow night will consist of Edward Cooper, James (for a ball is nothing without *him*), Buller, who is now staying with us, and I. I look forward with great impatience to it, as I rather expect to receive an offer from my friend in the course of the evening. I shall refuse him, however, unless he promises to give away his white coat.

I am very much flattered by your commendation of my last letter, for I write only for fame, and without any view to pecuniary emolument.

Edward is gone to spend the day with his friend, John Lyford, and does not return till to-morrow. Anna is now here; she came up in her chaise to spend the day with her young cousins, but she does not much take to them or to anything about them, except Caroline's spinning-wheel. I am very glad to find from Mary that Mr. and Mrs. Fowle are pleased with you. I hope you will continue to give satisfaction.

How impertinent you are to write to me about Tom, as if I had not opportunities of hearing from him myself! The *last* letter that I received from him was dated on Friday, 8th, and he told me that if the wind should be favourable on Sunday, which it proved to be, they were to sail from Falmouth on that day. By this time, therefore, they are at Barbadoes, I suppose. The Rivers are still at Manydown, and are to be at Ashe to-morrow. I intended to call on the Miss Biggs yesterday had the weather been tolerable. Caroline, Anna, and I have just been devouring some cold souse, and it would be difficult to say which enjoyed it most.

Tell Mary that I make over Mr. Heartley and all his estate to her for her sole use and benefit in future, and not only him, but all my other admirers into the bargain wherever she can find them, even the kiss which C. Powlett wanted to give me, as I mean to confine myself in future to Mr. Tom Lefroy, for whom I do not care sixpence. Assure her also, as a last and indubitable proof of Warren's indifference to me, that he actually drew that gentleman's picture for me, and delivered it to me without a sigh.

Friday   At length the day is come on which I am to flirt my last with Tom Lefroy, and when you receive this it will be over. My tears flow as I write at the melancholy idea. Wm. Chute called here yesterday. I wonder what he means by being so civil. There is a report that Tom is going to be married to a Lichfield lass. John Lyford and his sister bring Edward home to-day, dine with us, and we shall all go together to Ashe. I understand that we are to draw for partners. I shall be extremely impatient to hear from you again, that I may know how Eliza is, and when you are to return.

With best love, &c., I am affectionately yours, J. Austen

To Cassandra Austen
Tuesday 8 January 1799

Jane's letters often allow insight into her personality, showing her to be as amusing in her everyday life as in her novels. This one also reveals details of early writing.

My dear Cassandra

You must read your letters over *five* times in future before you send them, and then, perhaps, you may find them as entertaining as I do. I laughed at several parts of the one which I am now answering.

Charles is not come yet, but he must come this morning, or he shall never know what I will do to him. The ball at Kempshott is this evening, and I have got him an invitation, though I have not been so considerate as to get him a partner. But the cases are different between him and Eliza Bailey, for he is not in a dieing way, and may therefore be equal to getting a partner for himself. I beleive I told you that Monday was to be the ball night, for which, and for all other errors into which I may ever have led you, I humbly ask your pardon.

Elizabeth is very cruel about my writing music, and, as a punishment for her, I should insist upon always writing out all hers for her in future, if I were not punishing myself at the same time.

I am tolerably glad to hear that Edward's income is so good a one – as glad as I can be at anybody's being rich besides you and me – and I am thoroughly rejoiced to hear of his present to you.

I am not to wear my white sattin cap to-night, after all; I am to wear a Mamalouc cap instead, which Charles Fowle sent to Mary, and which she lends me. It is all the fashion now; worn at the opera, and by Lady Mildmays at Hackwood balls. I hate describing such things, and I dare say you will be able to guess what it is like. I have got over the dreadful epocha of mantua-making much better than I expected. My gown is made very much like my blue one, which you always told me sat very well, with only these variations: the sleeves are short, the wrap fuller, the apron comes over it, and a band of the same completes the whole.

I assure you that I dread the idea of going to Bookham as much as you do, but I am not without hopes that something may happen to prevent it.

Theo has lost his election at Balliol, and perhaps they may not be able to see company for some time. They talk of going to Bath, too, in the spring, and perhaps they may be overturned in their way down, and all laid up for the summer.

Wednesday   I have had a cold and weakness in one of my eyes for some days, which makes writing neither very pleasant nor very profitable, and which will probably prevent my finishing this letter myself. My mother has undertaken to do it for me, and I shall leave the Kempshott ball for her.

You express so little anxiety about my being murdered under Ash Park Copse by Mrs. Hulbert's servant, that I have a great mind not to tell you whether I was or not, and shall only say that I did not return home that night or the next, as Martha kindly made room for me in her bed, which was the shut-up one in the new nursery. Nurse and the child slept upon the floor, and there we all were in some confusion and great comfort. The bed did exceedingly well for us, both to lie awake in and talk till two o'clock, and to sleep in the rest of the night. I love Martha better than ever, and I mean to go and see her, if I can, when she gets home. We all dined at the Harwoods' on Thursday, and the party broke up the next morning.

This complaint in my eye has been a sad bore to me, for I have not been able to read or work in any comfort since Friday, but one advantage will be derived from it, for I shall be such a proficient in music by the time I have got rid of my cold, that I shall be perfectly qualified in *that* science at least to take Mr. Roope's office at Eastwell next summer; and I am sure of Elizabeth's recommendation, be it only on Harriet's account. Of my talent in drawing I have given specimens in my letters to you, and I have nothing to do but to invent a few hard names for the stars.

Mary grows rather more reasonable about her child's beauty, and says that she does not think him really handsome ; but I suspect her moderation to be something like that of W— W—'s mama. Perhaps Mary has told you that they are going to enter more into dinner parties; the Biggs and Mr. Holder dine there to-morrow, and I am to meet them. I shall sleep there. Catherine has the honour of giving her name to a set, which will be composed of two Withers, two Heathcotes, a Blachford, and no Bigg except herself. She congratulated me last night on Frank's promotion, as if she really felt the joy she talked of.

My sweet little George! I am delighted to hear that he has such an inventive genius as to face-making. I admired his yellow wafer very much, and hope he will chuse the wafer for your next letter. I wore my green shoes last night, and took my *white fan* with me; I am very glad he never threw it into the river.

Mrs. Knight giving up the Godmersham estate to Edward was no such prodigious act of generosity after all, it seems, for she has reserved herself an income out of it still; this ought to be known, that her conduct may not be overrated. I rather think Edward shows the most magnanimity of the two, in accepting her resignation with such incumbrances.

The more I write, the better my eye gets, so I shall at least keep on till it is quite well, before I give up my pen to my mother.

Mrs. Bramston's little moveable apartment was tolerably filled last night by herself, Mrs. H. Blackstone, her two daughters, and me. I do not like the Miss Blackstones; indeed, I was always determined not to like them, so there is the less merit in it. Mrs. Bramston was very civil, kind, and noisy. I spent a very pleasant evening, cheifly among the Manydown party. There was the same kind of supper as last year, and the same want of chairs. There were more dancers than the room could conveniently hold, which is enough to constitute a good ball at any time.

I do not think I was very much in request. People were rather apt not to ask me till they could not help it; one's consequence, you know, varies so much at times without any particular reason. There was one gentleman, an officer of the Cheshire, a very good-looking young man, who, I was told, wanted very much to be introduced to me; but as he did not want it quite enough to take much trouble in effecting it, we never could bring it about.

I danced with Mr. John Wood again, twice with a Mr. South, a lad from Winchester, who, I suppose, is as far from being related to the bishop of that diocese as it is possible to be, with G. Lefroy, and J. Harwood, who, I think, takes to me rather more than he used to do. One of my gayest actions was sitting down two dances in preference to having Lord Bolton's eldest son for my partner, who danced too ill to be endured. The Miss Charterises were there, and played the parts of the Miss Edens with great spirit. Charles never came. Naughty Charles! I suppose he could not get superseded in time.

Miss Debary has replaced your two sheets of drawing-paper with two of superior size and quality; so I do not grudge her having taken them at all now. Mr. Ludlow and Miss Pugh of Andover are lately married, and so is Mrs. Skeete of Basingstoke, and Mr. French, chemist, of Reading.

I do not wonder at your wanting to read 'First Impressions' again, so seldom as you have gone through it, and that so long ago. I am much obliged to you for meaning to leave my old petticoat behind you. I have long secretly wished it might be done, but had not courage to make the request.

Pray mention the name of Maria Montresor's lover when you write next. My mother wants to know it, and I have not courage to look back into your letters to find it out.

I shall not be able to send this till to-morrow, and you will be disappointed on Friday; I am very sorry for it, but I cannot help it.

The partnership between Jeffereys, Toomer, and Legge is dissolved; the two latter are melted away into nothing, and it is to be hoped that Jeffereys will soon break, for the sake of a few heroines whose money he may have. I wish you joy of your birthday twenty times over.

I *shall* be able to send this to the post to-day, which exalts me to the utmost pinnacle of human felicity, and makes me bask in the sunshine of prosperity, or gives me any other sensation of pleasure in studied language which you may prefer. Do not be angry with me for not filling my sheet, and beleive me yours affectionately,

J. A.

Written during a visit to Bath, Jane speaks much of the latest fashions. Jane was in fact a keen observer and admirer of fashion and talk of it often fills her letters.

To Cassandra Austen
Tuesday 11 June 1799

My dear Cassandra

Your letter yesterday made me very happy. I am heartily glad that you have escaped any share in the impurities of Deane, and not sorry, as it turns out, that our stay here has been lengthened. I feel tolerably secure of our getting away next week, though it is certainly possible that we may remain till Thursday the 27th. I wonder what we shall do with all our intended visits this summer! I should like to make a compromise with Adlestrop, Harden, and Bookham, that Martha's spending the summer at Steventon should be considered as our respective visits to them all.

Edward has been pretty well for this last week, and as the waters have never *dis*agreed with him in any respect, we are inclined to hope that he will derive advantage from them in the end. Everybody encourages us in this expectation, for they all say that the effect of the waters cannot be negative, and many are the instances in which their benefit is felt afterwards more than on the spot. He is more comfortable here than I thought he would be, and so is Elizabeth, though they will both, I beleive, be very glad to get away – the latter especially, which one can't wonder at *somehow*. So much for Mrs. Piozzi. I had some thoughts of writing the whole of my letter in her style, but I beleive I shall not.

Though you have given me unlimited powers concerning your sprig, I cannot determine what to do about it, and shall therefore in this and in every other future letter continue to ask your further directions. We have been to the cheap shop, and very cheap we found it, but there are only flowers made there, no fruit; and as I could get 4 or 5 very pretty sprigs of the former for the same money which would procure only one Orleans plumb – in short, could get more for three or four shillings than I could have means of bringing home – I cannot decide on the fruit till I hear from you again. Besides, I cannot help thinking that it is more natural to have flowers grow out of the head than fruit. What do you think on that subject?

I would not let Martha read 'First Impressions' again upon any account, and am very glad that I did not leave it in your power. She is very cunning, but I saw through her design; she means to publish it from memory, and one more perusal must enable her to do it. As for 'Fitzalbini,' when I get home she shall have it, as soon as ever she will own that Mr. Elliott is handsomer than Mr. Lance, that fair men are preferable to black; for I mean to take every opportunity of rooting out her prejudices.

Benjamin Portal is here. How charming that is! I do not exactly know why, but the phrase followed so naturally that I could not help putting it down. My mother saw him the other day, but without making herself known to him.

I am very glad you liked my lace, and so are you, and so is Martha, and we are all glad together. I have got your cloak home, which is quite delightful – as delightful at least as half the circumstances which are called so.

I do not know what is the matter with me to-day, but I cannot write quietly; I am always wandering away into some exclamation or other. Fortunately I have nothing very particular to say.

We walked to Weston one evening last week, and liked it very much. Liked *what* very much? Weston? No, *walking* to Weston. I have not expressed myself properly, but I hope you will understand me.

We have not been to any public place lately, nor performed anything out of the common daily routine of No. 13, Queen Square, Bath. But to-day we were to have dashed away at a very extraordinary rate, by dining out, had it not so happened that we did not go.

Edward renewed his acquaintance lately with Mr. Evelyn, who lives in the Queen's Parade, and was invited to a family dinner, which I beleive at first Elizabeth was rather sorry at his accepting; but yesterday Mrs. Evelyn called on us, and her manners were so pleasing that we liked the idea of going very much. The Biggs would call her a nice woman. But Mr. Evelyn, who was indisposed yesterday, is worse to-day, and we are put off.

It is rather impertinent to suggest any household care to a housekeeper, but I just venture to say that the coffee-mill will be wanted every day while Edward is at Steventon, as he always drinks coffee for breakfast.

Fanny desires her love to you, her love to grandpapa, her love to Anna, and her love to Hannah; the latter is particularly to be remembered. Edward desires his love to you, to grandpapa, to Anna, to little Edward, to Aunt James and Uncle James, and he hopes all your turkies and ducks, and chicken and guinea fowls are very well; and he wishes you very much to send him a printed letter, and so does Fanny – and they both rather think they shall answer it.

A plate from The Gallery of Fashion, *Niklaus von Heideloff, August 1799.*

A personal and revealing letter, written upon the death of her father in 1805, to her naval brother Francis. It is easy to see how much Jane admired her father and how close the family were.

'On more accounts than one you wished our stay here to be lengthened beyond last Thursday.' There is some mystery in this. What have you going on in Hampshire besides the *itch* from which you want to keep us?

Dr. Gardiner was married yesterday to Mrs. Percy and her three daughters.

Now I will give you the history of Mary's veil, in the purchase of which I have so considerably involved you that it is my duty to economise for you in the flowers. I had no difficulty in getting a muslin veil for half a guinea, and not much more in discovering afterwards that the muslin was thick, dirty, and ragged, and therefore would by no means do for a united gift. I changed it consequently as soon as I could, and, considering what a state my imprudence had reduced me to, I thought myself lucky in getting a black lace one for sixteen shillings. I hope the half of that sum will not greatly exceed what you had intended to offer upon the altar of sister-in-law affection.

Yours affectionately, Jane

They do not seem to trouble you much from Manydown. I have long wanted to quarrel with them, and I believe I shall take this opportunity. There is no denying that they are very capricious – for they like to enjoy their elder sister's company when they can.

To Francis Austen
Tuesday 22 January 1805

My dearest Frank

I wrote to you yesterday ; but your letter to Cassandra, this morning, by which we learn the probability of your being by this time at Portsmouth, obliges me to write to you again, having unfortunately a communication as necessary as painful to make to you. – Your affectionate heart will be greatly wounded, & I wish the shock could have been lessen'd by a better preparation; – but the Event has been sudden, & so must be the information of it. We have lost an Excellent Father. – An illness of only eight & forty hours carried him off yesterday morning between ten & eleven. He was seized on saturday with a return of the feverish complaint, which he had been subject to for the three last years; evidently a more violent attack from the first, as the applications which had before produced almost immediate releif, seemed for some time to afford him scarcely any. – On Sunday however he was much better, so much so as to make Bowen quite easy, & give us every hope of his being well again in a few days. – But these hopes gradually gave way as the day advanced, & when Bowen saw him at ten that night he was greatly alarmed. – A Physician was called in yesterday morning, but he was at that time past all possibility of cure – & Dr. Gibbs and Mr. Bowen had scarcely left his room before he sunk into a Sleep from which he never woke. – Everything I trust & beleive was done for him that was possible! – It has been very sudden! – within twenty four hours of his

death he was walking with only the help of a stick, was even reading! –
We had however some hours of preparation, & when we understood his
recovery to be hopeless, most fervently did we pray for the speedy release
which ensued. To have seen him languishing long, struggling for Hours,
would have been dreadful! & thank God! we were all spared from it. Except
the restlessness & confusion of high Fever, he did not suffer – & he was
mercifully spared from knowing that he was about to quit the Objects
so beloved, so fondly cherished as his wife & Children ever were. – His
tenderness as a Father, who can do justice to? – My Mother is tolerably
well; she bears up with great fortitude, but I fear her health must suffer
under such a shock. – An express was sent for James, & he arrived here this
morning before eight o'clock.—The funeral is to be on Saturday, at Walcot
Church. – The Serenity of the Corpse is most delightful! – It preserves the
sweet, benevolent smile which always distinguished him. – They kindly
press my Mother to remove to Steventon as soon as it is all over, but I do
not beleive she will leave Bath at present. We must have this house for
three months longer, & here we shall probably stay till the end of that time.

We all unite in Love, & I am affec'ly Yours
J A.

To Crosbie & Co.
Wednesday 5 April 1809

Gentlemen

In the spring of the year 1803 a MS. Novel in 2 vol. entitled Susan was sold
to you by a Gentleman of the name of Seymour, & the purchase money
£10. rec'd at the same time. Six years have since passed, & this work of
which I avow myself the Authoress, has never to the best of my knowledge,
appeared in print, tho' an early publication was stipulated for at the time
of sale. I can only account for such an extraordinary circumstance by
supposing the MS. by some carelessness to have been lost; & if that was
the case, am willing to supply you with another copy if you are disposed
to avail yourselves of it, & will engage for no farther delay when it comes
into your hands. It will not be in my power from particular circumstances
to command this copy before the Month of August, but then, if you accept
my proposal, you may depend on receiving it. Be so good as to send me a
Line in answer as soon as possible, as my stay in this place will not exceed
a few days. Should no notice be taken of this address, I shall feel myself at
liberty to secure the publication of my work, by applying elsewhere. I am
Gentlemen &c. &c.

M. A. D.

When her early version of Northanger Abbey *never appeared in print, Jane wrote to seek an answer from the publisher. Amusingly, she signed herself as Mrs Ashton Denis, so that the initials read as 'M.A.D'.*

Written to her brother Francis on the birth of his son,
Francis William. The letter not only indicates Jane's
affection for her family but shows she was as skilled
a poet as she was a novelist.

To Francis Austen
Wednesday 26 July 1809

My dearest Frank, I wish you joy
Of Mary's safety with a Boy,
Whose birth has given little pain
Compared with that of Mary Jane.—

May he a growing Blessing prove,
And well deserve his Parents' Love!—
Endow'd with Art's & Nature's Good,
Thy name possessing with thy Blood,
In him, in all his ways, may we
Another Francis William see!—
Thy infant days may he inherit,
Thy warmth, nay insolence of spirit,—
We would not with one fault dispense
To weaken the resemblance.

May he revive thy Nursery sin,
Peeping as daringly within,
His curley Locks but just descried,
With, 'Bet, my be not come to bide.'—

Fearless of danger, braving pain,
And threaten'd very oft in vain,
Still may one Terror daunt his soul,
One needful engine of Controul
Be found in this sublime array,
A neighbouring Donkey's aweful Bray.
So may his equal faults as Child,
Produce Maturity as mild!
His saucy words & fiery ways
In early Childhood's pettish days,
In Manhood, shew his Father's mind
Like him, considerate & kind;
All Gentleness to those around,
And eager only not to wound.

Then like his Father too, he must,
To his own former struggles just,
Feel his Deserts with honest Glow,
And all his self-improvement know.—
A native fault may thus give birth
To the best blessing, conscious Worth.—

As for ourselves, we're very well;
As unaffected prose will tell.—
Cassandra's pen will paint our state,
The many comforts that await
Our Chawton home, how much we find
Already in it, to our mind;
And how convinced, that when complete
It will all other Houses beat
That ever have been made or mended,
With rooms concise, or rooms distended.
You'll find us very snug next year,
Perhaps with Charles & Fanny near,
For now it often does delight us
To fancy them just over-right us.—

J. A.

Copy of a letter to Frank   July 26. 1809.

Jane valued and enjoyed her role as aunt, as her letter to her niece Anna Austen reveals. Anna shared her aunt's literary talents, and Jane seems to have offered her services as editor and reviewer.

To Anna Austen
Friday 9 September 1814

My dear Anna

We have been very much amused by your 3 books, but I have a good many criticisms to make – more than you will like. – We are not satisfied with Mrs. F.'s settling herself as Tenant & near Neighbour to such a Man as Sir T. H. without having some other inducement to go there; she ought to have some friend living thereabouts to tempt her. A woman, going with two girls just growing up, into a Neighbourhood where she knows nobody but one Man, of not very good character, is an awkwardness which so prudent a woman as Mrs. F. would not be likely to fall into. Remember, she is very prudent; – you must not let her act inconsistently. – Give her a friend, & let that friend be invited to meet her at the Priory, & we shall have no objection to her dining there as she does; but otherwise, a woman in her situation would hardly go there, before she had been visited by other Families. – I like the scene itself, the Miss Lesleys, Lady Anne, & the Music, very much. – Lesley *is* a noble name. – Sir T. H. you always do very well; I have only taken the liberty of expunging one phrase of his, which would not be allowable. 'Bless my Heart' – It is too familiar & inelegant. Your G. M. is more disturbed at Mrs. F.'s not returning the Egertons visit sooner, than anything else. They ought to have called at the Parsonage before Sunday. – You describe a sweet place but your descriptions are often more minute than will be liked. You give too many particulars of right hand & left. – Mrs. F. is not careful enough of Susan's health; – Susan ought not to be walking out so soon after Heavy rains, taking long walks in the dirt. An anxious Mother would not suffer it. – I like your Susan very much indeed, she is a sweet creature, her playfulness of fancy is very delightful. I like her as she is *now* exceedingly, but I am not so well satisfied with her behaviour to George R. At first she seemed all over attachment & feeling, & afterwards to have none at all; she is so extremely composed at the Ball, & so well-satisfied apparently with Mr. Morgan. She seem to have changed her Character. – You are now collecting your People delightfully, getting them exactly into such a spot as is the delight of my life; – 3 or 4 Families in a Country Village is the very thing to work on – & I hope you will write a great deal more & make full use of them while they are so very favourably arranged. You are but *now* coming to the heart & beauty of your book; till the heroine grows up, the fun must be imperfect – but I expect a great deal of entertainment from the next 3 or 4 books & I hope you will not resent these remarks by sending me no more. – We like the Egertons very well, we see no Blue Pantaloons, or Cocks & Hens; there is nothing to *enchant* one certainly in Mr. L. L – but we make no objection to him, & his inclination to like Susan is pleasing. – The Sister is a good contrast – but the name of Rachael is as much as I can bear: They are not so much like the Papillons as I expected, Your last chapter is very entertaining – the conversation on Genius &c. Mr. St. J.— & Susan

both talk in character & very well. – In some former parts, Cecilia is perhaps a little too solemn & good, but upon the whole, her disposition is very well opposed to Susan's – her want of Imagination is very natural. – I wish you could make Mrs. F. talk more, but she must be difficult to manage & make entertaining, because there is so much good common sence & propriety about her that nothing can be very *broad*. Her Economy and her Ambition must not be staring. – The Papers left by Mrs. Fisher is very good. – Of course, one guesses something. – I hope when you have written a great deal more you will be equal to scratching out some of the past. The scene with Mrs. Mellish, I should condemn; it is prosy & nothing to the purpose – & indeed, the more you can find in your heart to curtail between Dawlish & Newton Priors, the better I think it will be. One does not care for girls till they are grown up. – Your Aunt C. quite enters into the exquisiteness of that name. Newton Priors is really a Nonpareil. – Milton wd have given his eyes to have thought of it. Is not the Cottage taken from Tollard Royal?

Sunday 18th   I am very glad dear Anna, that I wrote as I did before this sad Event occurred. I have now only to add that your G.Mama does not seem the worse now for the shock. – I shall be very happy to receive more of your work, if more is ready; & you write so fast, that I have great hopes Mr. D. will come freighted back with such a Cargo as not all his Hops or his Sheep could equal the value of.

Your Grandmama desires me to say that she will have finished your Shoes tomorrow & thinks they will look very well; – and that she depends upon seeing you, as you promise, before you quit the Country, & hopes you will give her more than a day. – Yrs affec'ly

J. Austen

To Fanny Knight
Thursday 20 February 1817

As well as being fond of Anna, Jane was very close to her niece Fanny (see below, painted as an adult), who had also lost her mother. Both girls often sought their aunt's advice, in both their lives and their loves. This letter reveals much of Jane's true character and opinion.

My dearest Fanny,

You are inimitable, irresistable. You are the delight of my Life. Such Letters, such entertaining Letters as you have lately sent! – Such a description of your queer little heart! – Such a lovely display of what Imagination does. – You are worth your weight in Gold, or even in the new Silver Coinage. – I cannot express to you what I have felt in reading your history of yourself, how full of Pity & Concern & Admiration & Amusement I have been. You are the Paragon of all that is Silly & Sensible, common-place & eccentric, Sad & Lively, Provoking & Interesting. – Who can keep pace with the fluctuations of your Fancy, the Capprizios of your Taste, the Contradictions of your Feelings ? – You are so odd ! – & all the time, so perfectly natural – so peculiar in yourself, & yet so like everybody else! – It is very, very gratifying to me to know you so intimately. You can hardly think what a pleasure it is to me, to have such thorough pictures of your Heart. – Oh! what a loss it will be when you are married. You are too agreable in your single state, too agreable as a Neice. I shall hate you when your delicious play of Mind is all settled down into conjugal & maternal affections.

Mr. J. W. frightens me. – He will have you. – I see you at the Altar. – I have *some* faith in Mrs. C. Cage's observation, & still more in Lizzy's; & besides, I know it *must* be so. He must be wishing to attach you. It would be too stupid & too shameful in him, to be otherwise; & all the Family are seeking your acquaintance. – Do not imagine that I have any real objection, I have rather taken a fancy to him than not, & I like Chilham Castle for you; – I only do not like you shd marry anybody. And yet I do wish you to marry very much, because I know you will never be happy till you are; but the loss of a Fanny Knight will be never made up to me; My 'affec: Neice F. C. Wildman' will be but a poor Substitute. I do not like your being nervous & so apt to cry: – it is a sign you are not quite well, but I hope Mr. Scud – as you always write his name, (your Mr. *Scuds*: amuse me very much) will do you good. – What a comfort that Cassandra should be so recovered! – It is more than we had expected. – I can easily beleive she was very patient & very good. I always loved Cassandra, for her fine dark eyes & sweet temper. – I am almost entirely cured of my rheumatism; just a little pain in my knee now and then, to make me remember what it was, & keep on flannel. – Aunt Cassandra nursed me so beautifully! – I enjoy your visit to Goodnestone, it must be a great pleasure to you, You have not seen

Goodnestone, Kent, home of the Bridges family c.1826.

Fanny Cage in any comfort so long. I hope she represents & remonstrates & reasons with you, properly. Why should you be living in dread of his marrying somebody else? – (Yet, how natural!) – You did not chuse to have him yourself; why not allow him to take comfort where he can? – In your conscience you *know* that he could not bear a comparison with a more animated Character. – You cannot forget how you felt under the idea of it's having been possible that he might have dined in Hans Place. – My dearest Fanny, I cannot bear you should be unhappy about him. Think of his Principles, think of his Father's objection, of want of Money, of a coarse Mother, of Brothers & Sisters like Horses, of sheets sewn across &c. – But I am doing no good – no, all that I urge against him will rather make you take his part more, sweet perverse Fanny. – And now I will tell you that we like your Henry to the utmost, to the very top of the Glass, quite brimful. – He is a very pleasing young Man. I do not see how he could be mended. He does really bid fair to be everything his Father and Sister could wish; and William I love very much indeed, & so we do all, he is quite our own William. In short we are very comfortable together – that is, we can answer for *ourselves.* – Mrs. Deedes is as welcome as May, to all our Benevolence to her Son; we only lamented that we cd not do more, & that the £50 note we slipt into his hand at parting was necessarily the Limit of our Offering. – Good Mrs. Deedes! – I hope she will get the better of this Marianne, & then I wd recommend to her & Mr. D. the simple regimen of separate rooms. – Scandal & Gossip; – yes I dare say you are well stocked; but I am very fond of Mrs. C. Cage, for reasons good. Thank you for mentioning her praise of Emma &c. – I have contributed the marking to Uncle H.'s shirts, & now they are a complete memorial of the tender regard of many.

Friday I had no idea when I began this yesterday, of sending it before your Br went back, but I have written away my foolish thoughts at such a rate

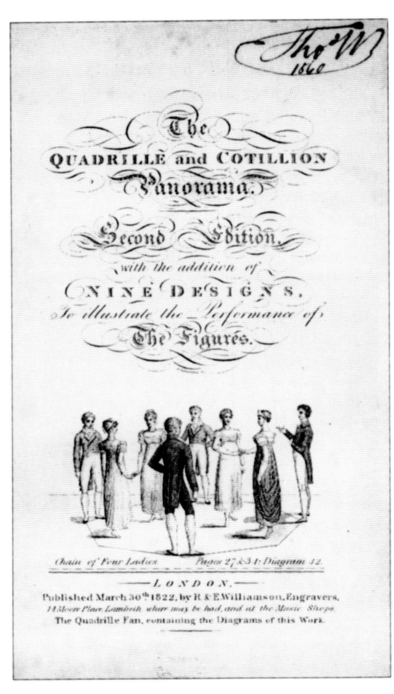

Title page of Wilson's The Quadrille and
Cotillion Panorama, *c. 1822, from the archives of
the Royal Academy of Dancing (Philip Richardson
Collection).*

that I will not keep them many hours longer to stare me in the face. – Much obliged for the *Quadrilles*, which I am grown to think pretty enough, though of course they are very inferior to the Cotillions of my own day. – Ben & Anna walked here last Sunday to hear Uncle Henry, & she looked so pretty, it was quite a pleasure to see her, so young & so blooming & so innocent, as if she had never had a wicked Thought in her Life – which yet one has some reason to suppose she must have had, if we beleive the Doctrine of original Sin, or if we remember the events of her girlish days.

I hope Lizzy will have her Play. Very kindly arranged for her. Henry is generally thought very good-looking, but not so handsome as Edward. – I think *I* prefer his face. – Wm. is in excellent Looks, has a fine appetite & seems perfectly well. You will have a great Break-up at Gm in the Spring, You *must* feel their all going. It is very right however. One sees many good causes for it. – Poor Miss C. – I shall pity her, when she begins to understand herself. – Your objection to the Quadrilles delighted me exceedingly. – Pretty well, for a Lady irrecoverably attached to *one* Person! – Sweet Fanny, beleive no such thing of yourself. – Spread no such malicious slander upon your Understanding, within the Precincts of your Imagination. – Do not speak ill of your Sense, merely for the Gratification of your Fancy. – Yours is Sense, which deserves more honourable Treatment. – You are *not* in love with him. You never have been really in love with him. – Yrs very affec'ly

J. Austen

Uncle H. & Miss Lloyd dine at Mr Digweed's today, which leaves us the power of asking Uncle & Aunt F.— to come and meet their Nephews here.

A Regency dance (above).

Pattern for a dancing dress, from Ackermann's Repository
February 1809 *(left).*

A Jane Austen Timeline

On the surface the society Jane Austen portrays in her novels seems to be one both peaceful and simplistic. Yet her novels are full of soldiers and sailors and show a rising middle class, as well as tensions between the old generation and the new. Jane's life time would span a number of significant historical events and in turn, she would be a part of an England that was witnessing a great social upheaval.

One of the most significant impacts on England during Austen's life were the events in France, on both a wider social and personal family scale. Born the year after King Louis XVI's accession to the French throne, Jane Austen would have been thirteen years old at the start of the French Revolution. The Revolutionary ideology threatened to disrupt British politics and social order, as well as causing trade difficulties that would impact the way British industry worked and even causing dramatic changes in its fashion. The traditions, rules and hierarchy of the Georgian period began to fade and give way to a new generation's values and beliefs and it would be this generation to which Austen's heroes and heroines would belong.

As the eighteenth century gave way to the nineteenth England would undergo even further change. In France, Napoleon Bonaparte had seized power and in 1804 he would crown himself Emperor. Europe would be again in turmoil and for Jane Austen the Napoleonic Wars came very close to home, with two brothers serving in the Navy and another in the Army during the period. When the Prince of Wales came to be Prince Regent in 1811, England's transformation would have been evident. The colonisation of the New World offered new prospects and the wars had turned young men of no consequence into respected gentleman of title. New money meant a new social hierarchy as well as a society that held a totally different set of morals and values to its predecessors. Even fashion had undergone a complete transformation, as the extravagant dress of the previous century was replaced with a new classical simplicity.

So though at first glance we may not see it, the world of Jane Austen's novels is one of great change. It is in Walter Elliot's arrogance and the way in which his disapproval of the naval career is at odds with the honesty and gentlemanlike behaviour of its officers. We find it Jane's subtle but effective mockery of social climbers like Mr Elton, or those with ideas above their station such as Caroline Bingley. Look closely and her novels are a keen observation of a new generation, a new order and a new century.

A coloured engraving of the French Revolution by an unknown artist (left).

1775   **1795**   **1796**   **1798**

Jane Austen

Lady Susan, Marianne and Elinor (early version of *Sense and Sensibility*)

Susan (an early version of *Northanger Abbey*)

Jane Austen born, seventh child of the Rector of Steventon

First Impressions (an early version of *Pride and Prejudice*)

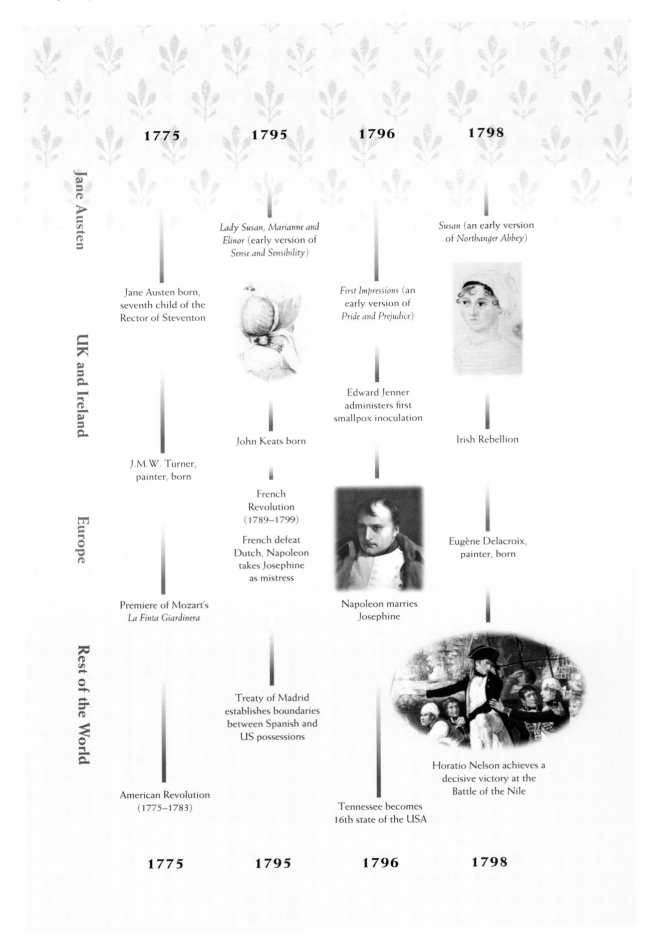

UK and Ireland

Edward Jenner administers first smallpox inoculation

John Keats born

Irish Rebellion

J.M.W. Turner, painter, born

Europe

French Revolution (1789–1799)

French defeat Dutch, Napoleon takes Josephine as mistress

Eugène Delacroix, painter, born

Premiere of Mozart's *La Finta Giardinera*

Napoleon marries Josephine

Rest of the World

Treaty of Madrid establishes boundaries between Spanish and US possessions

Horatio Nelson achieves a decisive victory at the Battle of the Nile

American Revolution (1775–1783)

Tennessee becomes 16th state of the USA

1775   **1795**   **1796**   **1798**

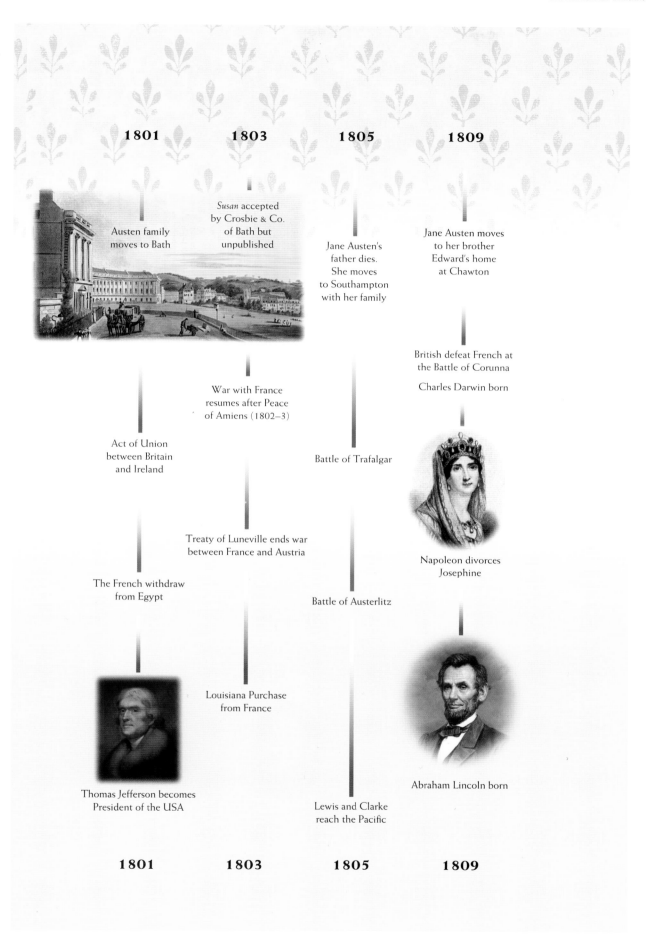

1801   **1803**   **1805**   **1809**

Austen family
moves to Bath

Susan accepted
by Crosbie & Co.
of Bath but
unpublished

Jane Austen's
father dies.
She moves
to Southampton
with her family

Jane Austen moves
to her brother
Edward's home
at Chawton

War with France
resumes after Peace
of Amiens (1802–3)

British defeat French at
the Battle of Corunna

Charles Darwin born

Act of Union
between Britain
and Ireland

Battle of Trafalgar

Treaty of Luneville ends war
between France and Austria

Napoleon divorces
Josephine

The French withdraw
from Egypt

Battle of Austerlitz

Louisiana Purchase
from France

Abraham Lincoln born

Thomas Jefferson becomes
President of the USA

Lewis and Clarke
reach the Pacific

1801   **1803**   **1805**   **1809**

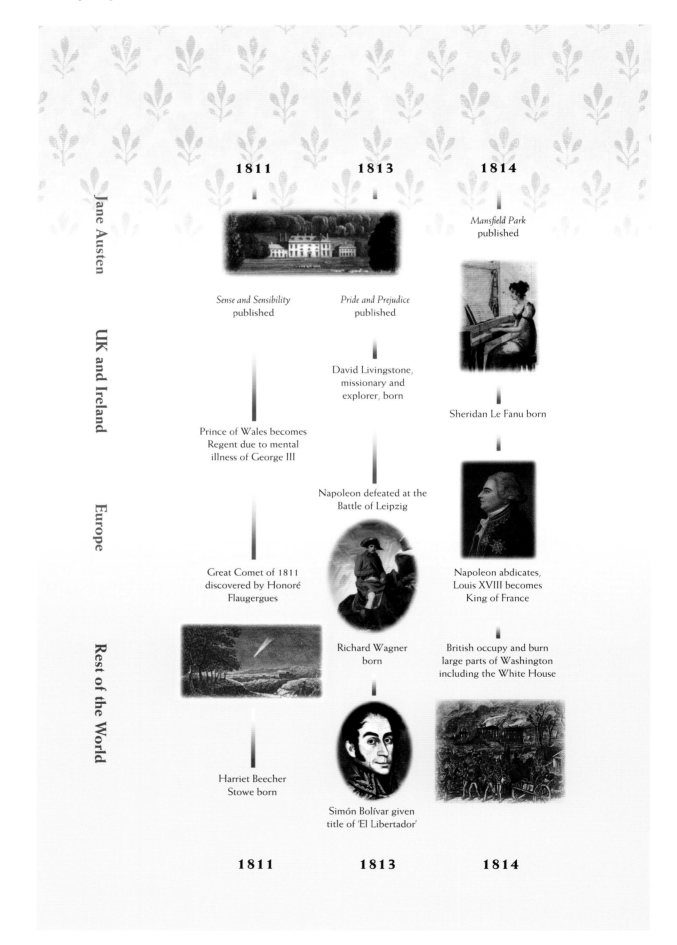

1811   **1813**   **1814**

Jane Austen

Mansfield Park
published

Sense and Sensibility
published

Pride and Prejudice
published

UK and Ireland

David Livingstone,
missionary and
explorer, born

Prince of Wales becomes
Regent due to mental
illness of George III

Sheridan Le Fanu born

Europe

Napoleon defeated at the
Battle of Leipzig

Great Comet of 1811
discovered by Honoré
Flaugergues

Napoleon abdicates,
Louis XVIII becomes
King of France

Rest of the World

Richard Wagner
born

British occupy and burn
large parts of Washington
including the White House

Harriet Beecher
Stowe born

Simón Bolívar given
title of 'El Libertador'

1811   **1813**   **1814**

1816   **1817**   **1818**   **1871**

Jane Austen dies
at Winchester
leaving *Sanditon*
unfinished

Northanger Abbey
and *Persuasion*
published

*A Memoir of Jane
Austen* by J.E.
Austen Leigh
published

Emma published

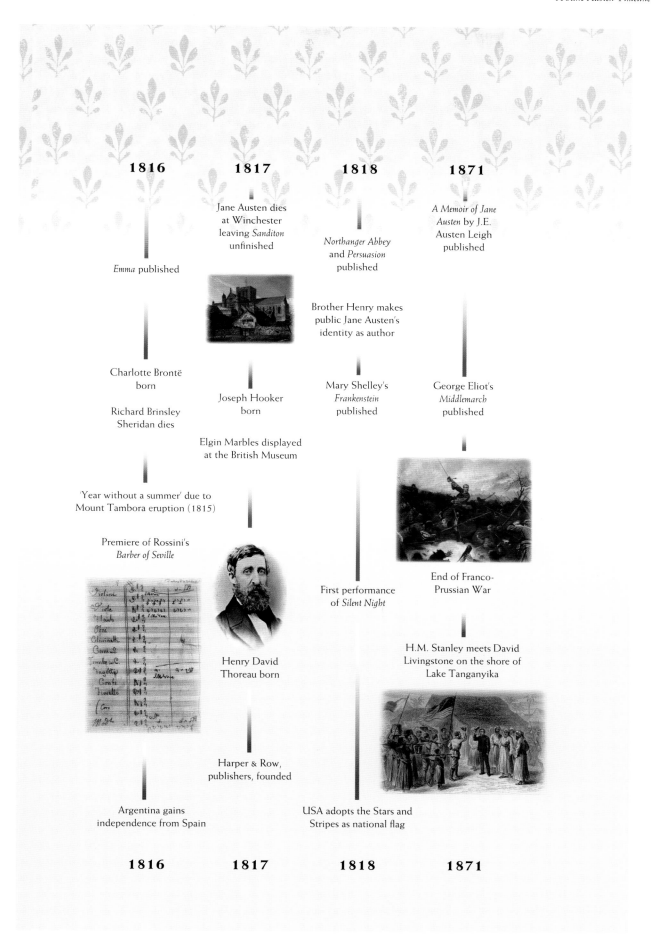

Brother Henry makes
public Jane Austen's
identity as author

Charlotte Brontë
born

Richard Brinsley
Sheridan dies

Joseph Hooker
born

Mary Shelley's
Frankenstein
published

George Eliot's
Middlemarch
published

Elgin Marbles displayed
at the British Museum

'Year without a summer' due to
Mount Tambora eruption (1815)

Premiere of Rossini's
Barber of Seville

End of Franco-
Prussian War

First performance
of *Silent Night*

Henry David
Thoreau born

H.M. Stanley meets David
Livingstone on the shore of
Lake Tanganyika

Harper & Row,
publishers, founded

Argentina gains
independence from Spain

USA adopts the Stars and
Stripes as national flag

1816   **1817**   **1818**   **1871**

Jane Austen's England

Though she sends Elizabeth Bennet to witness the beauty of the Peak District in *Pride and Prejudice*, Jane Austen herself never left the south of England. However, Austen was in no way a stationary woman and travelled frequently throughout her lifetime. The family often visited the coast for holidays, enjoying the sea air of towns such as Lyme Regis as well as trips to the great centres of society, Bath and London. Bath in particular was a significant location in Austen's life; she enjoyed her visits there as a teenager when she had Steventon to return to, but found living in the city very difficult. The villages of Steventon, and later Chawton, were where Jane felt most at ease, and they were the locations for most of her creativity.

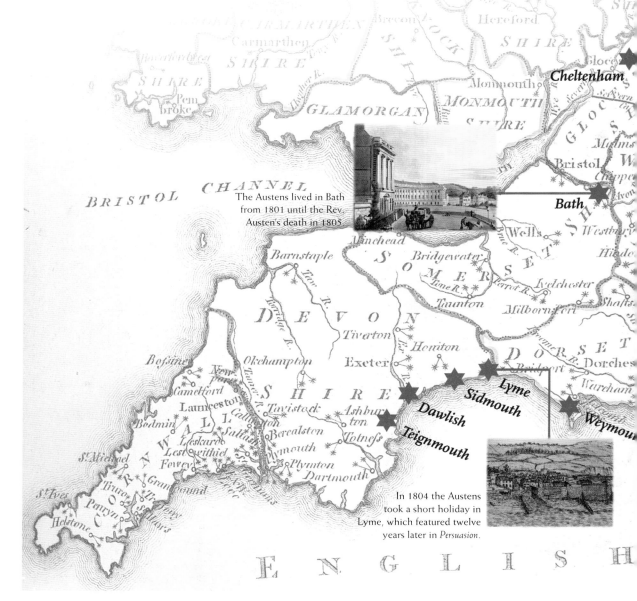

The Austens lived in Bath from 1801 until the Rev. Austen's death in 1805

In 1804 the Austens took a short holiday in Lyme, which featured twelve years later in *Persuasion*.

Though Hampshire would always be home for Jane, she did spend considerable periods away from home – particularly in her later life, when her brothers were settled with families of their own. Jane was often in Kent with her brother Edward, particularly after the death of his wife. The great house at Godmersham Park came to be one of Jane's favourite places, as well as giving her a valuable insight into the lives of the upper classes. Winchester too is a key, though sadly more sombre, location in Austen's life. It would be to Winchester that Cassandra took Jane to seek medical advice, and where she later died in the July of 1817. Winchester is now a point of pilgrimage for Austen fans, as her grave lies within the Cathedral.

Today one may follow in Jane's footsteps fairly swiftly, but for Jane these journeys would have been significantly longer. Austen's novels are full of discussions of carriages and preferable methods of transportation, as well as the dangers they still posed. The journey from Steventon to Bath, for example, would not have been a short one – it would have required a number of stops and would not have been particularly comfortable. Because of this many people often chose to travel as little as possible and, though Jane never left the south, she would generally have been considered a very well-travelled woman for her time.

The Steventon rectory (now demolished) was Jane Austen's home from her birth in 1775 until 1801.

Godmersham was owned by Edward Austen and frequently visited by Jane and Cassandra.

Southampton was home to the Austens from 1806 to 1809.

In 1809 Mrs Austen, Jane and Cassandra moved to Chawton, into a house provided by Jane's brother Edward.

Sense and Sensibility

Modern Interpretations
John Wiltshire

Sense and Sensibility was the first of Jane Austen's novels to be published (in 1811) and is arguably her least successful. With many brilliant scenes, from the introductory dialogue between Fanny Dashwood and her husband, in which she whittles his promise to his father down to nothing, to the surprise reappearance of Willoughby during Marianne Dashwood's illness, it is obviously a work of genius, but suffers from a certain clumsiness and often wooden eighteenth-century prose. More especially, there are problems with the balance between the two sister heroines – Elinor, who personates good sense, and Marianne, who embodies and expresses sensibility. Some critics believe Jane Austen definitely wants Elinor's point of view to have moral authority, whilst others respond much more enthusiastically to Marianne's fiercely romantic spirit. This seems to some to be the reverse of the author's design, or achievement. On the other hand, some believe that Jane Austen is giving a persistent critique of the 'sensible' adjustment to society that Elinor advocates.

Marilyn Butler, in *Jane Austen and the War of Ideas* (1975), presented the novel as an 'unremittingly didactic' text in which Jane Austen takes the conservative side in the ideological battles between novelists during the French Revolutionary and Napoleonic period, and hence claimed that the narrative is unequivocally sympathetic to Elinor. She argues that sensibility 'means sentimental (or revolutionary) idealism'. 'Sense' approximates to the traditional Christian personal and social ethic, 'sensibility' to a modern individualist ethic in two different manifestations, Marianne's and Lucy's (and by linking Lucy with Marianne, Butler tars her with the same self-seeking, egotistic brush). Jane Austen shows, through a series of carefully organised comparisons, the destructiveness of Marianne's romantic and 'progressive' ideas, Butler suggests. The importance of Christian self-examination and the pursuit of 'objective morality' is presented through the novel's innovative representation of Elinor's conscientious inner life. More recently, Sarah Emsley has continued a reading of the novel in didactic terms, though arguing that Austen shows both sisters 'aspiring to the ideal of virtuous behavior' (*Jane Austen's Philosophy of the Virtues*, 2005). On the other hand, Tony Tanner's essay of 1969 (reprinted in *Jane Austen*, 1988) read Marianne as a heroic victim of social conventions and false values. Claudia L. Johnson, in 1988 (*Jane Austen: Women, Politics and the Novel*), presented a view flatly in disagreement with Butler and much more akin to Tanner's, arguing that the novel 'assails the dominant ideology of its time' – patriarchal society. The novel is 'unremitting in its cynicism and iconoclasm', a critique of the bourgeois family, and an exposure of the self-deception and conventionality, not only of its villain, but its male heroes too.

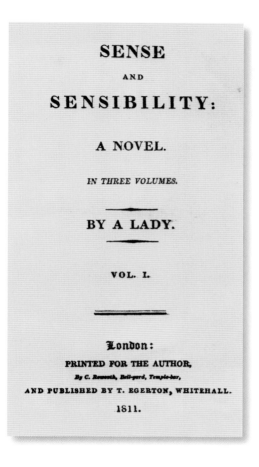

SENSE

AND

SENSIBILITY:

A NOVEL.

IN THREE VOLUMES.

BY A LADY.

VOL. I.

London:
PRINTED FOR THE AUTHOR,
By C. Roworth, Bell-yard, Temple-bar,
AND PUBLISHED BY T. EGERTON, WHITEHALL.
1811.

A Hampshire landscape at Selborne by Samuel Grimm (1733–1794).

Such modern criticism of *Sense and Sensibility* has its origins in D. W. Harding's article 'Regulated Hatred' (1940: reprinted in *Regulated Hatred and Other Essays on Jane Austen*, 1998). Harding argued that a close reading of Austen's novels shows signs of 'the eruption of fear and hatred into the relationships of everyday social life'. Their ironic technique disguises these emotions, because the preservation of civilised decorum is more important to the author than direct self-expression. This argument lies behind Tanner's essay, which demonstrated that this novel dramatises a contest between genuine feeling and the constraints of social life. The problem at its heart, he argued, is 'how much of an individual's inner world should be allowed to break out in the interests of personal vitality and psychic health'. Is the price of a civilised society – a community – the repression of authentic feeling and candid speech? The novel is energised by a genuine dialectic (which Harding had grounded in Jane Austen's own personal dilemma) between the youthful, romantic Marianne Dashwood, and her cautious, conservative sister, Elinor. Tanner developed this approach through a brilliant contrast between the 'muffled scream' that Marianne emits when she is brutally rejected by Willoughby at the very centre of the novel, and the 'screens' that Elinor Dashwood is so good at making – a metaphor, as he shows, for her impulse to hide and contain Marianne's displays of feeling. 'Between Marianne's compulsion to scream and Elinor's instinct to screen, Jane Austen brings home to us some of the problems and paradoxes involved in life in society as she knew it.'

Marianne is thus a 'self-authenticating figure of protest' whose illness in the latter part of the novel displays the cost of her passionate, and idealistic, rebellion against the exigent realities of ordinary life. For Johnson and other critics, these 'realities' would translate into patriarchy and its limitation of the possibilities and opportunities open to intelligent women. Helen Scott in *Love's Madness* (1996) similarly understands the novel to be searching for a language in which to depict the cost of women's conformity, and focuses on Marianne as a variation of the 'love-mad woman' found in other literature of the period. Eve Kosovsky Sedgwick's influential essay 'Jane Austen and the Masturbating Girl' (1991) also focuses on Marianne's symptomatic behaviour, treats the figure sympathetically, and has been widely influential. But it is clear, too, that the novel presents her illness as an occasion for reform: she confesses as much to Elinor, and even begins to speak in the accents of her sensible Christian sister. Throughout *Sense and Sensibility* Elinor is brought closer to the reader than Marianne, and therefore it can be said to support her view of wise conduct, but if most readers take the younger sister's part, they are responding to the strong vein of subversion or rebellion that is manifest in *Sense and Sensibility*'s depiction of the social world that surrounds them both. As Roger Gard argues in *Jane Austen's Novels: the Art of Clarity* (1992), the 'axis' of sense and sensibility in the novel is complicated by another whose poles are decent concern for others and, at the other extreme, boorishness, banality and the pursuit of self-interest at all cost. Yet the novel's depiction of a social world of barren trivia does enhance the readers' affinity with the sisters – to sympathise with Marianne's rejection of social forms, and to respect Elinor's capable and independent judgement. The trouble is that it prompts the reader to criticise Marianne's responses to a society which it shows, at the same time, to eminently deserve those very responses.

Moreland Perkins' *Reshaping the Sexes in Sense and Sensibility* (1998), a book-length study, is a most interesting and stimulating recent interpretation of this novel. Whilst admitting that 'most right-minded readers' are, and are meant to be, on 'the side' of the 'social rebel' Marianne, Perkins reads the novel as Elinor's story. He argues that 'in constructing Elinor, Austen opposes the patriarchally imposed concept of genteel feminine gender'. Elinor is presented as an accomplished intellectual, a woman who enjoys the exercise of her mind, is capable of subjecting her own feelings to rational analysis, without losing touch with them, and displays the 'principled scepticism' that her era associated with the masculine gender. Edward Ferrars, on the other hand, is endowed with many of the characteristics associated with the female. His 'reticent domesticity', his self-deprecation and subservience to his family, all combine to subvert, or 'reconstruct', the conventional ideal of masculinity – making him, as the performance of Hugh Grant in 1995 suggested, a virtual new age guy.

Willoughby and Marianne, from Sense and Sensibility.

This film of *Sense and Sensibility* (1995), with script by Emma Thompson and directed by Ang Lee, is one of the more successful of the Austen film adaptations. There was a BBC adaptation of the novel broadcast in 1985, but by contrast it is wooden and tedious. The Thompson/Lee film is certainly a more generous work than the novel. 'Most of the laughter in *Sense and Sensibility* is hollow,' comments Rachel M. Brownstein in her section on the book in the *Cambridge Companion to Jane Austen* (1997). Neither of the heroines takes any pleasure in their neighbours' silly jokes. In the film the audience is invited to laugh along with Sir John Middleton and Mrs Jennings, whose warmth and benevolence are unmistakable. Thompson's script expands the comic potential in what is sometimes a dour, even censorious narrative, in which distress plays a much larger role than in any other of Austen's published writings. For long stretches of the book Elinor is troubled about Edward Ferrars's behaviour to her; Marianne is made ill by Willoughby's treatment, and the comedy, which centres around near-caricature figures, is often sour. A number of them – Fanny Dashwood and her weak husband; the Palmers, a mutually uncomprehending couple in the vein of the Bennets; Anne Steele, Robert Ferrars – are simply offered to the reader as objects of dislike, embodiments of stupidity, uncultivated folly and mercenary self-interest. Even Lucy Steele, vivid in her slyly persistent self-interest, is hardly developed, the reader's view of her always mediated through Elinor's sufferings at her hands. Mrs Jennings is an exception. It gradually becomes clear that she is a warm-hearted and generous woman, and that Marianne's intolerant views of her are unjust, but not before the reader has been treated to an extended display of her garrulous lack of tact.

One way in which the script reworks the novel is in the matter of children. Young children, such as the unruly toddler Walter Musgrove in *Persuasion*, who climbs on Anne Elliot's back and won't let go, occur in several of

"Why was he to ruin himself and their poor little Harry?"

Austen's novels, but only in *Sense and Sensibility* are they mentioned at some length and with what one might call old-maidish intolerance. Passage after passage displays the Middletons and the Steeles drooling over and spoiling the little dears. The film deletes all of these scenes, and instead develops the figure of the third, and youngest, Dashwood sister, Margaret, who hardly has anything to do in the novel. An active, imaginative eleven-year-old, Margaret is gifted with perception and an independent spirit. Her innocently pertinent remarks puncture the decorum that governs genteel behaviour with a comic effect attractive to modern audiences. (Austen's is the pre-romantic view that children need discipline and education, Thompson's the post-romantic view of them as free spirits.) The script uses Margaret in a series of amusing incidents with Edward Ferrars. The friendship between the two is one of the ways Edward's credentials are established and helps to make the rather pallid, anxious figure of the novel charming. The entirely invented scene in which Margaret is lured from her hiding place – with the atlas under the library table – by Elinor and Edward's impromptu comic dialogue about the source of the Nile deftly suggests how well these two adults might get on – and that they share the same sense of humour.

In 'Conservative Austen, Radical Austen: *Sense and Sensibility* from text to screen' in *Adaptations* (1999), however, Julian North revisits the conservative versus 'subversive' debate that surrounds this text and argues that the film 'erodes' the distinction between sense and sensibility and 'smoothes over ideological conflicts within the novel'. But it could be argued that the film in fact corrects many of the text's weaknesses. Colonel Brandon is unsatisfactory to most readers, and his introduction into the novel in Chapters 7 and 8 as an older man, 'silent and grave', is almost entirely through the disparaging eyes of Marianne. In Lee's film his entry is managed carefully: an anonymous figure is first seen riding up to the front entrance of the house; then his silhouette, unreadable against the light behind, enters the house; gradually, as the camera tracks back with his progress through the rooms, he comes into focus, his face intermittently lit, partially shadowed, until he emerges into the light, lured by the accompanying sound of Marianne's singing. He stands, silent and grave indeed, but imbued by these cinematic means with a powerful presence, which is picked up in Elinor's quick glance at this male standing in the doorway mesmerised by the girl at the piano. Throughout the film, Brandon retains the mysterious potency created through this entrance, an effect increased by his broken hints at a painful past.

Brandon is shadowy in the novel and Elinor throughout is a figure of suppressed emotion. 'Her feelings were strong; but she knew how to govern them,' the reader is told in the first chapter. For most of the book, though, Elinor's feelings are less obvious than her unremitting control – a result of the contrast with Marianne. It is true, as North argues, that Marianne is presented dramatically, whereas Elinor is revealed to the reader through her inner meditations, and that this distinction is blurred in the film – inevitably, perhaps. But in the novel, Elinor is not merely a stoic figure. It is part of Jane Austen's purpose to delay overt revelation of Elinor's strength of feeling till towards its close. As Perkins points out, for much of the text, we are often told of Elinor's deep feeling, but it is only in three late scenes that we are shown it convincingly. The first two emphatic representations of her emotional life – her sharing of Marianne's suffering at Willoughby's hands, and then the scenes of near despair as she watches alone over Marianne's sickbed – are followed immediately by her encounter with Willoughby, unable to keep away from the woman he really loves. In this remarkable scene, Elinor is shown to respond to his physical charm, and even allows his sexual allure temporarily to influence her judgement of his conduct. But their encounter, which expands the reader's sense of Elinor's emotional life, partially redeems the villain, and complicates the whole of the novel's emphasis on companionate love and marriage, is omitted from the film.

If Elinor is to become a sympathetic presence, though, the movie needs to show that Marianne's harsh criticisms of her sister's lack of romantic feeling are unfair. It does this by providing scenes in which Elinor and Edward are clearly attracted to one another. But this is not enough, and needs to be supplemented by indications of Elinor's emotional life. One scene which is directed to this purpose parallels Brandon's later introduction. Edward Ferrars walks through Norland house to find Elinor standing alone in the doorway, her back to the camera, listening to Marianne playing the piano. She is weeping: 'That was my father's favourite.' Edward gives her his handkerchief with which to dry her eyes. Much later, when under Lucy Steele's attack, she is seen in her bedroom, from behind, using Edward's handkerchief, with his initials embroidered on it, again. This certainly has the effect of making Elinor more akin to Marianne than she appears to be in the novel, but in these and other scenes it is important that her outbreaks of emotion are observed only by the camera.

The suppression of feeling is, in fact, a leading motif of the film, perhaps most remarkably in the scene when Elinor performs the task, painful to her and potentially embarrassing to both of them, of disclosing Brandon's gift which will enable Edward to marry Lucy. This is shot with a stable unmoving camera: Elinor and Edward face each other in silhouette. The screenplay for the film gives the actors many hints ('his eyes full of growing comprehension', 'his eyes full of sadness'). But instead of the close-ups these suggest, which would have explored both the characters' uneasy emotions, the camera holds its distance. The direction of the film replicates the control which they themselves exert. This control over powerful feelings gets its dramatic pay-off when Edward comes to Barton Cottage and reveals that it is his brother Robert who has in fact married Lucy. In the novel, 'Elinor could sit no longer. She almost ran out of the room, and as soon as the door was closed, burst into tears of joy.' Decorum – those screens around private feelings that Tanner showed are omnipresent in the novel – is still kept up. In the film, Elinor has no such self-control: as Edward finishes speaking she slumps into a nearby chair and bursts into 'tears of joy', hysterical at first, but turning into joyousness. Perhaps the alteration from the novel makes, as North suggests, 'Elinor become Marianne', but this relief from

Their landlord – called to welcome them.

"For shame, Willoughby. Can you wait for an invitation here?"

prolonged misery, this climactic bursting out of repressed emotion, is an entirely credible and gratifying release, as much to the audience as to the character. It has been earned, personally and cinematically.

The film does not ignore the ideological debates, which structure both the novel and its subsequent criticism. Indeed, these are transfigured in its controlling moral motif. It opens with a grim scene in which a dying Mr Dashwood, with intense urgency, extracts from his son a promise to look after his mother and sisters. In the subsequent satiric sequence, this is progressively turned into nothing. John Dashwood's broken promise to his father (not an all-pervasive 'patriarchy') leaves the sisters in near-poverty and is the premise of both the novel's and film's later action. Later, Lucy Steele exacts a promise from Elinor that she will tell no-one of her engagement to Edward, and therefore Elinor, whose heart is broken, cannot confide in, and in effect must deceive, her sister. Her fortitude, which Sarah Emsley sees as the leading virtue promoted by the novel, is tested here. Marianne's reproach that she 'communicates nothing' is the more bitter to Elinor because she cannot break silence without breaking her promises to others. The film cannot make manifest the intellectual abilities which are so much a part of Austen's conception of Elinor, but the working out of this theme gives her stature. When Edward obliquely confesses his feelings for Elinor (though he accepts that he now must marry Lucy) he says, 'Your friendship has been the most important of my life.' She replies, 'You will always have it.' 'Forgive me,' he responds, and she uses this hint at his feelings for the film's most telling moment of moral authority: 'Mr Ferrars, you honour your promises – that is more important than anything else. I wish you – both – very happy.' Keeping their promises exacts a painful cost from each of them, all the more painful because it is, here as elsewhere, unspoken. This gives austere dignity to a film which has been sometimes thought a sentimental adaptation of a problematic and challenging novel.

Regency Life
Maggie Lane

Crime and Society

Neither the great gulf that lay between rich and poor, educated and uneducated, nor (to modern sensibilities) the injustices of colonialism, transportation, slavery and war, provoked Jane Austen to protest in her fiction. Famously, she was not that kind of writer. She set out to entertain and, as a by-product, to offer moral guidance in conducting personal and social life – but she never wanted to change the structure of society. What she advocated was for each member of society, wherever they found themselves, to behave to those above, around and below with kindliness, respect and sensitivity. In no novel more than *Sense and Sensibility* are the pressures of society on the individual more palpable, or the right response to those pressures more minutely examined.

Jane Austen was well placed to observe her society, belonging to the literate, middling classes, poor and insignificant in herself but with family connections to those with, or close to, real power. The society she portrays and knew so well offered a degree of social mobility, as individuals could rise (or fall) by their own efforts. Yet the structure itself stayed much the same. It was a pyramid, with wealth, rank and prestige concentrated at the top, and new money derived from trade making constant incursions, via marriage or purchase of land, into layers that part welcomed, part resisted – but was certainly refreshed by – its ambition.

Beneath the Royal family itself – with whom Jane Austen once had dealings in the shape of a command from the Prince Regent to dedicate her next novel to him (which she did with some reluctance) – came the nobility: 'Dukes, Marquisses, Earls, Viscounts and Barons' as Jane herself correctly listed them in order of rank in a letter to her niece Anna. These comprised some three hundred families, and their fictional counterparts are almost wholly absent from Austen's work.

Next in prestige came the landed gentry. In 1803 there were 540 baronets and 350 knights, both ranks carrying the title 'Sir' with the man's Christian name, and 'Lady' with his surname for his wife. (When a Lady is addressed by *her* Christian name, she is the *daughter* of nobility, such as Lady Anne Darcy in *Pride and Prejudice* who has married a plain Mr Darcy.) Baronet was an hereditary title, passing from father to son, while knight died with the man on whom – probably for some service to his monarch – it had been conferred. In *Sense and Sensibility*, Sir John Middleton is the holder of a baronetcy. With such a connection on their mother's side, as well as their paternal forbears' landed estates, the Dashwood sisters, for all their present poverty, belong effortlessly to a rank in which ladies do not earn their own living, or travel in a public stagecoach, or can be made to feel inferior in breeding or manners.

Titled families are in the minority in Jane Austen's novels; most of her characters are at the level of the 6,000 landed squires, and 20,000 private and professional gentlemen, who together made up about 1.4 per cent of the national population and enjoyed about 15.7 per cent of its wealth at the turn of the eighteenth century. These are the families that automatically socialised together within a country neighbourhood – nobody who possessed the right status could opt out – and who varied their country lives by occasional visits to London or Bath, where any rusticity was polished away as everybody observed and imitated one another. These too were the literate and leisured classes, for whom conduct books and novels provided additional instruction on the mores of their kind.

Despite the fact that everybody had their place, and knew their place, and knew within a few moments of meeting somebody else *their* exact place in this body of English gentry – there was no sense of status. Rather, in Jane Austen's novels, as in the society they so faithfully reflect, there is a constant perception of each person jostling to assert their position or to forge ahead and drag their families with them, while looking down on and blocking those beneath. *Sense and Sensibility* is full of such strains and stresses. Mrs Ferrars and her daughter Fanny are the worst snobs, but everybody is infected to some extent. The vulgarity of the Steele sisters is a matter of scorn to their counterparts, the equally impoverished Dashwoods. Of course the Steeles are on the make and the Dashwoods are not – but still, no allowance is made for the difficulties of the former's circumstances. Mrs Jennings, whose wealth comes from her late husband's trade, is similarly vulgar, and is equally deplored (even while her hospitality is accepted) by Marianne, but Mrs Jennings' good heart wins the affection of first Elinor, then even Marianne. Lack of breeding can be alleviated by a generous spirit, which is one lesson the novel teaches.

The term 'class' was first used in 1753, when five classes had been mooted: the nobility, the gentry, the genteel trades, the common trades and the peasantry. The difference between the genteel and common trades was that the former required some capital, education and manners. A common tradesman – as, from her low-class name, we assume Biddy Henshaw's father to have been in *Sense and Sensibility* – might, of course, accumulate enough wealth to launch his children into a higher class. The phrase 'middle classes' was first used in 1797 and 'working classes' in 1813. But more usually during the period in which Jane Austen was writing, the term for the different levels in society was 'orders' or 'ranks'. These terms have a more fixed connotation than class, which is relatively fluid. 'The lower orders' for the people of Jane Austen's world encompassed not only what we think of as the working classes doing manual labour on the land or (unknown to Jane Austen) in factories, but the people who were encountered and taken for granted every day in their own homes – their army of servants.

Beneath the deserving poor, who laboured for their keep, came the paupers and criminal classes. These figure very little in Jane Austen's fiction, though their existence is felt as the dark underside in that generally joyous novel, *Emma*. In Jane Austen's lifetime, the number of crimes which carried the death penalty rose from 160 to 225, as successive governments panicked at the rising rate of lawlessness brought on, for the most part, by poverty and destitution. Anyone over the age of seven who was found guilty of one of these crimes, many of them exceedingly petty, could be hanged. From 1788 the sentence was often transmuted to transportation to the penal colonies of Australia, and although this was for a fixed term, very few ex-prisoners would have had the means for getting back to their homes and families.

It is a quite extraordinary fact that Jane Austen's own aunt, the wealthy Mrs Leigh Perrot, was in 1800 arrested, gaoled and tried at the Taunton Assizes for the theft from a Bath shop of lace worth one shilling and that, had she been found guilty, she could have been hanged but would almost certainly have been transported. Her devoted husband actually made arrangements to sell all his property and accompany her to the other side of the world. Mrs Austen offered her daughters to support their aunt at her trial; Mrs

Leigh Perrot declined, declaring it would cut her to the heart to have two young ladies gawped at in court. This is how close Jane Austen herself came to being witness to the brutal criminal justice system of her time.

In her novels, this side of life is largely ignored. In *Sense and Sensibility*, poverty is the genteel poverty of the Steeles and the Dashwoods, and crime itself is, in fact, confined to the gentry classes. That is, a crime is committed by Colonel Brandon when he challenges Willoughby to a duel. Duelling had become a crime in the reign of George III, though of 172 known duels in that reign, resulting in 91 deaths, only eighteen cases had ever been brought to trial, and only two men had been executed. Nevertheless, the upright, honourable Colonel Brandon is the only one of Jane Austen's heroes to engage in a criminal activity.

Elsewhere in *Sense and Sensibility* the murky underworld of Georgian life is suggested by the fall from polite society of the two Elizas, mother and daughter. Once a highly respectable young woman and loved by Colonel Brandon himself, the elder Eliza slips into prostitution as the only way to keep herself; her illegitimate daughter, the other Eliza, though afforded some protection by Colonel Brandon, is living at the margins of society and finds herself pregnant and abandoned by her seducer, Willoughby. For Jane Austen and her contemporaries, it really was a truth universally acknowledged that for a woman one false step could lead to ostracism and penury; Marianne herself later realises, with a shudder, that it was not impossible when she loved Willoughby that she too might have fallen into the same trap. As Jane Austen observes elsewhere (in *Mansfield Park*) the penalties for sexual transgression were widely different for men and women – at least in this world.

Landscape and the Picturesque

One of the factors pushing more and more of the population into poverty and crime was enclosure of the open fields and common land that had once provided the peasantry with subsistence farming. Though enclosure led to many improvements in agriculture including increased yields to feed the growing population, on an individual level, it could be disastrous. Families who had once been self-sufficient in food, however meagre, and however hard their lives, were now forced into labouring for a master, employed and often even housed at his whim. The potential for all the social ills of dislocation, vagrancy, starvation, poaching, theft and extreme punishment was very great. 'Poverty has very much sensibly increased: the husbandmen come to the parish [i.e. for aid], for want of employment,' reported Arthur Young in his *General Report on Enclosure*, 1808.

In *Emma* Jane Austen gives us a portrait of prosperous farming with a human face, and there can be no doubt that she viewed enclosure, and the application of intelligent minds to the business of farming, favourably. But she was not unaware of its consequences when handled inhumanely. Hence in *Sense and Sensibility* we encounter the wealthy John Dashwood, who has already shown meanness to his half-sisters, planning to boost his income

She could have no doubt of it being Edward's face.

yet more by enclosing Norland Common. Not wrong in itself, perhaps, but we know that it is likely to be wrong in his hands, and that he will have no care at all for the poor people whose livelihood he is taking away. We can be certain that they will be left to shift for themselves – certainly, if his wife has anything to do with it (and she will!). Enclosing land, together with politics and breaking horses, is the topic of conversation among the gentlemen at Mrs Ferrars' dinner party when the ladies retire.

If landscape can be said to belong to one of three categories – natural, cultivated for production, and cultivated for aesthetic pleasure – then ideas about all three sorts were changing during Jane Austen's lifespan. As Acts of Enclosure were passed, land that had once been waste or semi-waste came into cultivation; the new landowners planted hedges round their fields, and clumps of trees for shelter and timber. This is the kind of landscape that Jane Austen herself seems to have most appreciated: productive land, kept in good trim. Then there was the ornamentation of land, which was slightly more questionable in her view. Again, the John Dashwoods are the offenders in *Sense and Sensibility*, rooting up the old walnut trees (productivity) to make way for glasshouses and flower beds (fashion).

In contrast, Colonel Brandon is a good steward of his inheritance, Delaford. Mrs Jennings describes this estate as 'a nice old-fashioned place, full of comforts and conveniences; quite shut in with great garden walls that are covered with the best fruit trees in the country'. A particularly well-balanced estate, drawing its author's approval, is Cleveland, the country home of Thomas Palmer, MP. It has a productive kitchen garden, greenhouse and poultry-yard. But its extensive grounds, which Jane Austen makes sure to tell us is not a park – that is, not entitled by Act of Parliament to keep deer – makes a further contribution to landscape, typical of the mid-eighteenth century, when the fashion was to beautify grounds with classical buildings. A Grecian temple on the horizon attracts Marianne's attention and causes her to walk too far in wet grass. Typically, Marianne seeks out what is wildest and furthest away from the rest of mankind.

Marianne is the character with the most ardent response to nature and landscape in any of the novels; for her it is part of the sensibility on which she so prides herself as being superior to most other people. In this, Jane Austen distances herself from Marianne, taking a more rational stance. She gives some of this rationality to Elinor, who remarks dryly after one of Marianne's raptures, 'It is not everyone who has your passion for dead leaves.' The early chapters of *Sense and Sensibility* have much to say – some of it mocking – about appreciation of landscape. In a memorable passage, Edward Ferrars, who stands for common sense, engages Marianne in a lengthy debate on a subject which was a hot topic with the reading public in the 1790s when the novel was conceived.

According to her brother Henry, Jane Austen herself was 'a warm and judicious admirer of landscape, both in nature and on canvas'. In the same short biographical notice about his sister published shortly after her death,

Henry says, 'she was early enamoured of Gilpin on the Picturesque.' Here he identifies the source of the fashion to which Jane Austen responds in all her early novels, but in *Sense and Sensibility* most of all.

William Gilpin, a clergyman and amateur artist, published a series of books between 1782 and 1800 – Jane's childhood years – assessing the scenery of the wilder parts of Britain in terms of 'that kind of beauty that would look good in a picture'. This is the meaning of his term 'picturesque'. He favoured the rough and the rugged over the smooth and the tamed. Running concurrently with improvements in agriculture, the picturesque movement opened people's eyes to the value – aesthetic, not practical – of *un*cultivated land.

It was as if having manipulated nature to their own advantage more than any other generation before them, people wanted to get back to nature in the raw – at least when they were on holiday, if not around their own homes. Gilpin's sketching tours included the Lake District, the Highlands of Scotland, South Wales and the Wye Valley, the West of England and the Isle of Wight, rejecting tidy farms and seeking out mountains, forests and moors. These books, introducing new ideas to a large swathe of the literate classes – including the Austen family – set off a craze for sightseeing travel, and brought a new appreciation of the natural beauty of their own country, the wilder parts of which had formerly been regarded as at best worthless, at worst hostile and dangerous. Now they were ready to be thrilled by a little danger. Gilpin captured the spirit of the age. The Austens might never have taken seaside holidays in the West Country if they had not read William Gilpin.

She immediately left the room

His writing is full of technical terms with regard to drawing, and he was strict as to composition. For example, something like a gnarled tree should occupy the side of the picture, drawing the eye in; and if cattle were introduced in the middle distance, to give a sense of perspective, they should be grouped in threes or fives, never twos or fours. His concepts engaged Jane Austen's deep but not uncritical interest. While she received from Gilpin valuable impressions and information about parts of her country she was never likely to see, and while she was certainly in favour of looking discriminatingly at her surroundings, she was quick to note what was ridiculous in his more extreme pronouncements. All three of the novels written by her in the 1790s introduce discussion of his ideas.

In *Pride and Prejudice*, Elizabeth Bennet and her uncle and aunt plan a trip (later curtailed) to the Lakes, and do get to view the natural wonders of Derbyshire. They are among the first 'tourists' in literature. Elizabeth also makes a knowing remark, when invited by Darcy and the two Bingley sisters to join them on a path, 'No, no; stay where you are. You are charmingly group'd and appear to uncommon advantage. The picturesque would be spoilt by admitting a fourth.'

In *Northanger Abbey*, Catherine Morland is instructed by Henry Tilney on the elements of picturesque scenery when they walk up Beechen Cliff above Bath: 'He talked of foregrounds, distances and second distances – sidescreens and perspectives – light and shades; and Catherine was so hopeful a scholar that when they gained the top of Beechen Cliff, she voluntarily rejected the whole city of Bath as unworthy to make part of a landscape.'

Henry is not a natural bore or a pedant. Jane Austen puts this jargon into his mouth to make fun of it. Marianne laments that too much discussion of landscape has become a mere jargon and refers to Gilpin, though not by name. Edward Ferrars, a less witty and subversive hero than Henry, seems to express his author's views: 'I like a fine prospect, but not on picturesque principles. I do not like crooked, twisted, blasted trees. I admire them much more if they are tall, straight and flourishing. I do not like ruined, tattered cottages. I am not fond of nettles, or thistles, or heath blossoms. I have more pleasure in a snug farmhouse than a watch-tower – and a troop of tidy, happy villagers please me more than the finest banditti in the world.'

This last detail is a sly reference to the Italian landscape paintings which had first inspired Gilpin to look at his own country with a painter's eye. For Jane Austen, not only is the happiness of the population paramount, but England should look like England: what in *Emma* she calls 'a sweet view, sweet to the eye and to the mind. English verdure, English culture, English comfort' – her ideal.

Geographical Settings
Caroline Sanderson

Sense and Sensibility opens in the English county of Sussex, where the family of Dashwood has 'long been settled' at the large estate of Norland Park. Successive generations of the family have lived there 'in so respectable a manner, as to engage the general good opinion of their surrounding acquaintance'. So it is a huge wrench when the wife and daughters of Mr Henry Dashwood decide to quit 'that beloved spot' for ever, following his untimely death. 'Dear, dear Norland!', exclaims Marianne Dashwood on their final evening in Sussex, 'when shall I cease to regret you! – when learn to feel a home elsewhere!'

At first they have no intention of leaving Sussex. With her son John Dashwood and his wife Fanny already installed at Norland, however, Mrs Dashwood struggles to find a house in the neighbourhood 'that at once answered her notions of comfort and ease, and suited the prudence of her eldest daughter, whose steadier judgement rejected several houses as too large for their income'. Heavily influenced by the 'narrow-minded and selfish' Fanny, John neglects to make adequate provision for his mother and half-sisters, leaving them only five hundred a year between them to live on. 'What on earth can four women want for more than that? They will live so cheap! … I am sure I cannot imagine how they will spend half of it,' the avaricious Fanny remarks.

It is not financial considerations, however, which finally make Mrs Dashwood determined to leave Sussex, but rather Fanny's offensive behaviour when she realises that her brother Edward Ferrars is growing increasingly attached to Elinor. 'To quit the neighbourhood was no longer an evil; it was an object of desire; it was a blessing, in comparison of the misery of continuing her daughter-in-law's guest.' She immediately accepts the timely offer from her cousin, Sir John Middleton of 'a small house on very easy terms', almost two hundred miles away in Devon.

The house, Barton Cottage, lies on Sir John's Barton Park estate, which, we are told, is 'within four miles northward of Exeter', Devon's principal town. Such is the distance from Norland to Barton by road that the Dashwood's furniture – including Marianne's 'handsome pianoforte' – is all sent round by water. Despite their sadness at having left Norland, their first sight of the Barton Valley is a cheering one. 'It was a pleasant fertile spot, well wooded, and rich in pasture.' The situation of Barton Cottage also meets with their approval. 'High hills rose immediately behind, and at no great distance on each side, some of which were open downs, the others culti-vated and woody. The village of Barton was chiefly on one of these hills, and formed a pleasant view from the cottage windows. The prospect in front was more extensive; it commanded the whole of the valley, and reached into the country beyond.' Thus Jane Austen paints a picture of the verdant landscape typical of this part of Devon, with its rolling hills and deep wooded valleys known locally as coombes. Barton – the ancient West Country name for the principal farm of a parish – is a common place-name in this part of the world.

With what indignation such a letter as this must be read by Miss Dashwood

Were her detailed descriptions of Barton inspired by Jane Austen's own visits to Devon? We know for certain that she made two visits to the county in 1801 and 1802, a few years after the writing of *Sense and Sensibility* was completed in 1798. However, she did make revisions to the novel from 1809 onwards, prior to its publication in 1811. The Austens had a family friend in Devon – the Revd Richard Buller, son of the Bishop of Exeter, and a former pupil of Jane's father, Mr George Austen. From 1799 to 1806, Buller was vicar of Colyton, a village a few miles from the coast in East Devon, close to the border with Dorset. Shortly after his marriage in 1800, Jane writes amusingly of having received a 'most affectionate' letter from him. 'I was afraid he would oppress me by his felicity & his Love for his Wife, but this is not the case; he calls her simply Anna, without any angelic embellishments for which I respect & wish him Happy.' Jane also writes that Revd Buller is 'very pressing in his invitation to us to come & see him at Colyton, & my father is very much inclined to go there next Summer. It is a circumstance that may considerably assist the Dawlish scheme.'

In the late eighteenth century, Dawlish, a former fishing village on the south coast of Devon, some fifteen miles from Exeter, was developed as a seaside resort, and it continues to attract holidaymakers today. The Austens holidayed there in 1802: in a letter to her niece Anna, written in 1814, Jane Austen remarks that the library at Dawlish 'was particularly pitiful & wretched 12 years ago and not likely to have anybody's publication'. Jane's ambivalent attitude towards Dawlish extends to *Sense and Sensibility*. It is

Sidmouth in Devon, where the Austens stayed in 1801.

the town chosen by Robert Ferrars and Lucy Steele for their honeymoon, where they pass 'some months in great happiness for (Lucy) had many relations and old acquaintance to cut'. Earlier, when Elinor is introduced to Robert Ferrars for the first time in London, he expresses great surprise that 'anybody could live in Devonshire without living near Dawlish'.

The Austens also stayed at Sidmouth, another south Devon resort, in 1801. According to Austen family legend, it was during one of these Devon holidays that Jane met a man whom she felt that she could love. The story came from her sister Cassandra, years after Jane's death, and was recorded by her niece Caroline Austen in a letter to her brother James Edward Austen-Leigh in 1869. 'In Devonshire an acquaintance was made with some very charming man – I never heard Aunt Cass speak of anyone with such admiration – she had no doubt that a mutual attachment was in progress between him and her sister. They parted – but he made it plain that he should seek them out again – & shortly afterwards, he died!'

Though seventeen-year-old Marianne Dashwood has already declared 'that I shall never see a man whom I can really love. I require so much!', Devon has a painful affair of the heart in store for her too. Once the Dashwoods are settled at Barton Cottage, they begin to explore the local area, which abounds in beautiful walks. They soon discover Allenham, 'an ancient, respectable looking mansion,' which reminds them of Norland. When Marianne twists her ankle whilst hurrying home in the rain, she is rescued by Willoughby, a relative of Mrs Smith, the old lady to whom Allenham belongs. Willoughby has an estate called Combe Magna in the neighbouring county of Somerset, and he later makes Marianne a present of a horse he has bred here.

Rising hastily walked for a few minutes about the room

As Marianne and Willoughby become inseparable, an excursion is arranged to Whitwell, the house of Colonel Brandon's brother-in-law, which lies twelve miles from Barton and has 'highly beautiful grounds', including a lake to sail on. The excursion has to be cancelled at the eleventh hour, however, when Colonel Brandon is called to London on urgent business. He rides to the nearby town of Honiton fifteen miles away, where he picks up the mail coach to London. Little do those in the disappointed excursion party suspect that he has at last received news of his ward, Eliza, who disappeared from Bath eight months before in the company of Willoughby. He later abandoned her, destitute and pregnant with his child. Not long afterwards, Willoughby is himself compelled to leave for London, after Mrs Smith gets wind of his entanglement with Eliza. When Willoughby refuses to make an honest woman of her, Mrs Smith dismisses him from 'her favour and her house'.

Soon after Willoughby has departed, leaving Marianne distraught, in Devon, Edward Ferrars arrives at Barton Cottage having spent a fortnight with friends near Plymouth, some forty miles to the south. Marianne is greatly taken aback that Edward has been in the county for a whole two weeks without riding over to see Elinor. Then, Sir John Middleton's sister-in-law, Charlotte, comes to stay at Barton Park with her husband. Mr and Mrs Palmer live at Cleveland in Somerset, which, we are told, is about thirty miles from Willoughby's home at Combe Magna. Mrs Palmer tries to persuade Elinor and Marianne to spend part of the winter season in London, as was the custom for the landed gentry. 'I shall be quite disappointed if you do not. I could get the nicest house in the world for you, next door to our's in Hanover-square,' enthuses Charlotte. Elinor and Marianne politely decline the invitation.

Meanwhile, during the course of a morning excursion to Exeter, Sir John's mother-in-law Mrs Jennings meets by chance two ladies to whom she is related – Miss Anne and Miss Lucy Steele – , and immediately invites them to stay at Barton Park. Through their obsequious behaviour, the Miss Steeles quickly ingratiate themselves with Lady Middleton. Lucy Steele wastes no time in revealing to Elinor her secret engagement to Edward Ferrars, whom she had come to know during the four years he was a pupil of her uncle, Mr Pratt at Longstaple. It was with the Miss Steeles that Edward had been staying, prior to his arrival at Barton Cottage.

Mrs Ferrars

The Miss Steeles remain at Barton Park for almost two months, celebrating Christmas with the Middletons. With the New Year just around the corner, however, Mrs Jennings decides to return to London, and invites Elinor and Marianne to accompany her. 'I would have every young woman of your condition in life acquainted with the manners and amusements of London.' This time, they are more easily persuaded, particularly Marianne who is desperate to see Willoughby again. The journey to London takes three days by chaise. Since the death of her husband, 'who had traded with success in a less elegant part of the town,' Mrs Jennings 'had resided every winter in a house in one of the streets near Portman-square'. The house is in Berkeley Street, now Upper Berkeley Street, and is 'handsome and handsomely fitted up'.

Willoughby's London lodgings are in Bond Street, still a smart shopping street today, just as it was in Jane Austen's time, when fashionable young men about town were known as 'Bond Street loungers'. A whole day having passed with no word from Willoughby, Marianne is restless and distracted during their shopping expedition, particularly in Bond Street itself where she 'could with difficulty govern her vexation at the tediousness of Mrs Palmer … who dawdled away her time in rapture and indecision'. It is from Bond Street that Willoughby later writes his cruel letter to Marianne, in which he professes himself quite unaware of any intimacy between them. Much later we discover that the words are actually those of Miss Sophia Grey, his heiress wife to be, which she has forced Willoughby to copy.

'Here I am once more in this Scene of Dissipation & vice, and I begin already to find my Morals corrupted,' wrote Jane Austen from London in August 1796, in one of her earliest surviving letters. She was staying in Cork Street, just around the corner from Bond Street, en route for Rowling in Kent, the home of her brother Edward. At that time, coaches from the west and south of England set their passengers down at the White Horse Cellar in Piccadilly. The White Horse was close to Burlington House, an eighteenth-century mansion, which, with its later Victorian facade, is now home to the Royal Academy. Just to the north of Cork Street, now renowned for its art galleries, is Conduit Street, where Sir John and Lady Middleton have their London residence, and to the south, back towards Piccadilly, is Sackville Street, home of Gray's, the jeweller's shop where Elinor is 'carrying on a negociation (*sic*) for the exchange of a few old-fashioned jewels of her mother'.

Gray's is very busy when the Dashwoods visit. 'All that could be done was to sit down at that end of the counter which seemed to promise the quickest succession; one gentleman only was standing there, and it is probable that Elinor was not without hope of exciting his politeness to a quicker dispatch.' The gentleman, however, who turns out to be none other than 'coxcomb' Robert Ferrars, spends a further quarter of an hour 'examining and debating … over every toothpick-case in the shop'. Elinor, who does not recognise Edward's brother, never having met him, is left with the 'remembrance of a person and face of strong, natural, sterling insignificance, though adorned in the first style of fashion'.

Colonel Brandon hears confirmation of Willoughby's marriage in a stationer's shop in Pall Mall, close to his own lodgings which are in St James's Street. This area of London was popular with officers, being close to the War Office, the Admirality and St James's Palace, King George III's official London residence. Shortly afterwards, the Miss Steeles arrive in town to stay with a cousin at Bartlett's Buildings in Holborn, a relatively unfashionable part of town to the east, close to the City of London and home, then as now, to many legal chambers. Before long, however, Lucy and her sister are invited to stay in the much more fashionable location of Conduit Street with Lady Middleton. Elinor and Marianne's brother John, his wife Fanny and their son Harry are the next arrivals in town. Though it was customary to call on close friends and family at the first opportunity, John Dashwood still has not called in Berkeley Street after two days. He is forced to make his excuses when he bumps into his sisters by chance in Gray's. 'I wished very much to call upon you yesterday … but it was impossible, for we were obliged to take Harry to see the wild beasts at Exeter Exchange.' This was a famous menagerie of animals, situated on the north side of the Strand.

The John Dashwoods have taken 'a very good house' for three months in Harley Street, best known today for its numerous private medical practices. Completely unaware of Colonel Brandon's attachment to Marianne, John Dashwood congratulates Elinor on having secured his affections, and 'the prospect of a very respectable establishment in life'. He is already planning a trip to Colonel Brandon's country home, Delaford in Dorset: 'I think I can answer for your having Fanny and myself among the earliest and best pleased of your visitors.' Elinor does her best to disabuse him of the notion, but without success.

When Lucy Steele's engagement to Edward Ferrars becomes public, Elinor gets the inside story from Lucy's elder sister, Nancy, whom she meets whilst out walking on a sunny Sunday morning with Mrs Jennings in Kensington Gardens. The Gardens were the grounds of Kensington Palace, a royal residence last lived in by William III a century earlier, which had been open to the public by permission of George III. Marianne has declined to join her sister in the walk because she is afraid of meeting Willoughby in such a public place. Jane Austen herself knew the Gardens: in a letter of 1811, she mentions a pleasant Sunday stroll there when 'everything was fresh and beautiful'. Elinor learns from Nancy Steele that Edward is currently lodging in Pall Mall, but plans to go to Oxford to begin his ordination shortly.

'With her large talking over the business'

By the second week of March the Dashwood sisters have been in London for more than two months and Marianne is impatient to leave town and return to Devon. 'She sighed for the air, the liberty, the quiet of the country; and fancied that if any place could give her ease, Barton must do it.' Fortunately, Mrs Jennings plans to leave town at the end of March with her daughter, to stay at the Palmers' country home at Cleveland in Somerset, and invites Elinor and Marianne to accompany them. Once at Cleveland, which lies 'within a few miles of Bristol', the Dashwood sisters will only require one long day's journey to bring them the eighty miles home to Barton.

The three-day journey to Cleveland – the name of which recalls the real town of Clevedon close to Bristol – is taken at a stately pace since Mrs Palmer now has a two-month-old baby. As soon as they arrive, Marianne, feeling 'all the happy privilege of country liberty', resolves to spend her days 'wandering from place to place in free and luxurious solitude', and sighing over the fact that Combe Magna lies less than thirty miles away. All those walks in long and wet grass, however, give Marianne a heavy cold which results in a violent fever. Concerned about the possibility of infection, Mrs Palmer takes her baby to stay with a relation of Mr Palmer's who lives a few miles the other side of Bath.

Willoughby hears of Marianne's illness from Sir John Middleton, whom he meets in the lobby of the Theatre Royal in London's Drury Lane. Desperate for news, he sets out for Somerset the following morning at eight o'clock, stopping once only at Marlborough in Wiltshire to take a quick snack of cold beef and a pint of porter. By eight o'clock that evening, Willoughby is hammering on the door at Cleveland, having travelled around 120 miles in 12 hours, an astonishing feat for those days. When Marianne is finally well enough to return home with Elinor and her mother in Colonel Brandon's carriage, they take a leisurely two days over the journey of eighty miles as a precaution against any relapse in Marianne's condition.

Fresh air and walks in the Devon countryside around Barton soon restore Marianne to health and some degree of contentment. And as for Elinor, her happiness is about to be assured via a most unexpected twist. The Dashwoods' manservant, having been sent one morning to Exeter on business, sees 'Mr Ferrars' and his new wife, the former Miss Lucy Steele,

The gardener's Lamentations upon blights

stopping in a chaise at the door of the New London Inn. Before long it is revealed that Lucy has in fact married Edward's younger brother Robert. Edward is thus free to propose to Elinor, which he does with alacrity.

Mr and Mrs Edward Ferrars are soon settled at Delaford in Dorset, Edward having been given the living there by Colonel Brandon. Earlier in the novel, Jane Austen has subtly described Delaford in some detail, knowing as she does that it is the future home of both Dashwood sisters. For Mrs Jennings, Delaford is 'exactly what I call a nice old fashioned place, full of comforts and conveniences … and the parsonage-house within a stone's throw'. It is in her opinion 'a thousand times prettier than Barton Park'. The novel thus concludes with the reader safe in the knowledge that Elinor and Marianne will be very happy in Dorset, especially as, 'though sisters, and living almost within sight of each other, they could live without disagreement between themselves, or producing coolness between their husbands.'

A Modern Perspective
Josephine Ross

'Her feelings were strong, but she knew how to govern them.'
Sense and Sensibility, Chapter 1

Over the centuries, devotees of Jane Austen's fiction have included many of the most famous and eminent literary figures of every era – from Sir Walter Scott and the poets Coleridge and Southey in her own time, to Martin Amis, Carol Shields and Fay Weldon in ours. One leading author who decidedly did not share their opinions, however, was the great Victorian novelist Charlotte Brontë. Writing to a friend in 1850, she observed blightingly, 'The Passions are perfectly unknown to her; she rejects even a speaking acquaintance with that stormy sisterhood.' She could not have had Jane Austen's first-published novel, *Sense and Sensibility*, in mind when she passed that cool judgement on the 'authoress' who – some 40 years before – had given the world the archetypal teenage rebel, Marianne Dashwood, whose wild, passionate pursuit of love, freedom and self-fulfilment drives her to misery, near-breakdown, and the brink of death. In the debate between 'sense' and 'sensibility' (or reason and unbridled feeling), Jane Austen comes down on the side of sense; but *Sense and Sensibility* is nonetheless written with intensity, from the heart, and is the work of an author with a far more than 'speaking acquaintance' with the 'stormy sisterhood'.

First published in 1811, *Sense and Sensibility* in its final form was evidently revised from an earlier manuscript, a novel-in-letters begun some time in the 1790s with the title *Elinor and Marianne*. Some aspects of the work bear striking parallels with Jane Austen's own life-experiences. Like the Dashwood sisters, Elinor and Marianne, who, on their father's death, have to leave their comfortable life in a large and 'elegant' country mansion to take up residence with their mother in a cramped cottage provided by a charitable relation, the Austen sisters – who had grown up in some style and comfort at their father's rectory of Steventon – were, by 1811, living on an income of £500 a year, in a cottage provided by their brother, who had inherited extensive property. In their devotion to one another, Jane Austen and her beloved elder sister, Cassandra, decidedly resembled Elinor and Marianne Dashwood. There, however, most of the likenesses ended. Cassandra Austen apparently possessed not only the intelligence, prudence and self-command of Elinor, but also the markedly-superior beauty of Marianne; while Jane, for all her wit and at times irreverent outlook, had none of the disdain for social convention of the hot-headed younger sister. And both the Austens, evidently, shared Elinor's approach to life and relationships in general, which Jane Austen sums up, early in the novel, in the comment, 'Her feelings were strong; but she knew how to govern them.' It is an attitude that will stand this highly-sympathetic heroine in good stead, as the narrative unfolds.

*Miss Dashwood...
I entreat you to stay*

The influence of the Romantic movement, in all its aspects, was gathering pace during Jane Austen's lifetime. In 1774, a year before her birth, the great German author Goethe had published his landmark novel, *The Sorrows of Young Werter*, setting off a wave of 'Werter Fever' throughout Europe; in 1812, a year after *Sense and Sensibility* appeared, Lord Byron's verse epic *Childe Harold* caused a publishing sensation, and set impressionable young women everywhere swooning for darkly-brooding, tormented heroes with troubled lives and unorthodox loves. In the years between, the passion for Nature stimulated by the writings of eighteenth-century philosopher Jean-Jacques Rousseau had continued to flower, notably through the lyrical works of poets such as Cowper, Thomson and (Jane Austen's favourite) Crabbe; while the 'Picturesque' movement had spread through art, architecture and landscape, to be taken up with enthusiasm by travel-writers and tourists. A series of best-selling guide-books by the artist William Gilpin, in which he described and illustrated regions of wild natural beauty, had promoted a fashionable taste for untamed, rugged scenery; and the classical sites of Greece and Rome began to give way, as favoured destinations, to the mountains of Switzerland, and the majestic English lakes beloved of Wordsworth and his coterie. 'What are men to rocks and mountains!' exclaims Lizzy Bennet in *Pride and Prejudice*, as she embarks on a tour of the Derbyshire Peak District; and in *Sense and Sensibility*, ardent, impulsive Marianne Dashwood has almost as great a devotion to the principles of 'Picturesque beauty' as to her ideals of heroic manly beauty.

Two men whom she considers very far from ideal are Colonel Brandon (one of the family's new acquaintances, on their removal to Barton Cottage) and Edward Ferrars, their sister-in-law's brother, whose growing relationship with Elinor is assumed to be leading towards marriage. The former, a quiet, dignified ex-soldier, 'the wrong side of 35', is dismissed by Marianne as hopelessly old and staid; the latter, being reserved to the point of shyness and wholly undemonstrative in his tastes and manners is – she freely admits – not the type of romantic lover she could ever envisage for herself, fond though she is of him. Matter-of-factly, Jane Austen states, 'He was not

Colonel Brandon was invited to visit her.

handsome, and his manners required intimacy to make them pleasing.' But, as ever the author is requiring the reader to look below surface appearances, and the attractions of 'air and address', to find the realities beneath. The tender, albeit guarded, emotion with which Elinor speaks of Edward tells a different story. To Marianne's reproaches that 'his figure is not striking', and 'his eyes want all that spirit, that fire' which she considers indispensable in a lover, Elinor gently responds, 'His person can hardly be called handsome, till the expression of his eyes, which are uncommonly good, and the general sweetness of his countenance are perceived.' Touchingly, she concludes, 'At present ... I think him really handsome.'

Most regrettable, to Marianne, is Edward's refusal to share her artistic tastes. There are some charming exchanges between them, as he teases her about her Romantic attitudes to books, poetry and landscape. Their dialogues illustrate both their own characters and the contemporary debate – so interesting to Jane Austen herself, and her readers – over 'Reason' (or sense) and 'Feeling' (sensibility) as opposing influences in eighteenth- and early nineteenth-century art and literature. In particular, Edward banters with Marianne about landscape, and her devotion to the tenets of William Gilpin – 'him who first defined what Picturesque beauty was', as Marianne calls him. According to Jane Austen's brother, in an early biographical note, the author herself from 'a very early age' was 'enamoured of Gilpin on the Picturesque'; and there is more than one reference to his precepts in her fiction – as when Lizzy Bennet in *Pride and Prejudice*, invited to walk with Mr Darcy and the two Bingley sisters, declines to join them, laughingly declaring, 'No, no, you are charmingly group'd, and ... the Picturesque would be spoiled by admitting a fourth.' Her reference is to the rule that cattle, or figures in a landscape, should always be shown in uneven numbers, ideally three or five. Other principles, based on 'that which would look well in a picture', involved features such as clumps of artfully uncultivated trees and foliage, set, if possible, against a background of rearing hills and tumbling waterfalls, seen under a stormy sky, or through a soft, misty haze. 'Rocks and promontories, grey moss and brushwood ... are all lost on me,' Edward jokes to Marianne, adding 'I do not like ruined, tattered cottages. I am not fond of nettles, or thistles.' His own 'idea of a fine country', he explains, 'unites beauty with utility'. (Unconsciously, this Jane Austen character is here anticipating one of the great Victorian authorities on art and design, William Morris, whose statements concerning form and function would influence British, and western, culture, long after the writings of Gilpin had passed into antiquity.)

Marianne counters, in private, with eloquent criticisms of Edward's lack of proper 'feeling', singling out, indignantly, his failure to express 'rapturous delight' at Elinor's drawing-skills, and – most of all – lamenting his 'spiritless' and 'tame' performance when reading aloud to the family. 'But you *would* give him Cowper,' her mother gently remonstrates; and the reader is once again left in no doubt as to Edward's true taste, and good sense, when she points out, 'He would have done more justice to simple and elegant prose,' rather than the florid effusions of one of the most Romantic of the popular poets.

Alongside discussions of literature, and landscape, the role of manners in early nineteenth-century society is a central theme of *Sense and Sensibility*. Like many a teenager, past or present, Marianne – scorning conventions of all kinds – rejects the strict codes of social conduct on the self-justifying grounds of obeying her own sincere instincts, rather than following society's stuffy dictates. 'Upon Elinor, therefore, the whole task of telling lies when politeness required it, always fell,' Jane Austen notes, with silky urbanity. Marianne's refusal to oblige her hostess by joining a card-game at a party – saying brusquely, 'You know I detest cards' – is rude, but perhaps forgivable; the selfish folly of her behaviour in flouting the proprieties governing a young lady's behaviour with a male 'admirer' is not. As Jane Austen makes clear, in being determined to obey her heart, not her head, Marianne will cause great pain to others – but no one will suffer more from her wilful rebelliousness than herself.

The role of good manners – ultimately a system based on regard for the welfare of others, which may impose certain restraints on individual freedom of expression – is a subject examined with great sensitivity and perception in *Sense and Sensibility*. Codes of behaviour are shown as existing to protect dignity and promote respect, both for self, and for fellow human beings. The great comic character of this novel, Sir John Middleton's kind-hearted, but vulgar mother-in-law, Mrs Jennings, who loves to make personal remarks on such intrusive topics as pregnancy, and young ladies' real, or fancied, 'admirers', is unaware how much pain her well-meant 'raillery' on the subject of a certain 'Mr F.' will cause Elinor, as Edward Ferrars' reluctance to declare his feelings becomes increasingly puzzling and distressing to her.

No doubt in reaction to Mrs Jennings' unbridled vulgarity, the elder of her two well-married daughters, Lady Middleton, has developed an icy shell of insipid formality and 'elegance', and shows an adherence to the details of etiquette which is decidedly unattractive. Colonel Brandon, by contrast, demonstrates a natural, instinctive, and highly-sympathetic form of 'gentlemanlike' good breeding which marks him out as an attractive character (for all Marianne's scorn that he wears a flannel waistcoat against the cold, in her eyes the mark of a dull old bachelor). In an exquisite vignette, the two contrasting impulses behind observing formal good manners are displayed in Chapter 12 when Mrs Jennings teases Elinor Dashwood about 'Mr F.': Lady Middleton, considering such talk ill-bred, turns the conversation by observing that 'it rained very hard' – a subject on which she is quickly joined by Colonel Brandon who – ever 'mindful of the feelings of others' – can see that Elinor is upset. 'And much was said on the subject of rain by both of them,' the passage ends, ingenuously. Talking about the weather may be banal, but if it spares another person's embarrassment, it may be a sign of 'sensibility', not merely 'sense'.

The great Romantic rebel of Marianne has, of course, no patience with such tedious niceties. Encouraged by her sweet-natured, if somewhat foolish, mother (whom she resembles in many ways), and undeterred by the cautions of her wise elder sister, she rushes headlong into what she perceives to be a real-life romance when the man of her dreams, the handsome, spirited, lively young Mr Willoughby, enters her life. She is too head-over-heels in love to observe the protocols of formal courtship. Their relationship begins – most unconventionally – with close physical contact, when she injures herself while out walking: he, coming upon the scene like 'the hero of a favourite story', sweeps her up in his arms and carries her home. Begun thus uninhibitedly, their relationship continues so. Willoughby calls Marianne by her Christian name (normally permitted only between engaged couples, or through family connections such as Edward Ferrars' connections through his sister's marriage, to the Dashwoods). He whisks her away in his curricle, on their own, causing gossip among grooms and servants (in which Mrs Jennings gleefully joins); he cuts off a lock of her hair, as a keepsake; most improperly, he shows her – furtively – round the house which he will one day inherit, without introducing her to its owner, who is in residence at the time. And on every occasion the pair dance together, sing together, sit side by side at dinner and whisper together afterwards, ignoring their companions, in a way that – Elinor tells her sister caustically – 'has already exposed you to some very impertinent remarks', and arouses the general belief that they are engaged. When no formal declaration of Willoughby's actual intentions comes – thus jeopardising Marianne's reputation, as well as her happiness – Elinor can only watch, worry and try, unsuccessfully, to warn.

At the same time, her own, curiously parallel, experience, as she waits for a proposal from Edward, is causing her deep inner turmoil; but in behaving (unlike Marianne) with calmness and 'sense', she is able to keep – for much of the novel – from upsetting either herself or her family too greatly. When the cause of Edward's reticence becomes clear, it is an honourable one: he has been trapped in youth into an engagement with a pretty, but sly, mercenary and socially ambitious young woman, Mrs Jennings' distant relation, Lucy Steele. Though long weary of the obligation, he must keep to it, for the sake not merely of formal, public manners, but of every principle of honour and duty. No gentleman worthy of the name can break off an engagement, since to do so might cast a slur on the lady's virtue, damaging her reputation as well as her prospects. While struggling with her feelings, Elinor can only glory in his conscience, and character, while never ceasing to love him.

Willoughby's reasons for not fulfilling the general expectation, that he and Marianne are engaged, have no such justification. Having made no formal commitment to marry her – such as society's 'rules' would require, given their intimacy – he freely jilts her, when faced with the temptation of marrying an heiress, and thereby restoring his fortunes. Marianne's initial incredulity, and then despair, on discovering that the tender lover whom she has regarded as the chivalric 'hero of a favourite story' is closer in character to a storybook villain is truly heartrending. Having always wallowed, sentimentally, in displays of feeling, she now falls into a depth of grief which is pitiful for her family to see, and moving for us to read.

Even Charlotte Brontë would surely have acknowledged Jane Austen's profound knowledge of 'the Passions', as she evokes the agonies of this betrayed young woman – whose follies, so forgivable, of trusting and loving too well, will lead her to the edge of madness and even death. Dying for love is in the true tradition of novels such as Goethe's *Werter*, but no avowedly Romantic novel could outdo in livid intensity some of the scenes in *Sense and Sensibility* as when, seeing 'Marianne stretched on the bed, almost choked by grief, one letter in her hand and two or three others lying by her', Elinor, silently, 'seating herself on the bed, took her hand, kissed her affectionately several times, and then gave way to a burst of tears … scarcely less violent than Marianne's'. Phrases such as 'the anguish of her heart', 'lost in sobs', and 'misery such as mine has no pride!' will surely give the lie to Charlotte Brontë's assertions.

Marianne Dashwood's emotions are now expressed in ways which show remarkable psychological perception on the part of the author, as she becomes unwilling to eat (foreshadowing the 'anorexia' diagnosis so well-known in the twenty-first century among troubled teenage girls) and allows her depression and self-neglect almost to kill her. Her insistence, as she nurses her grief, on taking 'twilight walks' where there was 'something more of wildness than in the rest, where the trees were the oldest, and the grass was the longest and wettest' – coupled (as Jane Austen points out, prosaically) with the 'imprudence of sitting in her wet shoes and stockings' – brings on, in her weakened state, an illness which is nearly fatal. The recognition, on her recovery, of the misery which, through the 'extreme of languid indolence and selfish repining' she has inflicted on those who truly love her does as much as anything to make Marianne 'discover the falsehood of her own opinions and … counteract by her conduct her most favourite maxims'.

One of the happiest of men.

It is a satisfying irony (as she comes to realise) that Colonel Brandon, far from being stuffy and dull, has in many respects lived the life of the 'hero of a favourite story'. Parted in youth from the woman he loved, on the eve of their elopement, he has tracked her descent through prostitution and penury, to rescue her from a pauper's deathbed; he has brought up her bastard child as his 'ward', facing the slurs of the world thereby; on this girl's seduction and pregnancy, at the hands of none other than the faithless Willoughby himself, the Colonel – in defiance of the law, as well as his own safety – has called the young libertine out, and fought a duel with him. Yet again, Jane Austen shows the dangers of judging by 'first impressions', and outward appearances. People governed by sense – Elinor; Edward; Colonel Brandon – may lead lives of intense inner passion, ruled by noble ideals; a young charmer such as Willoughby may, conversely, be led by his unchecked impulses into the most unheroic, and un-'feeling' conduct.

Charlotte Brontë was wrong in her assessment of her great literary predecessor: Jane Austen was well-acquainted with sensibility, as well as sense. But when it came to 'the Passions', that 'stormy sisterhood', her attitude might be summed up in her own comment on Elinor Dashwood, one of her favourite heroines: 'Her feelings were strong; but she knew how to govern them.'

Principal Characters

Elinor Dashwood is the sensible and reserved eldest daughter of Mr and Mrs Henry Dashwood. Her 'advice was so effectual, possessed of a strength of understanding, and coolness of judgement, which qualified her, though only nineteen, to be the counsellor of her mother'. She becomes attached to Edward Ferrars, the brother-in-law of her elder half-brother, John.

Marianne Dashwood is the romantically inclined and eagerly expressive second daughter of Mr and Mrs Henry Dashwood. She is the object of the attentions of Col. Brandon and John Willoughby. 'Marianne's abilities were, in many respects, quite equal to Elinor's. She was sensible and clever; but eager in every thing; her sorrows, her joys, could have no moderation. She was generous, amiable, interesting: she was every thing but prudent.'

John Dashwood is the son of Henry Dashwood by his first wife. Rich by inheritance and by marriage 'he was not an ill-disposed young man, unless to be rather cold hearted, and rather selfish, is to be ill-disposed'. He agrees to help his stepmother and half-sisters in a neighbourly way, thereafter feeling somewhat guilty about his lack of generosity.

Henry Dashwood is a wealthy gentleman who dies at the beginning of the story. The terms of his estate prevent him from leaving anything to his second wife and their children. He asks John, his son by his first wife, to look after the financial security of his second wife and their three daughters.

Fanny Dashwood is the wife of John Dashwood, who dotes on her, and sister to Edward and Robert Ferrars. 'Mrs John Dashwood was a strong caricature of himself – more narrow-minded and selfish'. She is opposed to any connection between her brother Edward and Elinor.

Mrs Dashwood is the second wife of Henry Dashwood, and mother of Elinor, Marianne and Margaret, who is left in difficult financial straits by the death of her husband. She had 'an eagerness of mind … which must generally have led to imprudence'.

Margaret Dashwood is the youngest daughter of Mr and Mrs Henry Dashwood. 'She did not, at thirteen, bid fair to equal her sisters at a more advanced period of life.'

Sir John Middleton is a distant relative of Mrs Dashwood who, after the death of Henry Dashwood, invites her and her three daughters to live in a cottage on his property in Devonshire. 'A good-looking man, about forty,' he delights in having young people around him.

Mrs Jennings is Sir John Middleton's mother-in-law, 'a good-humoured, merry, fat, elderly woman, who talked a great deal, seemed very happy, and rather vulgar. She was full of jokes and laughter, and before dinner was over had said many witty things on the subject of lovers and husbands'. She wins Elinor's heart by her nursing of Marianne through her dangerous fever.

Lady Middleton was 'not more than six or seven and twenty; her face was handsome, her figure tall and striking, and her address graceful. Her manners had all the elegance which her husband's wanted … though perfectly well-bred, she was reserved, cold and had nothing to say for herself beyond the most commonplace enquiry or remark'. She is primarily concerned with mothering her four spoilt children.

Edward Ferrars is the elder of Fanny Dashwood's two brothers. He forms an attachment to Elinor Dashwood. His prior engagement to Lucy Steele, the niece of his tutor, has been kept secret owing to the expectation that his family would object and, indeed, he is disinherited. He becomes a clergyman and is offered a church living through Col. Brandon's influence. Released from his engagement by Lucy's elopement he proposes to Elinor.

Robert Ferrars is the younger brother of Edward Ferrars and Fanny Dashwood, 'very unlike his brother – silly and a great

coxcomb'. His mother's favourite, he succeeds in retaining much of the fortune that might have been forfeit after his elopement with Lucy Steele.

Mrs Ferrars is the mother of Fanny Dashwood and Edward and Robert Ferrars. She is the widow of a rich man, and controls her children's fortunes.

Colonel Brandon is a close friend of Sir John Middleton, a bachelor 'on the wrong side of five-and-thirty'. Brandon had fallen in love with his father's ward, but could not marry her because she was intended for his older brother. He was sent abroad and, while gone, the girl suffered numerous misfortunes, finally dying penniless and disgraced, and with a natural daughter, who Col. Brandon takes in.

Lucy Steele is a young, distant relation of Mrs Jennings, who has been secretly engaged to Edward Ferrars. She assiduously cultivates the friendship of Elinor Dashwood. Sir John Middleton declares that she 'is monstrous pretty, and so good humoured and agreeable', a judgement she subsequently belies.

John Willoughby is a nephew of a neighbour of the Middletons. 'His manly beauty and more than common gracefulness' charm Marianne. He seduces and abandons Eliza Williams, whose guardian, Col. Brandon, later fights a duel with him. He falls in love with Marianne, but is forced by mounting debts to relinquish her in favour of Sophia Grey, an heiress with fifty thousand pounds.

Charlotte Palmer is the daughter of Mrs Jennings and the younger sister of Lady Middleton, 'her kindness recommended by so pretty a face, was engaging; her folly, though evident, was not disgusting, because it was not conceited'. She is forgiving of her boorish husband.

Mr Palmer is the husband of Charlotte Palmer who is running for a seat in Parliament in spite of his idleness and rudeness. 'A grave-looking young man of five or six-and-twenty, with an air of more fashion and sense than his wife, but of less willingness to please.'

Anne/Nancy Steele is Lucy Steele's plain elder sister, who frequently embarrasses her.

Sophia Grey is a wealthy heiress who John Willoughby woos after he is disinherited in order to retain his comfortable lifestyle.

Miss Morton is the daughter of the late Lord Morton, whom Mrs Ferrars wants her eldest son, Edward, to marry.

Mr Pratt is private tutor to Edward Ferrars. An uncle of Lucy Steele.

Pride and Prejudice

Modern Interpretations
John Wiltshire

Pride and Prejudice remains Jane Austen's most popular novel. Still widely read, admired and loved two hundred years after its first publication, it continues to inspire readers, critics and film-makers. More films have been made of this book in fact than of all the other Austen novels together – a testimony both to its appeal as the foundational 'romantic' text in English, and to the tantalising challenge of representing the relationship of the two protagonists.

Visual reinterpretations of *Pride and Prejudice* include the 1940 version with Greer Garson and Laurence Olivier, which was followed by no less than four BBC serials (1952, 1958, 1967, 1980 – the last with a script by Fay Weldon), before the wildly successful BBC 1995 version with script by Andrew Davies, and the almost equally successful film of 2005 directed by Joe Wright. *Bride and Prejudice* (2004), which transfers the plot to modern India and replaces the class tensions in the narrative with cross-cultural ones, includes some scenes that follow Austen's dialogue quite closely. On the other hand, *Pride and Prejudice: a latter-day comedy*, released in 2003 by Excel Entertainment, is a clumsy attempt to update the novel as a teen comedy in the wake of *Clueless*. Many other recent popular films borrow from the novel's plot and allude to *Pride and Prejudice*; they include *You've Got Mail* (1998), *Bridget Jones's Diary* (2001) and *Becoming Jane* (2007).

Pride and Prejudice has always in fact been the novel of Jane Austen's most amenable to adaptation, and stage versions were popular before its conversion into film. This is because it is in many ways already the most dramatic, even theatrical, of Austen's books. It opens with a witticism, followed smartly by a dialogue. The dialogue is a masterpiece of exposition. 'You want to tell me,' says Mr Bennet to his wife, 'and I have no objection to hearing it': a perfect invitation for the recounting of the key facts the reader needs. We are not to know where this dialogue takes place (in the drawing-room, the garden, the bedroom?). This absence of precise scene-setting is common in the novel, and remarkable when compared with the careful choreography and detailing of the characters' positions and movements in the later books. Mr and Mrs Bennet could be speaking on a bare stage. Other signs of theatrical influence were spotted by one of the novel's first reviewers, who compared Elizabeth Bennet to Shakespeare's Beatrice in *Much Ado About Nothing*, and wrote that, 'The character of Wickham is very well portrayed; – we fancy, that our authoress had Joseph Surface before her eyes when she sketched it.' (Surface is the plausible, but actually scheming, brother of the hero in Sheridan's *The School for Scandal* – a comedy in which Jane Austen herself had performed. One of the play's key scenes takes place in the family portrait gallery.) The influence of eighteenth-century comedy on the repartee

A still from Bride and Prejudice.

1 Sydney Gardens from John Claude Nattes' Bath *(opposite).*

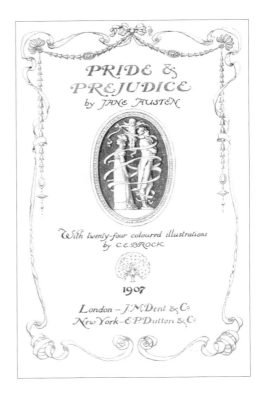

between the central characters in *Pride and Prejudice*, as on caricature figures, like Mary or Mrs Bennet, is plain. Two books which throw light on these aspects were published in 2002, by Paula Byrne and Penny Gay, both with the title *Jane Austen and the Theatre*.

Pride and Prejudice is not a play, though. It entwines three different narrative threads: the romantic story of Elizabeth and Darcy, the family narrative of the Bennets, and the broader social drama to which Pemberley – and all that it stands for – is the key. Criticism of the novel, as well as its visual representations, has to contend with a question that involves all of these. What makes the ultimate marriage of Elizabeth and Darcy plausible? What convinces readers that the obstacles to their reconciliation – personal, family, and class obstacles – are overcome? What makes readers accept and rejoice in what historians insist is a fantasy marriage between the lower gentry and the very rich? Film-makers and readers give very different answers to these questions. The novel's theatricality diminishes markedly in its second half, as more of the action takes place either in Elizabeth's internal life or (what amounts to the same thing) her encounter with Darcy's house and its grounds, an incarnation and visual representation of his character and civic role. Dealing with these aspects of the novel tests a film-maker's grasp of *Pride and Prejudice*'s complex narrative strands.

Modern criticism of *Pride and Prejudice* begins with Reuben Brower's 'Light and Bright and Sparkling', published in *The Fields of Light* (1951). This was the first essay to examine closely the exchanges between Elizabeth and Darcy, and explain why they are so fascinating. 'What most satisfies us in reading the dialogues in *Pride and Prejudice* is Jane Austen's awareness that it is difficult to know any complex person, that knowledge of a man like Darcy is an interpretation and a construction, not a simple absolute,' he suggested. Brower's essay stressed the way these interchanges prepare the reader for Darcy's interest in Elizabeth. 'Mr Darcy's politeness, his repeated questions, his gallantry, if interpreted favourably, indicate his increasing warmth of feeling,' whilst Elizabeth's replies, 'being more ambiguous than she supposes,' increase his fascination. In common with most readings of this period, the essay celebrates the 'triumph' of the novel in terms of 'balance'.

Robert Polhemus, in *Erotic Faith* (1990), makes equally perceptive comments on the relationship between Darcy and Elizabeth, taking as a key Darcy's avowal that he 'admired' Elizabeth from the first 'for the liveliness of your mind.' He connects the romance, however, with the family narrative. Elizabeth has learned ironic banter from her beloved father, and Polhemus suggests how 'the parental third person' is present in her interaction with Darcy. She 'relishes punishing Darcy's original pride and prejudice [because] they are so like qualities in her father that she, the father's favorite, might resent but could not directly rebel against.' The outcome of her avowal of her love for Darcy is a transformation of Elizabeth's relation with her father, for he now, begging her to think twice about it, speaks to her with an impassioned concern which frees them both from ironic indirection. These writers illuminate the reciprocal intellectual attraction between Elizabeth and Darcy, but ignore Elizabeth's 'fine eyes' and healthy flush, as well as Darcy's stare, which in the novel (as in the film versions) is repeatedly brought to our attention.

As with all of Jane Austen's novels, *Pride and Prejudice* has been subject to revisionist feminist criticism in recent decades. Earlier critics had praised the satisfying nature of the marriage conclusion. Here the higher gentry or wealthy landed class is reconciled with the lower, or, to put it another way, a decadent quasi-aristocracy (symbolised by Darcy's alternative marriage partner, Miss Anne Darcy – 'sickly and cross') is renewed and revived through marriage with vigorous 'new blood'. It was common to praise the success with which Austen persuades the reader that the unlikely marriage was a necessary culmination of her narrative. On the contrary, Susan Fraiman in a chapter called 'The Humiliation of Elizabeth Bennet' in *Unbecoming Women* (1993) argues interestingly that the heroine becomes diminished in the course of the novel's action, that 'Darcy woos away not Elizabeth's "prejudice," but her judgment entire' so that the marriage conclusion is therefore a capitulation to convention. Darcy's views are shown to be objective, Elizabeth's condemned for being subjective. Elizabeth is an outspoken girl 'entering a world whose voices drown out her own.' Likewise, Maaja Stewart in *Domestic Realities and Imperial Fictions* (1993) stresses the 'patterns of power that render Elizabeth completely helpless' in a world where men have both sexual and political prerogatives, and even a heroine as vivacious, witty and intelligent as Elizabeth succumbs to its pressures.

"*I think him very disagreeable*".

As Ashley Tauchert comments, 'The problem of the Austen happy ending for autonomous female subjectivity is pronounced in feminist interpretation' (*Romancing Jane Austen*, 2003). Both of these feminist critics pay particular attention to the scene at Pemberley in which Elizabeth returns, fascinated, to Darcy's portrait. There, Fraiman argues, Elizabeth turns herself into 'the object' of Darcy's gaze, thus making her capitulation to the 'perverse' demands of patriarchy clear to the wary reader. 'When she visits Pemberley and understands Darcy's power,' Stewart too writes, 'she looks at his portrait and directs his gaze – which she had earlier avoided – upon herself, thus subjecting not only their shared experience but also herself to his interpretation.' Replying in effect to such critics, Tauchert argues that Elizabeth's 'autonomy of will' is established 'by the narrative turn' between the first and second proposals. Elizabeth's 'No' to the first establishes her freedom, which prepares the conditions for the second proposal and a reconciliation between herself and Darcy on quite different terms. Similarly, John Wiltshire in *Recreating Jane Austen* (2000) argues that Elizabeth's rejection of Darcy precipitates Darcy's recognition of her as an independent person, and that this parallels and matches her own gradual recognition of him in his family, social and political dimensions.

Adapted from a stage play by Helen Jerome, the first film made of *Pride and Prejudice*, released in 1940, compresses the action to one or two settings.

They solaced their wretchedness
by duets after supper.

This version entirely omitted the Pemberley sequence so vital to the novel and to modern interpretations, never alluded to Darcy's role as great landowner, and generally played fast and loose with historical authenticity. The relationship between the two protagonists has its hiccups, but throughout the action the emphasis seems to be on their enjoyment of each other's company, and their difference in social status is underplayed. Whether or not one agrees that Elizabeth is fascinated by the spectacle of Darcy's wealth and power she encounters at Pemberley, the film's Elizabeth has certainly no interest in Darcy's money. Lady Catherine, in a final scene, threatens to cut Darcy off without a penny, and Elizabeth vows to marry him anyway. Greer Garson's Elizabeth is a romantic Hollywood heroine, after all.

As Sue Parrill suggests in *Jane Austen on Film and Television* (2002), this film belongs to the genre of 'screwball comedy'. Olivier however brings a distinction to the portrayal of Darcy that succeeds in overcoming the clumsy maladapted dialogue and situations. In one scene, Darcy is showing Elizabeth how to shoot arrows at a target: she worsts him by hitting the bull's eye every time. Darcy capitulates and apologises for his previous arrogance. This seems to be a reworking of an incident at Rosings in which Elizabeth at the piano delivers Darcy a little homily about learning to please other people. The subtlety that is missing from the film's dialogue is partly compensated for in Olivier's smiling responses to Elizabeth's pertness – an enigmatic or inscrutable half-smile that brings alive some of the ambiguity that, as Brower demonstrated, makes the encounters between the characters in the novel so fascinating.

The 1980 BBC serial is much more faithful to the novel's action but it has little to sustain a contemporary viewer's interest over its six episodes. A doe-eyed, lisping Elizabeth and a Darcy with blankly handsome face are not its weakest aspects. There is an important early dialogue in the novel, when Elizabeth, quick to divert attention from her mother's ill manners, jokes about the sonnet as a means for destroying love. Darcy responds with, 'I have been used to think of poetry as the food of love.' Elizabeth caps his response with a joke about poetry driving away any ordinary affection. This is one tiny moment in the novel that establishes some affinity, or even some reciprocal feeling, between the two protagonists. It ends with Darcy smiling at Elizabeth's witticism. The film presents this as a series of talking heads, first one, then the other: the effect is to destroy any possibility of relationship between the two, and Darcy's responsive smile is omitted. Far too many scenes are filmed frontally, leaving the actors little to do but stand around, hands genteelly clasped. However, the film does take Elizabeth to Pemberley, and as Linda V. Troost argues in 'Filming Tourism, Portraying Pemberley' (*Eighteenth-Century Fiction*, 2006) it attempts to treat the class dimensions of the novel seriously, making Darcy very obviously a cut above the heroine. The film includes the portrait scene at Pemberley, and registers Elizabeth's changing mind, but through the medium of a voice-over that is an awkward redaction of her complex responses in the novel. 'How stark you look in your portrait. But I remember your warmth, and would soften that look,' she declares. In the book she discerns a smile in the portrait that she now realises had often been on his face, though this film has never shown it.

No wonder the BBC wanted to remake *Pride and Prejudice* in 1995. This well-known version, directed by Simon Langton, amplifies the text by deliberately including much more material focusing on Darcy by a writer with a long-standing interest in male sexual infatuation. The scene in which Darcy, fresh from his bath, stares out at Elizabeth romping with a dog leaves the viewer in no doubt that she arouses his erotic interest. Otherwise his glowering stares would be difficult to interpret (though the camera's fascination is hint enough). The film's most celebrated sequence takes place at Pemberley, where, as Troost points out, Elizabeth's contemplation of his portrait is intercut with shots of Darcy's arrival on horseback at the estate, already presenting 'the new Darcy' Elizabeth is perceiving. 'Elizabeth gazes at his romantic portrait as Darcy dives into a lake in an attempt to cool his ardour.' But the novel's representation of Darcy's attraction to Elizabeth is much more complex, and his role as responsible citizen and landowner comes into this as well. By reducing Darcy's attraction to Elizabeth to infatuation, the script and film tends to ignore the self-revision that his character must perform before their renewed encounter at Pemberley.

In contrast to the most recent adaptation, this version immediately stresses, in a dialogue between Elizabeth and Jane, just how dysfunctional and unhappy their parents' marriage is. The dreadful embarrassment that Elizabeth suffers when her family displays itself in serial bad manners at the Lucas party in Chapter 18 is very vividly conveyed. In Wright's film (2003), by contrast, that family are happy, Mr Bennet is kind to Mary even when he has to stop her performance at the piano, and Mr and Mrs Bennet enjoy each other's company. Mrs Bennet, an appalling figure in 1995 (as in the novel) is played sympathetically, and her match-making abilities are applauded by her husband. (Emma Thompson is credited with a role in the film's script; this shift is akin to the transformation of the Middletons in her *Sense and Sensibility*.) And the film offers a quite different reading of Darcy. This is a shy, anguished man, tormented by his love of Elizabeth, and convincingly proud throughout. He is not presented to the audience as a sexual object; instead passionate attraction between the protagonists is imaged in a scene in which the film takes leave of the realism that has governed its mode so far, and in a slow motion, almost surrealist, sequence follows the two figures, locked in a dance-movement that utterly isolates them from the surrounding crowd. This notion of the two held together by a mutual attraction that is beyond words substitutes for the pleasure in verbal crossing swords which communicates their relationship in the novel.

Pemberley is ludicrously exaggerated into Chatsworth, that 'stream of some natural importance' of the novel swelled into the celebrated lakes and fountains of that palace. Elizabeth is shown bemusedly wandering through the famous sculpture gallery, surrounded by statues, some of them priceless

He was full of joy and attention.

Canovas, in polished white marble. In this beautifully conceived, filmed and edited sequence, takes merge and fade into each other, and communicate a visual equivalent of absorbed, dreamlike, contemplation. A bust of a veiled woman takes Elizabeth's attention: she moves on to a figure of a fallen gladiator, the camera showing the statue from the back, and allowing the viewer to imagine her glance as it passes over the exposed body. Then the camera moves up the polished torso of another white male figure, drawn into a kind of visual caress by its lustrous beauty. She then sees a bust of Darcy. The camera, positioned behind, allows the viewer to see in her face the mixture of desire and regret that the film has already suggested must be present in her feelings. The statue carries little suggestion of the smile that, in the novel, Elizabeth detects on the face in the portrait. Instead it is a clarified and symbolic representation of that inscrutable quality in Darcy's stares upon which both the novel and the other films insist. Elizabeth is still facing this image, which has acquired purity and beauty within this setting, when the housekeeper and the Gardiners come upon her; and with the housekeepers' words, 'This is he,' the music reaches a climax.

As she drifts through other rooms, Elizabeth's hands touch and caress various *objects d'art*. 'In the alchemy of love, the material and the immaterial can be transmuted,' Polhemus wrote, commenting on the estate's fusion of physical substance and the ideal. She hears faint sounds of piano music and is lured to the room where, as she perceives in a mirror through a half-open door, Georgina Darcy is playing. Suddenly, Darcy is present in the reflected glass, and the smile which was absent in the statue – and has been absent throughout the film – is brought wonderfully to life on his face as he laughs and romps about with his sister. The film thus retrieves a motif in the novel and turns it to its own account. This is not a solution to the problem of representing Elizabeth's thoughts as she contemplates the portrait. There could be no visual solution to this, nor to the novel's technical achievement in leading to that point. Instead, this is a rethinking of the 'erotic destination of the narrative' which, as the film's refusal of the portrait suggests, transforms it entirely. As this uneven but intelligent version demonstrates, the multifaceted text of *Pride and Prejudice* is still open to many interpretations, critical and visual alike.

Regency Life
Maggie Lane

Music and Dance

In Jane Austen's life and the lives of her characters, music and dancing held an important place. These twin arts occupied many an empty hour, whether in practising – a mainly female activity – or in performing, when the sexes came together for the evening. Though dancing, singing and playing an instrument might well have been pleasurable for their own sakes, they served an unspoken function in allowing women to demonstrate their skills and graces in public. They also maximised the opportunities for potential marriage partners to meet, to converse and become acquainted.

Significantly it is at a public ball that Elizabeth Bennet, portionless daughter of the minor gentry, first encounters Fitzwilliam Darcy, owner of a large estate and the eye-watering income of ten thousand pounds a year. His rejection of her as a dancing partner, resulting from his pride; and *her* consequent prejudice against him, set going one of the most entertaining love stories in the English language. The story begins with a dance and proceeds rather *like* a dance, as hero and heroine advance and retreat in a series of ever more intricate moves.

Nowhere in Jane Austen's writing are music and dance more pervasive than in *Pride and Prejudice*, which depicts a highly communal way of life – Mrs Bennet boasts that they dine with four and twenty families – where neighbours rely on one another for their evening entertainment, and judge one another on their performance. In this novel, not only do many scenes take place in a ballroom or clustered round a piano, but music and dancing are frequently the subject of conversation.

The music that occupies the characters in *Pride and Prejudice* is of the home-grown variety. Though in *Northanger Abbey* and *Persuasion* characters attend public concerts in Bath, and though even in the country professional musicians would have been engaged for full-scale balls at assembly rooms such as Meryton's and large private houses such as Netherfield, in the main Jane Austen's people make their own music. Rather, her women do. It is almost an obligation on young women of the gentry class to sing and play. It is their 'work' – the contribution they make to social life in return for being kept. Jane Austen herself was the provider of music in her family circle, having been taught to play the piano and to sing by William Chard, assistant organist at Winchester Cathedral, whom her father paid to visit Steventon Rectory. She was remembered, by her nephews and nieces, to have had a sweet singing voice.

The ability to play music denoted a young woman as being genteel, leisured, accomplished; it was a credit to her upbringing and a lure to potential husbands. The fact that many women gave up music once married – notably Mrs Elton in *Emma* – is telling, though some older married or unmarried women, Jane Austen among them, kept up the piano in order to play when the younger generation wished for an impromptu dance.

"You must allow me to present this young lady to you as a very desirable partner."

There is much debate about 'accomplishments' in *Pride and Prejudice*. The hypercritical Miss Bingley claims that a woman 'must have a thorough knowledge of music, singing, drawing and dancing' to deserve to be called accomplished. She and her married sister sing duets. Elizabeth can sing and play competently, but not brilliantly. Her performance is 'pleasing, but by no means capital'. Like another slightly wayward heroine, Emma Woodhouse, she admits she does not practise enough. But Elizabeth can rise to the occasion when called on to entertain the company at Rosings, for example, without either false modesty or showing off. Mary, the plain

"Excuse my interference:
it was kindly meant."

one of the Bennet family, practises avidly and performs whenever she has the opportunity, in a rather pathetic attempt to be noticed. But Mary is deceived as to her own abilities. 'Her voice was weak, and her manner affected.' Her performance at Netherfield excites Miss Bingley's derision, and brings on one of her father's most famous put-downs: 'That will do extremely well, child. You have delighted us long enough.'

Georgiana Darcy 'practises very constantly' on the pianoforte and is adding the harp to her acquirements. The harp was a fashionable instrument learnt only by the richest or most indulged young women – Mary Crawford in *Mansfield Park* and the Musgrove sisters in *Persuasion* are other harpists, and according to Mrs Elton in *Emma*, a governess who can teach the harp as well as the piano can command a higher salary. Georgiana is lonely, and playing seems to be a solace and an occupation, rather than a means of showing off, for her. She 'sings and plays all day long,' evidently for her own pleasure. She is one of the true music-lovers of the novels: others are Marianne Dashwood in *Sense and Sensibility*, Jane Fairfax in *Emma*, and Anne Elliot in *Persuasion*; all are in their different ways misunderstood, and music seems to have been a release for them.

'There are few people in England, I suppose, who have more true enjoyment of music than myself, or a better natural taste. If I had ever learnt, I should have been a great proficient,' boasts Lady Catherine de Bourgh ridiculously, though she is not beyond talking all through Elizabeth's performance. She is shocked that not all of Elizabeth's sisters have musical accomplishments. 'Why did you not all learn? You ought all to have learned. The Miss Webbs all play, and their father has not so good an income as yours.' For Lady Catherine music is not a matter of enjoyment and aptitude, but a social indicator.

Gentlemen never play a musical instrument in Jane Austen's world: that would denote loss of caste. Male instrumentalists of her time were confined to professionals, or 'hirelings' as she once referred to them in a letter, and did not rank with ladies and gentlemen, however cultured they were. A young woman of the gentry who fell in love with her music teacher brought a great deal of disapproval down on both their heads, as several real-life cases attest. This prohibition did not extend to use of the voice. In the novels gentlemen occasionally sing, not solo but to accompany a lady. Frank Churchill sings with Jane Fairfax in *Emma* and a mixed group sings glees in *Mansfield Park*. In *Pride and Prejudice* Colonel Fitzwilliam *perhaps* sings with Elizabeth at Rosings – the narrative is not quite clear as to whether he only listens or joins in – but the pompous Mr Collins declares, 'If I were so fortunate as to be able to sing, I should have great pleasure, I am sure, in obliging the company with an air; for I consider music as a very innocent diversion, and perfectly compatible with the profession of a clergyman.'

Mr Collins equally has no objection to dancing. 'A ball of this kind,' he says, speaking of Mr Bingley's ball at Netherfield, 'given by a young man of character, to respectable people,' is unlikely to have 'any evil tendency,' and far from objecting to dancing himself, he engages the unsuspecting Elizabeth for the first two dances. When they happen, 'Mr Collins, awkward and solemn, apologising instead of attending, and often moving wrong without being aware of it, gave her all the shame and misery which a disagreeable partner for a couple of dances can give.'

The country dances of the period, in which couples stand opposite each other in two long rows and work their way down the set, certainly called for a high level of attention to the movements of everybody else, as well as lightness of toe, which poor Mr Collins lacked. To learn a variety of steps, to move when required and be still when required, to make polite conversation while remaining alert to the demands of the dance, called for a fair degree of mental and physical self-command. This is why Sir William Lucas can remark complacently, 'There is nothing like dancing after all. I consider it one of the first refinements of polished societies,' and why Darcy's riposte, 'Every savage can dance,' though true, is not really fair.

English country dancing had evolved to demonstrate the polish, elegance and decorum of formal eighteenth-century manners. All eyes would be on the couple working their way down the set. Mr Bingley, for example, 'was quite struck with Jane as she was going down the set,' asks to be introduced to her, and ends by marrying her. Dancing has served its purpose here. As screen dramatisations of *Pride and Prejudice* have delighted in showing us, the pattern of taking a few steps, exchanging a few words – perhaps spoken over the shoulder or under an uplifted arm – was highly conducive to engaging the interest of the opposite sex.

Jane Austen herself loved dancing, as her surviving letters attest. 'There were twenty dances, and I danced them all, without any fatigue.' The fun was not only in the possibility of romance, but in dressing up, the pleasures of exercise – rare for a woman – and meeting up with one's female friends. Jane and her sister Cassandra regularly attended the Basingstoke assemblies, held throughout the winter months at Basingstoke Town Hall. These would have the 'country town' tone of the Meryton Assembly which Darcy finds so intolerable. Not surprisingly he also despises the impromptu dance held in an ordinary house after dinner, such as the one at Lucas Lodge where Mary plays 'Scotch and Irish airs' for her exuberant younger sisters to dance to.

Jane Austen enjoyed many an impromptu dance at the homes of relations and neighbours, but she also danced at the more sophisticated assemblies of Southampton and Bath when staying in those cities, and she attended the rather grand balls that were occasionally given by local aristocrats Lord Portsmouth and Lord Bolton in a spirit of condescending hospitality to their country neighbours. In *Mansfield Park* such a ball is given by Sir Thomas Bertram, and in *Pride and Prejudice* the nearest equivalent is Mr Bingley's ball, complete with formal invitations and, to warm departing guests, the obligatory white soup.

Country Dancing (detail) at a Cotillion Ball at the New Assembly Rooms, Bath. Plate X from Comforts of Bath *by Thomas Rowlandson, 1798.*

"I am persuaded ...... my proposals will not fail of being acceptable."

Meals and Manners

The meals that punctuated the day in Jane Austen's lifetime depended for their timing on where one stood in the social scale. Fashionable people, especially those from London, dined later than their less sophisticated country counterparts, who preferred their main meal cooked and eaten by natural light. Those who dined early required supper, while those who dined late needed something to fill the gap at midday.

Even breakfast varied in its timing. In *Pride and Prejudice* it is notable that breakfast is over at Longbourn when Elizabeth receives Jane's note from Netherfield informing her that she is unwell. Elizabeth debates with her parents, waits for Kitty and Lydia to put on their outdoor clothes, walks the three miles to Netherfield – and finds the fashionable ladies there only just about to begin breakfast.

Breakfast in Jane Austen's time was a delicate meal of bread, toast or buns and tea, coffee or chocolate drunk from fine china. What we think of as the full English breakfast was rarely served before Victorian times except at inns or to members of the family about to set off on a lengthy journey. The only evidence of 'cooked' breakfast in the novels is the cold pork bones and broken eggshells left behind by Henry Crawford and William Price when they leave Mansfield Park early in the morning for London. Of course, men were expected to have bigger appetites. Georgiana Darcy travels on an empty stomach, arriving at Pemberley to 'a late breakfast'.

When Jane Austen mentions a midday meal in the private houses of her characters, vague phrases such as 'the cold repast' or 'a collation' or simply 'the sandwich tray' are employed. The word 'luncheon' is used just once in the novels, and that is in association with an inn. Elizabeth and Jane Bennet having travelled back from London, Lydia and Kitty meet them with the family carriage at the George Inn in an unnamed town, and order 'the nicest cold luncheon in the world', which consists of 'a sallad [*sic*] and cucumber' and 'such cold meat as an inn larder normally affords'.

Nobody is ever invited to lunch at a specified hour, not only because the word was not current, but because this cold food is produced at any time to suit, and it is taken not in the dining room but in whichever room the family use for sitting in the morning. Even at Pemberley, which has an abundance of rooms, daytime food is offered in the saloon, the room assigned to receive morning visitors. When Elizabeth and Mrs Gardiner pay their morning call to the ladies of Pemberley they are shown into the saloon where the first awkward attempts at conversation are relieved by 'the entrance of the servants with cold meat, cake, and a variety of all the finest fruits in season'.

Especially in households humbler than Pemberley, once the food had been brought into the room by servants, it could be managed by the family. Although there is a waiter in attendance at the George Inn, Lydia takes on the job of dressing the salad. Lady Catherine, deigning to take some refreshment at Hunsford Parsonage, 'seemed to do it only for the sake of finding out that Mrs Collins's joints of meat were too large for her family,' which suggests they were carved on the spot by the assiduous Mr Collins. Cold food and little or no work left the servants free to concentrate on the all-important dinner.

Dinner, at whatever hour it was served, marked the end of 'morning' with its largely separate occupation for the two sexes, who came together for the 'evening' in a complete change of costume. Entrance to the dining room was in strict order of precedence, a precisely calculated combination of social status, marital status and age. The Bennet girls have evidently filed into the dining room after their mother in order of age all their lives, even when only the family is present; thus towards the end of the novel Elizabeth is sickened to observe her youngest sister, Lydia, 'walk up to her mother's right hand, and hear her say to her eldest sister, "Ah! Jane, I take your place now, and you must go lower, because I am a married woman."'

Host and hostess sat at the head and foot of the table, with the most important guests at their side. At Rosings there *is* no host, and as Mr Collins is more 'at home' there than Sir William Lucas, the only other male guest, 'He took his seat at the bottom of the table, by her ladyship's desire, and looked as if he felt that life could furnish nothing greater.'

In a large party, many are left to choose their own place. At Longbourn, Mrs Bennet refrains from inviting Bingley to occupy the place of principal male guest next to herself, because she is anxious he should sit by Jane. It is Darcy, therefore, who is invited to take the seat next to Mrs Bennet, much to the discomfiture of them both. Mrs Bennet has to leave the rest, including Mr Bingley, to chance: 'Jane happened to look round, and happened to smile; it was decided. He placed himself by her.'

In a decided difference from today, all the dishes comprising a 'course' would be on the table together – soup, fish, joints of meat, poultry, vegetables. Cookery books of the period often carry diagrams suggesting how the dishes might be arranged on the table to achieve a pleasing balance. Gentlemen helped their neighbours to the dishes they could reach, and servants carried round others by request. While ordinary family dinners would probably consist of just this one course, when company came a second course would be provided. This might include some new joints of meat, but the emphasis this time round was on lighter savoury concoctions like fricassees and patties, together with a selection of fruit tarts, jellies and creams. Mrs Bennet, always proud of her housekeeping, in planning a dinner for Bingley and Darcy, 'did not think anything less than two full courses, could be good enough for a man, on whom she had such anxious designs, or satisfy the appetite and pride of one who had ten thousand a year.'

When all had eaten sufficient, the ladies would withdraw to the drawing-room (the origin of its name), leaving the gentlemen to their port and conversation. If this was the hour most looked forward to by many of the men, it could be the most tedious for the women, with neither male

Sent by his daughter to announce her engagement

'She saw Mr Darcy with him': Darcy and Bingley (Hugh Thomson).

company nor alcohol to enspirit the scene. Even Elizabeth is known to flag. 'Anxious and uneasy, the period which passed in the drawing-room, before the gentlemen came, was wearisome and dull to a degree, that almost made her uncivil.' Conversely, the absence of men to attract might actually improve the manners of the ladies, Bingley's sisters for example. At Netherfield, 'Elizabeth had never seen them so agreeable as they were during the hour which passed before the gentlemen appeared.'

In the early novels, of which *Pride and Prejudice* is one, the gentlemen return *en masse*, shepherded by their host. At Mrs Philip's, the visiting soldiers all appear, in Elizabeth's eyes, 'superior to the broad-faced stuffy uncle Philips, breathing port wine, who followed them into the room.'

The arrival of the men was the signal for the ladies of the house to make tea. Some guests might even be invited *just* to drink tea, joining the family and more honoured guests *after* dinner, without seeming to feel slighted. 'Drinking tea' in Jane Austen's novels always denotes this after-dinner occasion, never the afternoon tea with which we are familiar, and which the Victorians introduced. Making tea usually devolved on the younger, marriageable ladies of the house, presumably because it showed off their pleasant manners and dainty movements. At Longbourn, Jane makes the tea and Elizabeth pours the coffee. Though the ceremony was known as 'drinking tea', coffee was also offered at Netherfield, Rosings and Mrs Philips's as well as at Longbourn.

After a period of music, cards or conversation, the last refreshment of the day was supper, which had been a substantial, hot meal when dinner was early, but for fashionable people had now dwindled to an elegant snack on a tray. Mrs Philips demonstrates her vulgarity when she promises her guests 'a nice comfortable noisy game of lottery tickets, and a little bit of hot supper afterwards'. Her sister, Mrs Bennet, also offers supper, and is disappointed when the party from Netherfield will not stay for it. The only supper acceptable to the most elegant in society is quietly at home by themselves, the exception being at a private ball, when it is absolutely essential to replenish the energy expended in dancing, and fortify the body against a cold drive home late at night. 'A private dance, without sitting down to supper, was pronounced an infamous fraud upon the rights of men and women,' says the narrator in *Emma*. This is why Bingley jokes about his housekeeper having to make 'white soup enough,' for all his guests.

A lady taking tea, silhouette by Charles Rosenberg (1745–1844).

Geographical Settings
Caroline Sanderson

Of all the journeys which take place in *Pride and Prejudice*, perhaps the most important is that which brings Elizabeth Bennet to Derbyshire. Elizabeth's aunt and uncle, Mr and Mrs Gardiner, originally propose to their much-loved niece that she accompany them on a summer tour of the Lake

District. In the event, Mr Gardiner's business commitments prevent them from travelling so far north. Elizabeth, who had 'set her heart on seeing the Lakes' is disappointed but agrees to go with them on a tour of Derbyshire, which Mrs Gardiner, who had once lived in the county, was eager to see again.

In the late eighteenth century such tours of English beauty spots and country houses were all the rage, as wealthy British travellers rediscovered the glories of their own land. Travel to the continent, where doing the Grand Tour had been an accepted part of the education of rich young men born into the landed gentry, had become difficult and dangerous following the outbreak of war with France in 1793. On the journey north from the Bennet's home in Hertfordshire, Elizabeth and the Gardiners visit the historic towns of Oxford, Blenheim, Warwick, and Kenilworth, which still feature on many tourist agendas today. Once in Derbyshire, they take in 'the celebrated beauties of Matlock, Chatsworth, Dovedale or the Peak'.

Her ladyship, with great condescension, arose to receive them.

After visiting all the other 'principal wonders of the county', the Gardiners decide to take in Pemberley, the home of Mr Darcy, which is a mere five miles from their lodgings in the fictional town of Lambton. They are especially keen to see the grounds, which are reputed to have some of the 'finest woods in the country'. Elizabeth, nervous of meeting the master of the house, is 'distressed' at the prospect. 'She felt she had no business at Pemberley, and was obliged to assume a disinclination for seeing it. She must own that she was tired of great houses after going over so many, she really had no pleasure in fine carpets and satin curtains.' She is a little reassured when the chambermaid at their lodgings in Lambton tells her that the Darcy family are not yet down for the summer. Despite this, when the excursion takes place, her spirits are 'in a high flutter'.

Pemberley does not disappoint. 'They gradually ascended for half a mile, and then found themselves at the top of a considerable eminence, where the wood ceased, and the eye was instantly caught by Pemberley House, situated on the opposite side of a valley, into which the road with some abruptness wound. It was a large, handsome stone building, standing well on rising ground, and backed by a ride of high woody hills … Elizabeth was delighted. She had never seen a place for which nature had done more, or where natural beauty had been so little counteracted by an awkward taste … at that moment she felt, that to be mistress of Pemberley might be something!'

From this moment, Elizabeth's opinion of Mr Darcy, already softened by the letter, in which he explains his actions in separating Mr Bingley from Elizabeth's sister, Jane, and reveals Mr Wickham's true character, begins to undergo a dramatic transformation. A conversation with the housekeeper at Pemberley, Mrs Reynolds, casts him in a completely different light, as a munificent lord and master, and an affectionate brother to Georgiana. When Mr Darcy returns unexpectedly early to Derbyshire, his generous attentions to Elizabeth, and to her aunt and uncle further endear him to

"Will you do me the honour of reading that letter?"

all of them. Later of course, Darcy plays an important role in ensuring that Wickham makes an honest woman of Lydia Bennet after their elopement, tracing them to their London hideaway and paying off Wickhams's considerable debts. Mr Darcy and Elizabeth are finally united, but not before her future husband has helped bring about the engagement of Jane and Mr Bingley.

There is no evidence that Jane Austen herself ever made it as far north as Derbyshire. She travelled to Warwickshire with her mother and sister in 1806, where she stayed with her mother's cousin, Thomas Leigh at Stoneleigh Abbey, a grand mansion dating from Elizabethan times. Later the Austen ladies extended their tour of relatives to take in the village of Hamstall Ridware in Staffordshire, home of Jane's cousin, the Revd Edward Cooper. As far as we know, this was the furthest north Jane Austen ever travelled. Her descriptions of Derbyshire in *Pride and Prejudice*, therefore, were almost certainly based on geographical research rather than personal experience. In more than one TV and film adaptation of her novel, Chatsworth House, the magnificent seat of the Dukes of Devonshire near Bakewell, has played the role of Pemberley, but as Jane Austen also mentions Chatsworth by name in the novel, it is unlikely that she really had it in mind. In fact, though the locations Jane Austen uses in her novels have always excited speculation, the truth is that it's almost always impossible to pin down her inspirations for the great houses of which she writes – Mansfield Park, Pemberley, Northanger Abbey, Kellynch Hall, Hartfield – just as her characters cannot wholly be identified with people she actually knew. They are creations of her imagination, composites of places known to her: locations in the end, that existed only in her mind's eye.

Part of Jane Austen's inspiration for Pemberley may have come from a grand house in another part of England entirely, one that she knew extremely well as the future home of her brother Edward. Godmersham Park in Kent belonged to Edward's adoptive parents, Mr and Mrs Thomas Knight. Completed in 1732, Godmersham is a substantial red-brick mansion with a large park, which lies in a wonderfully Arcadian setting in the shadow of the North Downs. From a rise behind the house, it is possible to look down on a view very similar to that described in *Pride and Prejudice*: gentle wooded hills, grazing sheep and a patchwork of fields, with the pretty River Stour flowing through the middle.

Edward Austen first attracted the notice of the wealthy Thomas Knight and his wife when they visited their distant cousins the Austens during their wedding journey in 1779. The Knights were so taken with 12-year-old Edward that they invited him to accompany them on the rest of their journey. When it became clear that they were not going to have children of their own the Knights decided to adopt him as their heir. The adoption was formally agreed upon in 1783, and Edward Austen's life was transformed. Instead of going to university like his older brother James, he began training for the role of a landed gentleman. He was sent abroad on the Grand Tour and travelled for the next four years, spending a year studying in Dresden.

He was in Switzerland in 1786 and Rome in 1789, returning to England only in 1790, at the age of 23. At the end of the following year he married Elizabeth Bridges, the daughter of a Kentish baronet, Sir Brook Bridges of Goodnestone Park, near Canterbury. The newly-weds spent their early married life at nearby Rowling, a small country house owned by the Bridges family, moving to Godmersham in 1797, at about the time that Jane Austen was busy composing *Pride and Prejudice*. Jane made many subsequent visits to Godmersham to stay with her brother and his family of eleven children.

Kent is an important location in *Pride and Prejudice*, as it is home both to Elizabeth Bennet's obsequious cousin, Mr Collins, and Mr Darcy's imperious aunt, Lady Catherine de Bourgh. After Elizabeth Bennet's friend and neighbour from Longbourn, Charlotte Lucas, contains her aspirations and marries the preposterous Mr Collins ('I am convinced that my chance of happiness with him, is as fair, as most people can boast on entering the marriage state'), Elizabeth goes to stay with them at the parsonage in the Kent village of Hunsford. Together with Sir William Lucas, and Charlotte's younger sister, Maria, she travels via London and the home of her aunt and uncle Gardiner in Gracechurch Street, which we are told, quite precisely, is a journey of twenty-four miles. Gracechurch Street, which lies now, as it did then, in the commercial heart of the City of London, is a location much derided by Miss Bingley and Mrs Hurst, who lives in Grosvenor Street in the much more fashionable district of Mayfair. 'The Netherfield ladies would have had difficulty in believing that a man who lived by trade and within view of his own warehouses, could have been so well bred and agreeable.' All is 'joy and kindness' with the Gardiners in Gracechurch Street however, and Elizabeth's short stay in London passes 'most pleasantly away … in bustle and shopping, and the evening at one of the theatres'.

Mrs Reynolds informed them that it had been taken in his father's lifetime.

The next day, the second leg of the journey to Kent, and another twenty-five miles brings Elizabeth to Hunsford, which, Jane Austen tells us, lies close to the village of Westerham near Sevenoaks in Kent. Mr Collins goes into raptures as he describes the vista of Lady Catherine de Bourgh's grand residence, which his lowly parsonage affords. 'Of all the views which his garden, or which the country, or the kingdom could boast, none were to be compared with the prospect of Rosings.' Later, as they walk across the park, after Lady Catherine has condescended to ask them to dine, Elizabeth finds much to admire in the landscape and her view is only slightly affected by Mr Collins's 'enumeration of the windows in the front of the house, and his relation of what the glazing altogether had cost Sir Lewis de Bourgh'.

Enduring Mr Darcy's unwelcome first proposal during her stay with the Collins, Elizabeth remains in Kent for around six weeks. She and Maria Lucas return home in early May, despite Lady Catherine de Bourgh's protestations that the girls should stay until Lady Catherine herself plans to travel to London for a week in early June: ' … as Dawson does not object to the Barouche box, there will be very good room for one of you – and indeed if the weather should happen to be cool, I should not object to taking you both, as you are neither of you large.' Lady Catherine has to be content

Repton design for the pheasantry, Royal Pavilion, Brighton, 1808.

however with advising them to mention her name at The Bell in Bromley, Kent, where the post-chaise will stop to change horses. Within four hours, Elizabeth and Maria are back in Gracechurch Street, and, after spending a few days more in London, they set out with Jane for the 'town of — in Hertfordshire', where Mr Bennet's carriage, and their over-excited sisters Lydia and Kitty are waiting to meet them at an inn.

Lydia quickly reveals that the militia will be leaving nearby Meryton in a fortnight for an encampment near Brighton in Sussex. Until the 1750s, Brighton, then known as Brighthelmstone, was a small fishing village. Its rapid development as a seaside resort followed the publication in 1750 of a Latin treatise on the virtues of sea water, by Dr Richard Russel.

Russel's pronouncements, quickly translated into English, secured a wide readership. He hailed sea water as a cure-all for a wide variety of ailments, from gout to gonorrhoea, and as a result, sea-bathing became all the rage. Brighton owed much of its popularity to the presence of the Prince of Wales, later George IV, who frequented the town for several decades, and built the extraordinary Indian-style building known as Brighton Pavilion, still the town's most famous landmark today. Jane Austen was no admirer of the Prince. After his estrangement from his wife, Princess Caroline in 1813, she wrote, 'Poor Woman, I shall support her as long as I can because she is a woman and because I hate her husband.' Just two years later however, Jane Austen reluctantly obeyed a royal command and dedicated her novel *Emma* to the Prince Regent after he expressed admiration for her work. She sent a copy of the novel to James Stanier Clarke, the Prince's librarian at his London residence, Clarence House. Stanier Clarke wrote to thank her, adding that he had sent the book on to the Prince himself in Brighton. What the Prince thought of *Emma* or whether he even read it is sadly not recorded.

Following the outbreak of war with France in 1793, regiments of soldiers from all over England took turns in defending Brighton as its geographical position on the Channel coast made it vulnerable to attack. Jane Austen's brother Henry spent some time there with his own regiment, the Oxfordshire militia in 1793. Lydia is desperate to follow the soldiers and is ecstatic when her friend Mrs Forster, wife of the Colonel of the regiment, invites her to accompany them to Brighton for the summer. Elizabeth pleads with her father not to let Lydia go, but Mr Bennet agrees to the plan, commenting somewhat fatefully that, 'Lydia will never be easy till she has exposed herself in some public place or other.' For Lydia herself, 'a visit to Brighton comprised every possibility of earthly happiness. She saw with the creative eye of fancy, the streets of that gay bathing place covered with officers.'

When Lydia elopes from Brigthon with Wickham, the couple disappear without trace for several days, much to the alarm of the whole Bennet family. Eventually, they are traced to a house in London, where Wickham — with the provision of certain financial incentives — is finally prevailed upon to marry Lydia. The ceremony takes place at the church of St Clement's in the parish where Wickham has his lodgings. It is possible that Jane Austen was thinking of the same St Clement's church mentioned in the popular children's nursery rhyme, 'Oranges and Lemons', as it is located in Eastcheap, not far from the Gardiners' house in Gracechurch Street.

It is only in these later stages of the novel that we are given more precise clues as to the geographical location which Jane Austen envisaged for Longbourn, the Bennets' home in Hertfordshire. When news of their elopement first reaches the Bennets, Lydia and Wickham are first assumed to be heading for Scotland and the border town of Gretna Green, where marriages could be performed without parental consent under Scottish law. At that time, anyone heading north out of London in the direction of Scotland would have journeyed along the Great North Road, now the A1000 road that passes through Hertfordshire and merges with the A1 trunk road to the north. This route, writes Jane to Elizabeth, would have brought them within ten miles of Longbourn. The county of Hertfordshire lies immediately to the north of London, and today its southern towns merge indistinguishably with the suburbs of the metropolis. In the late eighteenth century however, Hertfordshire was still a rural place, renowned for its market gardens, which supplied London with vegetables, and for its malting industry. Colonel Forster attempts to trace Lydia and Wickham at inns in the Hertfordshire towns of Barnet and Hatfield but finds no sign of them. This suggests they are still in London and increases the family's fears that Wickham has no intention of marrying Lydia.

Her affections had been never without an object.

Though to our knowledge Jane Austen never visited Hertfordshire herself, she chose the county as the main setting for *Pride and Prejudice*. It is interesting to note that the Derbyshire militia was actually stationed in Hertfordshire during the winter of 1794–5, an event Jane Austen could have read about in the paper and taken inspiration from. As usual she is quite precise in describing the relative locations of the places that feature in the novel. Longbourn, we are told, is situated a mile from the market town of Meryton and three miles from Mr Bingley's home at Netherfield, distances which Elizabeth has no hesitation in walking. Longbourn is also close to another town, which Jane Austen does not name, referring to it only as 'the town of — in Hertfordshire'. Among the Hertfordshire towns that have been suggested as the models for Meryton and '—' are Hertford and Ware, both of which lie within striking distance of the Great North Road.

By the end of *Pride and Prejudice*, however, few of the main characters remain in Hertfordshire. After his marriage to Lydia, Wickham leaves the Derbyshire militia and joins the regular army, where he has the promise of an 'ensigncy in General—'s regiment'. Much to Mrs Bennet's chagrin, the Wickhams leave almost immediately for Newcastle in the far north of England, where the regiment is stationed, which means that mother and daughter may not meet again for a year or more. Later, when the peace is signed with France, they are to be found 'always moving from place to place in quest of a cheap situation'. Mr Bingley and his wife Jane remain at Netherfield for a year, before 'so near a vicinity to her mother and Meryton relations' ceases to be

Oh, papa, what news— what news?

desirable 'even to his easy temper or her affectionate heart'. The Bingleys leave Hertfordshire and buy an estate in a neighbouring county to Derbyshire. The move happily places Jane within thirty miles of Elizabeth, who is now mistress of Pemberley. And both Mrs Darcy and her husband remain on the 'most intimate terms' with the Gardiners, 'both ever sensible of the warmest gratitude towards the persons who, by bringing her into Derbyshire, had been the means of uniting them.'

A Modern Perspective
Josephine Ross

'I dearly love a laugh.'
Elizabeth Bennet, in *Pride and Prejudice*, Chapter 11

Today, almost two centuries after it first appeared in 1813, *Pride and Prejudice* is one of the most famous and popular novels in the English language. Constantly filmed, televised, reprinted and discussed, it is updated, downloaded, annotated and translated; the opening line, 'It is a truth universally acknowledged ...' features in every Dictionary of Quotations; its title and author are recognised throughout the world. Churchill, Kipling, Henry James and Nabokov were famous fans; no current school curriculum, or recommended reading-list, is complete without it. For a work first published in an edition of some 1,500 copies, which received few reviews and earned its author less than £200 in her lifetime, *Pride and Prejudice* has had an extraordinary and fittingly ironic fate.

Yet as the renown of Jane Austen's masterpiece has grown, so too has the level of myths and misconceptions surrounding it. Some commentators in the twenty-first century (mostly, though not invariably, male) have come to refer scoffingly to *Pride and Prejudice* as a 'heaving bosom' novel, full of bonnets and ballrooms, in which swooning heroines pursue rich husbands – while wider issues, such as the plight of servants and the working classes, and the horrors of the Napoleonic Wars, are wholly ignored. As always with superficial judgements based on lack of knowledge and easy assumptions, nothing could be further from the truth. *First Impressions* was, of course, the original title of this immortal novel of human relationships, ideas and errors; that *Pride and Prejudice* should itself have become the victim, in some quarters, of prejudiced opinions based on mistaken first impressions, is in itself a testimony to the author's genius, and understanding of human nature.

The notion that Jane Austen would ever have written a 'heaving bosom' novel, except in fun, is of course nonsensical. From her earliest years she derived much of her literary inspiration from a desire to mock, parody – and counter – the hilariously silly conventions of bad 'women's fiction' – swooning heroines, long-lost heirs, improbable coincidences, lurid love-scenes, and the rest. It was a genre she knew well. As a child growing up in the literary and academic surroundings of her father's Hampshire vicarage –

where jokes and books were two abiding Austen family passions – she was encouraged to read, and to read widely. From Georgian children's fables and school primers, with their instructive moral tales and lively woodcut illustrations (some of which she scribbled over and coloured in) she progressed to popular histories, plays, poetry, volumes of essays and, of course, the classic novels: Defoe's *Robinson Crusoe*; Sterne's *Tristram Shandy*; Fanny Burney's *Evelina*; above all, Richardson's vast novel-in-letters, *Sir Charles Grandison*, rarely read today, but Jane Austen's lifelong favourite. (According to her family, she referred to the characters as if they had been living friends.) At the same time as absorbing great writing, she revelled in what a pretentious character in her last, unfinished work *Sanditon* would sneeringly call 'The mere Trash of the common Circulating Library' – namely, Gothic horror stories and, above all, sentimental fiction, such as twenty-first-century critics (and fans) might know by such terms as 'Mills & Boon', 'soap opera' and 'bodice-ripper'. No parodist, past or present, has ever produced a funnier, or more accurate, response to the genre than Jane Austen's *Love and Freindship*, written in 1790, when she was only 15. Taking its (misspelt) title from Goethe's 1774 Romantic landmark *The Sorrows of Young Werter*, and its style from such eighteenth-century forerunners of Dame Barbara Cartland as the popular Georgian 'authoress' Agnes Maria Bennett, this glorious spoof-saga of thwarted love, larceny, mistaken identity and continual fainting-fits is – specifically and hilariously – everything that her mature fiction is not.

I talked to her repeatedly in the most serious manner.

In *Pride and Prejudice*, first drafted some five years later, and rewritten for publication in 1813, Jane Austen consciously set out to create real characters, believable situations and genuine moral dilemmas – a resolute intelligent heroine, and a hero who, first presented as a self-consciously haughty, Byronic stereotype, who has to be laughed and even embarrassed out of his Regency dandy ways as the novel progresses. No heroine was ever less given to swooning than clever, merry Elizabeth Bennet. Her character is established, in all its commonsense vitality and charm, in Chapter 7, when eager to reach her sister Jane, who has been taken ill while visiting the Bingleys at Netherfield Hall, she sets out across three miles of muddy fields, 'jumping over stiles and springing over puddles', to arrive with 'weary ankles, dirty stockings and a face glowing with the warmth of exercise'. Her snobbish hostesses are shocked by such disregard for conventional appearances, mocking her 'blowsy' hair and 'petticoat six inches deep in mud'. Their other guest, Mr Darcy, however, is struck by 'the brilliancy which exercise had given her complexion', and the heightened brightness of her eyes. Seeing her before in a ballroom, elegantly turned-out, he had dismissed her as 'tolerable, but not handsome enough to tempt *me*', and declined to dance with her. Now, he feels the first stirrings of attraction for this unaffected, spirited young woman who puts concern for her sister's welfare above any thought for her own appearance.

The idea that *Pride and Prejudice* is full of detailed descriptions of dress and looks is, of course, another fallacy. With the exception of Emma Woodhouse

As they hastily turned round —

in *Emma*, who is conventionally 'handsome' (but initially, unsympathetic, by design), none of Jane Austen's heroines is a classic beauty, let alone preoccupied with fashion. Two of them – Elinor Dashwood in *Sense and Sensibility* and Elizabeth Bennet herself – are shown as being outshone in good looks by a much lovelier sister, as is shy little Fanny Price by her beautiful cousins in *Mansfield Park*. Tomboyish teenage Catherine Morland in *Northanger Abbey* is elated to hear that she looks 'almost pretty today'; at the other end of the age spectrum, Anne Elliot in *Persuasion*, fading into her 30s, is flattered and surprised to find herself the object of a handsome stranger's interested glances. In every case, Jane Austen does no more than hint at the actual faces and figures involved – thus allowing every reader to form his or her own mental picture. Where Elizabeth Bennet is concerned, much of our information is artfully provided at second-hand, through the eyes of Miss Bingley, her jealous rival for Mr Darcy's affections. We may thereby draw our own conclusions when Miss Bingley declares, 'Her face is too thin; her complexion has no brilliancy; and her features are not at all handsome. Her nose wants character; there is nothing marked in its lines. Her teeth are tolerable, but not out of the common way; and as for her eyes, which have sometimes been called so fine …' Such ungenerous, unsisterly, downgrading of another woman receives its just reward (and put-down) when Mr Darcy coolly responds that he has come to regard Elizabeth Bennet as 'one of the handsomest women of my acquaintance'. Present-day surveys consistently show that few women are truly content with their own appearance; here, ahead of her time, Jane Austen is surely reassuring her female readers, of every era, that beauty is truly in the eye of the beholder; that personality counts; and that we may all possess more physical attractions than society's stereotypes (often media-led) might have us believe.

Fashion magazines such as *La Belle Assemblée*, subtitled *Bell's Court*, and *Fashionable Magazine*, were already well-established by the time *Pride and Prejudice* was written. With their enticing combination of society reports, embroidery patterns, features on science and the arts, and – above all – gorgeous illustrations of the latest 'Morning Promenade Gown' or 'New Spencer Jacket', such publications would have been familiar to the Bennet girls; and though Jane Austen never mentions them in her novels, she and her sister Cassandra must surely have glanced at them from time to time. Certainly her letters show that, though no beauty herself, she was passionately interested in dress – constantly reporting from Bath and London on her purchases of gowns, shoes, hats, gloves, stockings and fabrics; describing new clothes being made for her; and commenting on what others wore, down to details of hair and makeup. Had Jane Austen wished, in *Pride and Prejudice*, to write a forerunner of the 'Shopping and F(lirting)', or 'chicklit', genre as some modern detractors would claim, she was ideally qualified to do so. That she deliberately, and subtly, did not is yet another tribute to her art and powers as a novelist.

In fact, references to clothing in *Pride and Prejudice* are strikingly rare. When Elizabeth Bennet first appears, in Chapter 2, she is 'employed in trimming a hat'; but no hint as to its colour, or style, is given. The point being made is that even when at rest, and conversing, Lizzy is never idle-handed. Later in the novel, the sister who is her moral antithesis – noisy, empty-headed, self-indulgent Lydia, who indeed thinks of nothing but shopping and flirting – idles away a spare moment in buying a bonnet that she neither needs nor even likes. Again, no details of the bonnet are given; but since her sisters 'abused it as ugly', we may infer that it will end up discarded and unworn – a further proof of her profligacy. In another of the novel's scant mentions of clothing, Lydia's gleeful letter announcing her moral downfall, when she has eloped with Mr Wickham, includes a message to her lady's maid, 'to mend a great slit in my worked muslin gown'. It is not necessary to be a follower of modern Freudian psychology, or Symbolism, to recognise the point being made here – that Lydia is as careless of her clothes as of her good character. Her sister Elizabeth's petticoat, earlier muddied in a good cause, will wash easily; Lydia's tearing of a fine muslin gown will, however, have to be repaired by someone's painstaking labours and fine-stitching – just as her personal misconduct will have to be patched up, and invisibly mended, at some cost to Mr Darcy's purse; her family's mortified feelings; and her own, all-too-delicate reputation.

Witless Mrs Bennet has always indulged her heedless, frivolous youngest daughter; and their relationship is wonderfully evoked. Yet in some respects, the characterisation of this most fallible mother is another feature of *Pride and Prejudice* that is not always fully understood by today's readers. The well-worn charge, that Mrs Bennet thinks of nothing but marrying off her five daughters, is, of course, true, and the vulgarity and ambition she displays in pursuit of husbands for them are as culpable as they are comical. Yet there is a dramatic, and even poignant, motivating force behind her conduct that would have been recognisable to the novel's original readers.

From the outset, Jane Austen makes it clear that the high standard of living that the Bennet family are enjoying – complete with a carriage, servants, fine clothes, balls, and all the trappings of a charming house, supported by a good income – will come to an abrupt end on Mr Bennet's death, since under the system of 'entail' on property inheritance, every-thing he (and they) currently possess will pass, not to his children, since they are all daughters, but to the nearest male family member: in this case, their repellent cousin, Mr Collins. Apart from a small capital sum each, the Bennet sisters will be deprived in an instant of their home, lifestyle and – as relatively poor, dependent, single women – social status. With no employment available to well-bred females, except the dreary drudgery of governess-dom, it is crucial to their future welfare and security that they should obtain husbands who can support them. For all her 'follies and nonsense' in pursuit of her ends, Mrs Bennet is not a mere caricature: her cry 'Who is to maintain you when your father is dead? *I* shall not be able to keep you' comes from the heart, and should be heard and understood. It is the key to much of the action, and moral debate, in this profound novel of manners and mores.

A lady's toilette.

Whether almost any marriage at all is preferable to none, for a woman with no 'fortune', is a dilemma that would have been wholly familiar to the readers for whom *Pride and Prejudice* was written. Jane Austen herself was in no doubt at all. 'Anything is to be preferred or endured, rather than marrying without Affection,' she insisted in 1814, in a letter to her niece Fanny Knight; an almost identical exhortation appears in *Pride and Prejudice*, when the heroine's elder sister, Jane, exclaims, 'Oh Lizzy! Do anything rather than marry without affection!' Her plea is, of course, unnecessary. Lizzy has consistently shown – with some vehemence – that she has no intention of marrying for worldly reasons, of any kind. She has turned down, unhesitatingly, the offer from Mr Collins, which would have ensured her comfort and security, and made her the future mistress of her old family home; still more remarkably, she is downright scornful in rejecting Mr Darcy's first marriage proposal, dismissing it as almost an insult, and heedless of the wealth, grandeur, historic estate and position in society that an alliance with him would bring. 'How rich and how great you will be! What pin-money, what jewels, what carriages you will have!' exclaims an ecstatic Mrs Bennet, on learning of Lizzy's acceptance of Darcy, at the climax of the novel; yet all this her daughter has previously rejected so summarily that even the reader can scarcely pause to wonder at her decision.

The opposite approach is exemplified by Lizzy's best friend, Charlotte Lucas, who 'without thinking highly either of men or matrimony', decides that marriage must be her 'pleasantest preservative from want'. Intelligent, but plain, aged 27, and with 'little fortune', Miss Lucas baldly admits, 'I ask only a comfortable home', and for this reason alone, accepts the repellent Mr Collins. However rational, even understandable, this attitude, it shocks Lizzy to find that a woman whom she has previously respected 'would have sacrificed every better feeling to worldly advantage'; and their friendship effectively lapses. No relationship between the sexes can be more shameful than Lydia's wanton cohabitation with Mr Wickham, outside marriage; yet the words such as 'humiliating' and 'disgracing herself', which Jane Austen applies to Charlotte's behaviour, show clearly the author's moral stance: that marriage without love is almost as much to be deplored as physical love without marriage.

If marrying for mercenary reasons is (contrary to some critics' belief) utterly condemned by Jane Austen and her heroines, so too is snobbery, and deference for high birth and rank. An underlying theme of *Pride and Prejudice* is the question of what constitutes, and defines, a 'gentleman'. The fact that so-called 'good breeding' is not always a guarantee of good manners, or good behaviour, is one that both Darcy and Elizabeth have to confront. Darcy's odious aunt, Lady Catherine de Bourgh – domineering, vain and self-obsessed – may be the daughter of an earl, but she is shown to be no less embarrassing, and even ill-bred, in her way than Elizabeth Bennet's mother, and her aunt Mrs Phillips. Lizzy's father is understood to be a 'gentleman' by dint of birth and social position; but by laughing at, rather than curbing, the 'folly and indecorum' of his wife and younger daughters he has not behaved in a 'gentlemanlike fashion'. Nothing does more to make

Darcy reassess his own manners than Lizzy's charge that his first proposal to her was not 'gentlemanlike'; while she, in turn, learns a harsh lesson from the discovery that Mr Wickham, outwardly so handsome, plausible and 'gentlemanlike', is in fact a gambler, a liar and a libertine. Dispensing with both pride and prejudice, both hero and heroine have to learn to look below surfaces, to arrive at truths.

A factor that does much to change Elizabeth's opinion of Mr Darcy is his behaviour towards his servants, as well as his tenants, and the poor and under-privileged in general. Visiting his country estate, Pemberley, she is struck by the praise of his devoted housekeeper, who calls him 'the best master … that ever lived'. As Lizzy reflects with pleasure, 'What praise is more valuable than the praise of an intelligent servant?' The fact that servants play little active part in the narrative is proof, not that they and their lives were of no interest to Jane Austen, but that she was too realistic and truthful an author to set her fiction in any circles where she was not 'quite at home'. They are a constant, discreet presence in *Pride and Prejudice* but, as in life, they are largely kept in the background. That they have eyes and ears and private opinions is never in doubt, however. It is obvious that the 'two elegant ladies' who are the Bingley sisters' personal maids are as scornful as their mistresses of Lizzy's dishevelled appearance when she visits Netherfield Hall; and it is a source of shame to both Lizzy and Jane that their mother's lack of discretion ensures that the disgrace of Lydia's elopement with Mr Wickham cannot be kept from the household staff.

Gave him to understand that her sentiments had undergone so material a change—

The background of the Napoleonic Wars against which *Pride and Prejudice* unfolds needed no introduction or explanation for Jane Austen's contemporary readers. The novel is shot through with what, to them, were familiar references. At every ball there are officers, gorgeous in their scarlet 'regimentals'; the —th Militia are stationed in the Bennets' local town of Meryton to be in readiness for the long-threatened French invasion. Better even than flirting with officers on the High Street, for Lydia Bennet and her ilk, or even attending a grand military review, is the prospect of visiting Brighton camp, where Wellington's armies – drilling, marching, manoeuvring by day, dancing by night – awaited their orders to face death or glory abroad. Even sensible Lizzy Bennet almost has her level head turned by Mr Wickham, in his guise as an 'officer and a gentleman'. There is no mention of war's horrors in *Pride and Prejudice* because this is a comedy of manners, depicting life on the domestic front in Regency England, not the battle-front in ravaged Europe. As Jane Austen would write at the conclusion of her next novel, *Mansfield Park*: 'Let other pens dwell on guilt and misery.'

Reading *Pride and Prejudice* in print for the first time, in January 1813, she anticipated some of the ignorant criticisms it would receive. Claiming to have had 'some fits of disgust' with it, she wrote, 'It is rather too light, and bright, and sparkling; it wants shade,' musing that she should have included 'some solemn specious nonsense', such as a 'long chapter – on the history of Bonaparte'. Readers all over the world today can only share the joke with her down the centuries, while treasuring this peerless novel, and revering the genius of its immortal author.

Principal Characters

Elizabeth Bennet is the protagonist of the novel. She is the second of Mr and Mrs Bennet's five daughters. She is her father's favourite and inherits his intelligence and wit, which leads her into prejudice – 'I meant to be uncommonly clever in taking so decided a dislike to him, without any reason.' Initially misled by first impressions, she is put off by Mr Darcy's cold outward demeanor. However, she becomes wise and mature enough to overcome her prejudices.

Fitzwilliam Darcy is the central male character. He is 28 when the novel opens and 'soon drew the attention of the room by his fine, tall person, handsome features, noble mien and the report … of his having ten thousand a year'. He is an intelligent and shy man, who often appears haughty or proud to strangers but possesses an honest and kind nature underneath. Initially, he considers Elizabeth his social inferior, unworthy of his attention; but he finds that, despite his inclinations, he cannot deny his feelings for Elizabeth. His initial proposal of marriage is rejected because of his pride and Elizabeth's prejudice against him.

Mr Bennet is the head of the Bennet family. An English gentleman with an estate at Longbourn in Hertfordshire, he has five daughters. Unfortunately, his property is entailed to a male descendant, meaning it can only be inherited by his closest male heir (Mr Collins). Mr Bennet 'was so odd a mixture of quick parts, sarcastic humour, reserve, and caprice, that the experience of three-and-twenty years had been insufficient to make his wife understand his character'. He is closer to Jane and especially Elizabeth, his two eldest and most sensible offspring. He prefers the solitude of his study, neglecting the raising of his children, which leads to near-disaster.

Mrs Bennet née Gardiner, the daughter of a Meryton attorney, is the querulous and excitable wife of Mr Bennet. 'She was a woman of mean understanding, little information, and uncertain temper. When she was discontented, she fancied herself nervous. The business of her life was to get her daughters married; its solace was visiting and news.'

Mary Bennet is the third and plainest daughter. She works hard for knowledge but has neither genius nor taste, but a pedantic air and a conceited manner.

Jane Bennet, the eldest sister, is 22 at the start of the novel, and considered to be the most beautiful amongst her sisters. '"You were dancing with the

only handsome girl in the room," said Mr Darcy, looking at the eldest Miss Bennett.' The depth of her feelings is difficult to discern due to her reserved manner. She sees only the good in people. She falls in love with Charles Bingley, and is devastated when he breaks off their developing relationship without explanation.

Lydia and **Kitty Bennet**, 'the two youngest of the family … their minds were more vacant than their sisters'. The younger, Lydia, is her mother's favourite. She is 15 when the narrative begins, extremely flirtatious, naïve, headstrong and reckless. When Lydia's influence is removed, Kitty spends more time with her elder sisters becoming 'by proper attention and management less irritable, less ignorant and less insipid'.

Charles Bingley is the closest friend of Mr Darcy, who leases property near the Bennets' estate. He 'was quite young, wonderfully handsome, extremely agreeable, and, to crown the whole, he meant to be at the next assembly with a large party'. Unlike many of those in his circle, he is approachable and mingles easily in company the others consider beneath them. He is attracted to Jane Bennet, who reciprocates his feelings but is too shy and reserved to fully express them.

William Collins, a clergyman, is cousin to Mr Bennet and heir to the Longbourn estate. Collins is a pompous, narrow-minded sycophant who is excessively devoted and flattering to his patroness, Lady Catherine de Bourgh. Advised by Lady Catherine to find a wife, he initially selects Jane, transfers his affections to Elizabeth who refuses him, and then proposes to Elizabeth's friend Charlotte Lucas who manages him so well that he marvels at their unanimity … 'we seem to have been designed for each other'.

George Wickham is a dashing, charming and handsome young soldier who at first attracts the attention of Elizabeth Bennet. His father was the manager of the Darcy estate, Pemberley, and he grew up with Darcy and his sister and was a favourite of Darcy's late father. Wickham's charm conceals a conniving and dishonorable nature, and there is bitter enmity between him and Darcy.

Lady Catherine de Bourgh, Darcy's aunt and patroness of William Collins, was 'a tall, large woman, with strongly marked features, which might once have been handsome. Her air was not conciliating … whatever she said was spoken in so authoritative a tone as marked her self-importance'.

Georgiana Darcy is Fitzwilliam Darcy's younger sister. 'Miss Darcy was tall … though little more than sixteen her figure was formed and her appearance womanly and graceful … She was less handsome than her brother, but there was sense and good humour in her face, and her manners were perfectly unassuming and gentle.'

Charlotte Lucas, 'a sensible, intelligent young woman about twenty-seven, was Elizabeth's intimate friend'. Her one regret is the loss of Elizabeth's esteem when she marries Mr Collins.

Mansfield Park

Modern Interpretations
John Wiltshire

At the beginning of the twenty-first century, *Mansfield Park* is considered Jane Austen's most ambitious, most controversial, and possibly richest novel. It is certainly the novel which is most clearly embedded in a specific historical setting, as its opening words suggest. 'About thirty years ago', taken with the information in the subsequent paragraphs, cues the reader to expect a specifically contemporary narrative, one not unlike, perhaps, the novels of Maria Edgeworth, the best-selling author of the time. Edgeworth's work dealt with social and political issues, and *Mansfield Park* is increasingly read as a narrative that makes interventions into controversies of the decade in which it was written. This saw the rise of Evangelicalism, the abolition of the slave trade, and the continuing war against Napoleon enter a phase in which sea-power was decisive. In contemporary readings of the novel, the challenges and changes wrought by Evangelicalism, the slave trade, and the importance of the navy to Britain's prosperity all loom large.

Before about 1970, most commentary on the novel concentrated on the explication of what might be called its moral argument. Many essays – of which the most famous is Lionel Trilling's of 1955 – sought to explain how it was that Jane Austen had apparently reversed the system of values apparent in *Pride and Prejudice*, and instead of a healthy, vigorous heroine, Elizabeth Bennet, being played off against a 'sickly' rival, the cross and silent Miss Anne Darcy, presented a 'puny' and quiet heroine – Fanny Price – who is pitted against the witty and engaging Mary Crawford. Many readers, especially first-time readers, cannot understand why they are being asked to sympathise, and perhaps even identify with a character who is described by Tom Bertram, her cousin, as 'creepmouse'. They find Fanny prim and prudish, her cousin Edmund a bore. The Crawfords, on the other hand, seem witty and adventurous; so why, they wonder, is Jane Austen asking us to mistrust them, and to admire the solemn central pair?

The critical accounts of the 1950s and 1960s were essentially attempts to meet this challenge and defend the novel against readings like these. They usually emphasised that the charm of the Crawfords is only superficial, and explicated the qualities of integrity and moral principle the novel sees in both Fanny and her cousin. Trilling's claim that Fanny Price is a specifically 'Christian heroine' was endorsed. She was often portrayed, as for instance by Tony Tanner, as a kind of secular saint. 'She suffers in her stillness. For righteousness' sake,' Tanner wrote, in one of the most widely circulated essays on the novel (1966, 1986), failing to notice the restless 'jealousy and agitation' that the narrator emphatically attributes to her heroine.

Critics thus tended to focus on the portrayal and assessment of characters in the novel, at the same time as they defended *Mansfield Park* as a coherent,

"*Good, gentle Fanny!*"

An 'after' drawing by Humphry Repton of Harlestone Park in Northamptonshire, from Fragments on the Theory and Practice of Landscape Gardening, *1816 (opposite).*

131

The kind pains you look to persuade me out of my fears

even systematic defence of conservativism. They almost completely ignored the historical circumstances of the action. This was a critical tradition interested in psychological life, and in ethical questions. Though moral principle was extensively discussed, this was never considered in the very relevant context of the ongoing success of Evangelical writers in converting the ruling classes of England to a more 'serious' view of their religious and social duties in the years about which Jane Austen was writing. Much was made of the theatricals. Little was said about the Napoleonic Wars, and nothing at all about slavery.

From about 1975, though, this way of reading *Mansfield Park* was gradually superseded by accounts which gave more emphasis to its political dimensions. The first influential books to take this step were Marilyn Butler's *Jane Austen and the War of Ideas* (1975) and Alistair Duckworth's *The Improvement of the Estate* (1971). Butler argued that Jane Austen took the conservative, anti-Jacobin view in the 'war of ideas' that surrounded the actual war with revolutionary France and then with Napoleon, and that *Mansfield Park* is virtually a didactic novel. Fanny Price is sickly and 'debilitated,' but we are to expect this of heroines in the Christian tradition, and the novel is read as an allegory, almost as a morality play, with Fanny being faced with a choice between worldliness, represented by Henry Crawford and his estate, and spiritual integrity. Her sojourn in Portsmouth is described by Butler as her temptation in the wilderness.

'Improvement' is an important buzz-word in the first decade of the nineteenth century and is constantly used by characters in the novel, including Edmund. Duckworth argued that Jane Austen was deeply conservative, and that she used crucial episodes – the visit to Sotherton and the rehearsals for *Lovers' Vows* – to indicate that improvement, in the sense of cultural innovation and change, was destructive of long-established, cherished values. To 'improve' the estate – 'to have the avenue down,' as Rushworth thinks of it, is to destroy patriotic symbols of continuity. Duckworth simply assumes that Jane Austen was hostile to the landscaping practices of Humphry Repton. Reading *Mansfield Park* as a serious contribution to an ongoing cultural debate, made more urgent by the conflict with France, Butler's and Duckworth's books continued the tradition that attempted to account for the authority which the novel undoubtedly exerts by reading it as a text of moral earnestness. These accounts, which were progressive in one sense, because they made the novel's historical setting relevant to its interpretation, were regressive in another, because they saw the novel in close to didactic terms.

By the 1980s, feminist readings or re-readings came to dominate the criticism of Jane Austen, as they still do to a large extent today. Feminist critics tended to concentrate at first on the 'domestic politics' of the novels, and to investigate more searchingly how the broader controversies of the period were mirrored in their language and echoed in the small daily conflicts and decisions which they depict and scrutinise. In her *Jane Austen; Women, Politics and the Novel* (1988), Claudia L. Johnson implicitly took issue with

Butler's reading of *Mansfield Park* as a novel which endorsed conservative values. She aligned Jane Austen not with Burke, but with Burke's antagonists, specifically with Mary Wollstonecraft, author of the radical polemic *The Rights of Woman* (1792). Johnson underscored the extent to which Jane Austen invites the reader to criticise the patriarch of the family, and master of the estate, Sir Thomas, rather than to respect him, and argued that the novel's pervasive ironies act subversively, putting question marks over all behaviour, and seeing self-deception omnipresent in the self-justifications of almost all the novel's characters. This was not then a conservative text, but a radically questioning one.

This debate: is Jane Austen a 'conservative' or 'subversive' writer, first articulated in these terms by Duckworth, continues to animate contemporary accounts of *Mansfield Park*. The debate took on a radical new dimension when, in the 1980s, articles began to appear which called attention to the 'West Indian' connection. A previously little-noticed feature of the novel, the fact that, as mentioned in its very first pages, Sir Thomas has a 'West Indian estate,' began to loom large in critical accounts, since if he has an estate in Antigua, as comes out a little later, that estate, during the period of the novel, must be worked by slave labour. Is Sir Thomas a slave-owner, and does the family's standing and prosperity – 'all the comforts and consequences of a handsome house and large income,' mentioned in the novel's first sentence – rest upon the labour of slaves in England's distant colonial empire? 'Yes' was the firm answer given in by far the most influential of these critiques, the discussion of *Mansfield Park* published in Edward Said's *Culture and Imperialism* (1993). Jane Austen's novel looked very different when seen from a point of view outside England, Said argued. Sir Thomas does not merely direct his daughters' and his niece's lives and choices in order to further the prosperity of his 'house,' as Johnson and other critics had suggested: he brings the efficient autocratic ways of the slave-owner to his management of Mansfield – specifically in his cleaning up after what might be seen as the abortive rebellious take-over of the theatricals.

Even more influentially, Said suggested that the adoption and transportation of Fanny Price from her home in Portsmouth to distant Northamptonshire paralleled the transportation of slaves from Africa to the West Indies. Fanny, like a slave, was a property, brought to Mansfield to serve the needs of its inhabitants. It is clear, of course, that Fanny is not literally a slave, or even, strictly speaking, a servant, but there is plenty of material in the novel to support an argument that no-one is really concerned about her, that she is 'ill-used' (as her cousin Julia puts it at one moment), and that she is kept pretty constantly at (unpaid) 'work' – 'work' being the needlework that she is continually seen carrying out for both her aunts. The passage in which Fanny, at the bidding of her aunt Bertram, is described as 'standing and stooping in a hot sun' in the rose-garden could readily be read as a reminder of slavery, as it is for example in John Wiltshire's *Jane Austen and the Body* (1992). Said also called attention to the scene in which Fanny asks her uncle about 'the slave-trade,' which is followed by a 'dead silence' from

Indulged with his favourite instrument

the rest of the family. This occasion (which is only reported by Fanny to Edmund, not dramatised), became the key to many subsequent readings.

Brian Southam's *The Silence of the Bertrams* (1995), for example, another very influential critique, emphasised the Bertram family's dependence on their West Indian property. He argued that the silence of the family following Fanny's question implied their collective guilt. Southam brought the date of the abolition of the slave trade, which took place after thirty years of agitation, in 1807 firmly into debate about the novel. It can be argued that Fanny's question to her uncle presumes – as her cousin says – that he would like to be asked, and is therefore possibly an advocate for abolition (as were several prominent planters). Dating the action of the novel to 1812–13, Southam argues on the other hand, though, that Sir Thomas is meant to be understood as a vicious, tyrannical exploiter of slaves on his estates. Whether the novel suggests that their Antiguan estates are crucial to the Bertrams' fortune, though, is unclear and has been keenly disputed.

Said's claim that Fanny is an abused property, brought in to serve the needs of the Bertram family, provided later critics with another angle on which to approach the questions surrounding the novel's heroine. The consequences of her adoption, her removal from the brothers and sisters 'among whom she had always been important as play-fellow, instructress and nurse' and her relegation to a lonely unregarded status in the grand house, clearly affects her psychologically. It is because Edmund is the only one among the coldly indifferent Bertrams to give her any real attention that he becomes so important to her. Studies in recent years have often focused on Fanny's inner life, and on the struggles and jealousies resulting from her need to suppress her own desires. In readings like Mary Waldron's (*Jane Austen and the Fiction of her Time*, 1999) Fanny is far from the figure of upright integrity and impeccable judgement that she was in the 1950s. At the same time, the focus on Jane Austen's presentation of Fanny's inner life has interestingly been suggested by William Deresiewicz to demonstrate the influence of the early romantics, especially Wordsworth, on Jane Austen's mature understanding of the psychological processes which adapt one to loss and adversity (*Jane Austen and the Romantic Poets* 2004).

Nothing demonstrates more clearly in fact the continuing increase in the status of *Mansfield Park* among readers of Jane Austen than the variety of approaches that have been found productive in the last decades. This is partly because, compared to both *Pride and Prejudice* and *Emma*, the immediately preceding and immediately succeeding novels, *Mansfield Park* is a continuously referential text. (The Cambridge edition of the novel has twice as many notes as for *Emma*, a longer novel.) Besides many allusions to Britain's colonial empire, including the slave trade, it comments on the system of patronage, especially in the navy. There are several dialogues about the clergy which refer to reforms in the Anglican church brought about through the influence of Evangelical writers, who saw change in the church and the ruling classes as the key to national renewal. The chapters concerned with Sotherton intervene in the debates about landscape gardening so current in the years in which the novel was written – debates which are both political and aesthetic. The social range of *Mansfield Park* is also greater than any of the other novels. The Price family in Portsmouth are at the very bottom of the gentry scale, the family of the baronet Sir Thomas Bertram are at the top. Compelling issues of class and status are enacted in the novel's drama of Fanny's ambiguous adoption. Stimulating articles have been published which discuss all these aspects, as well as its affinities with later Victorian fiction. In many ways *Mansfield Park* is a 'condition of England' novel written before the phrase was invented.

He walked to the gate and stood there without seeming to know what to do.

More recently, a quite different area of controversy has opened up around the novel. First published in 1814, *Mansfield Park* was revised by the author for the 1816 edition published by John Murray. All subsequent editions have taken this as their base text, though some, like Chapman's frequently reprinted Oxford edition, have preferred occasional readings from 1814. Contemporary critics and editors, however, have argued that the 1814 text must be closer to Jane Austen's original manuscript, and is therefore to be preferred, as it is in Kathryn Sutherland's 1996 Penguin edition. One problem with this argument is that the 1814 version is full of printing errors, so that to trust its publisher and printers to transcribe correctly Jane Austen's intentions is to draw a long bow. Nevertheless, increased focus on the details of Jane Austen's texts has proved to be rewarding.

The Miramax film of *Mansfield Park* released in 1999 was influenced by recent criticism, and especially by its preoccupation with slavery and the slave trade. Directed by Patricia Rozema, the movie was praised by some critics because it was not inhibited by reverence or respect for the novel, and instead of Austen's reticent, quiet, physically weak heroine, presented the opposite – a Fanny in the mould of Elizabeth Bennet, outspoken, vigorous, even 'wild.' This Fanny confronted her uncle with his connivance in the slave trade, and a major focus of the film was on slavery as the background of the Bertrams' fortunes, with the house depicted as a crumbling mansion to underline the decadence of their idle aristocratic lives. In line with Rozema's feminism, Mrs Norris, who is the major exploiter of Fanny Price in the novel, and a powerful study in moral pathology, became inconsequential, and Sir Thomas instead took over the role of tyrant, depicted in sexual acts with his slaves, hated by his eldest son, and altogether a monstrous incarnation of patriarchy. The climactic sequences in which Fanny opens a door to find Henry and Maria having sex, and then discovers sketches which prove her uncle's corruption, were set in darkness. Fanny was allowed to accept the proposal of a Henry Crawford made much less predatory than in the novel, and – in a motif borrowed from Jane Austen's own acceptance and next-morning rejection of Harris Bigg-Wither – turn him down the next day.

Dubbed 'Wuthering Park' by Austen readers, the film was the first and only movie so far based on one of her novels to be a failure at the box office. It lost – and deserved to lose – most of the money that previous Austen successes had made. Yet it survives in a strange half-life among some Austen scholars. It is certainly true that its drastic surgery on the novel is a useful provocation to revisiting the text, but it is difficult to rid oneself of the suspicion that to take the film seriously is to reveal an incapacity to understand the text which the film attempts to subvert. Whilst the novel's deft movement between its different characters has long been understood as one of its great achievements, for example, the film's editing is conventional and clumsy. As recent critical investigations of the figure have shown, Fanny Price is a markedly original creation, as challenging for readers now as she was for Austen's contemporaries.

The ITV/WGBH film of 2007, with script by Maggie Wadey, went even further than the earlier version in replacing Jane Austen's heroine by one of its own. Fanny is now a dramatically healthy and buxom young woman, who runs about and laughs a lot, and whose attraction for Henry is her lack of inhibition. She pouts and scowls whenever Edmund shows interest in Mary, and answers back to Mrs Norris. There is no Portsmouth sequence (which is like *Hamlet* without the Ghost) and almost nothing is seen of Fanny's East room, important in both the novel and in Rozema's film. Clumsily filmed and lit, this version at least gets the period of the house right, and there is some subtlety in the portrayals of Sir Thomas and Lady Bertram.

The decision of the producers and directors of these films that Jane Austen's Fanny could not be made attractive to modern audiences, though, is a strange one. Several successful films, such as *Washington Square* directed by Agnieszka Holland and Peter Webber's *The Girl with a Pearl Earring* (2004), have featured silent, reticent, even apparently unattractive but, as in Jane Campion's *The Piano* (1993), determined heroines, like Austen's pioneering creation. These would also include the less-known reworking of *Mansfield Park* by Whit Stillman, in *Metropolitan* (1990). This film transposes much of the action of *Mansfield Park* to a group of young well-off New Yorkers in the 1980s. Its heroine, the quiet and morally scrupulous Jane Austen fan Audrey Rouget, falls in love with Tom, who is attracted by the more striking and passionate Serena, just as Fanny was in love with an Edmund infatuated with Mary Crawford. Morally dubious games are played in the absence of parents, into which Audrey is unwillingly drawn. More interestingly than these plot resemblances, the film plays with its own affinities to Austen, including conversations between Tom and Audrey in which Lionel Trilling's widely-known 1955 article on *Mansfield Park* is discussed. Tom reads *Persuasion* and finds Jane Austen, much to his surprise, amusing. Simultaneously, then, the film is adapting the novel and conducting a conversation with and about it, and about Jane Austen's relevance to lives lived centuries later. The richness of this text, often thought less immediately attractive, and more 'difficult' than Jane Austen's others, thus continues to feed both criticism and the creative reworkings of film and television adaptations.

Regency Life
Maggie Lane

The Church

As the established religion of the country, the Church of England was a powerful force in Jane Austen's time. Its Bishops sat in the House of Lords; the Universities and endowed schools were under its control; its doctrines were accepted by all but a tiny minority, and its wealth and property were amassing – witness the many lovely rectories of the period. This monoculture did much to create a cohesive society. The sectarian conflict that had torn the country apart was a thing of the past, and calm – some would say, complacency – in religious affairs prevailed. Energy and effort could increasingly be focused on the secular goals of commerce, invention, discovery and empire.

Traditionally, the church provided a house and income for younger sons of the gentry, those who had no landed estate to inherit. Not for nothing was a parish known as a living. No vocation was required of such men and, as in any profession, it was inevitable that some would be more conscientious than others. Boys were often intended for the church long before their personal inclinations or suitability could be known. They simply had to be reasonable scholars – in Latin and Greek. The only essential was a university degree. Indeed, the ancient universities of Oxford and Cambridge had been founded specifically to educate men for holy orders, and the vast majority of graduates in Jane Austen's time still went into the church.

Dr Grant himself went out with an umbrella

She herself came from clerical stock. Her mother's father had been a clergyman, so was her own father and her eldest brother, James. Another brother, Henry, took holy orders in middle age after the failure of his bank left him without a livelihood. An uncle, a nephew, her only male first cousin and numerous cousins-once-removed were men of the cloth. It was almost the default occupation for Austens and Leighs.

The Cathedrals, the Universities and the Crown all had livings to dispose of, and nepotism and string-pulling were of course rife. But the majority of livings were in the gift of private landowners, and reserved for members of the family. The Leighs – Jane Austen's maternal relations – owned many such, and distributed them about the family, including to her brother James. Holding multiple livings was perfectly acceptable in the climate of the times. While Mr Austen held two neighbouring livings which he could oversee himself, one of James's three parishes was never visited by him, it was so far away, and he relied on a curate to do the work. James did, however, after much soul-searching, decline the offer of a fourth living, on the grounds not of pluralism, but of simony – accepting a living with the promise to give it up when a younger relation was of an age to take it. The family connection who had made the offer – Lord Craven – was probably

"It would give me the greatest pleasure, but that I am (but meant) going to dance"

not told James's reason for refusal, but as a man of the world he would have been astonished that conscience might make a man decline any addition to his income.

Though most clergy were not rich – Mr Austen had an income of about £600 per annum, and James, despite his scruples, of £1,100, while Henry Austen could only obtain a curacy at £54.12s.0d when he was first ordained – they had the satisfaction of belonging by association to the ruling class. This gave Jane Austen herself a secure social status and enabled her to observe her society from the position of an insider. Not only was the clergyman in any village looked up to as one of the few educated men in the community, but he – and his family – took their place as of right, on social occasions and in local affairs, among the neighbouring landholders. In Steventon, where Jane grew up, her father was known to be related to the absent Squire, and was regarded as his stand-in.

It was from this thoroughly clerical background that Jane Austen created her inimitable gallery of clergymen, from the obsequious Mr Collins in *Pride and Prejudice* to the shallow Mr Elton in *Emma*, from the witty hero Henry Tilney in *Northanger Abbey* to the dull but worthy Edward Ferrars in *Sense and Sensibility*. With the exception of Mr Collins, who pontificates about christening and burying his parishioners, none of them has anything to say about the profession itself. It is only in *Mansfield Park* that the role and duties of a clergyman are seriously considered.

By the time Jane Austen came to compose *Mansfield Park*, a century of Georgian laxity in matters ecclesiastical was drawing to an end. To many in the rising generation, patronage, nepotism, pluralism, absenteeism and lack of independence from the landholder seemed glaring abuses crying out for reform. The Evangelical movement gathered momentum, with the twin objectives of combating indolence in the Church, and stirring up the population to greater spiritual awareness. Among the measures advocated by the Evangelicals were stricter Sunday observance, the revival of morning and evening family prayers, and constant reading of the Bible to bring religion to the forefront of people's daily lives.

At first Jane Austen was wary of Evangelicalism, seeing it as an attack on the mild churchmanship that formed the firm foundation of her own life, and which had served the country so well in ensuring stability and social cohesion. With her belief in the essentially private nature of religious faith, she was suspicious of any false or exaggerated emotion. 'I do not like the Evangelicals,' she stated baldly in 1809. Her own cousin, the Reverend Edward Cooper, was an Evangelical preacher, whose sermons were published; she found them too full of what she called 'regeneration' – a quality she distrusted.

By 1814, however, many had been won over by the evident piety and humanity of the movement, Jane Austen among them. 'I am by no means convinced,' she wrote to a niece, 'that we ought not all to be Evangelicals, & am at least persuaded that they who are so from Reason & Feeling, must be happiest & safest.' Her proviso is very characteristic. She was never to depart from her commitment to reason, seeing it as a guiding principle in every area of life. But the Evangelicals' call to higher standards of personal morality was exactly what had always suffused and motivated her own writing, despite its essentially comic tone.

Mansfield Park is the *least* comic of her six published novels; though it certainly has its moments of high humour, the overall tone is serious, even sombre. It was composed in the years 1813–14 and is her answer to a spate of not very subtle Evangelical novels then being published. Writing at the very height of her imaginative powers, Jane Austen creates characters in whose talk and behaviour the issues take on life and meaning.

Dr Grant appears as one of the worst of the old-style clergymen. As his sister-in-law, Mary Crawford, dryly remarks, 'A clergyman has nothing to do but to be slovenly and selfish – read the newspaper, watch the weather, and quarrel with his wife. His curate does all the work, and the business of his own life is to dine.'

She worked very diligently under her aunt's directions

Edmund Bertram is in the new mould. He defines the clergyman's role as 'the charge of all that is of the first importance to mankind, individually or collectively considered, temporally and eternally – which has the guardianship of religion and morals, and consequently of the manners which result from their influence.' He explains to a sceptical Mary, 'It will, I believe, be everywhere found, that as the clergy are, or are not what they ought to be, so are the rest of the nation.' It is notable that while in *Pride and Prejudice* Elizabeth has laughed at Mr Collins' pomposity (and we have laughed with her), here Edmund's pronouncements have his author's approval and are proof against Mary Crawford's subversive wit.

Edmund is not yet ordained when he has this discussion with Mary, but he has evidently thought deeply about his calling – even while admitting that the knowledge of a good family living kept for him has influenced him in his choice of profession. His view is that a clergyman leads by example. He must therefore live among his flock.

As Edmund's ordination draws nearer, Henry Crawford, even more cynical than his sister, and not having heard Edmund's own views on the matter, assumes he will enjoy his £700 a year income from the living but remain resident at Mansfield Park, only riding the eight miles to Thornton Lacey for 'a sermon at Christmas and Easter'. For a man of the world like Henry to make this assumption, such doings were evidently common practice.

Sir Thomas puts him right. Edmund knows, says his father, that 'human nature needs more lessons than a weekly sermon can convey, and that if he does not live among his parishioners and prove himself by constant attention their well-wisher and friend, he does very little either for their good or his own.' It is therefore a *practical* ministry that Jane Austen advocates, perhaps ultimately little different from what she had observed of her own father's good practice, yet chiming with the new seriousness of the age.

A portrait of garden designer Humphry Repton (1752–1818).

Houses and Gardens

'Every generation has its improvements,' says Mary Crawford mischievously, referring to leaving off family prayers in Sotherton chapel. But this could almost be the motto for *Mansfield Park*, since improvements of another kind – to houses and gardens – are a regular topic of conversation among the characters, and one of the great set pieces in the novel is the day at Sotherton where they are purposely gathered to discuss how its grounds might be improved.

Improving grounds was all the rage at this time. Henry Crawford is a great improver (though he hardly improves the lives of those he comes into contact with). He has remodelled the grounds of his own house, Everingham, at the age of twenty-one, and is now eager to turn his attention to other people's. Later in the novel he will dream up grandiose plans for Edmund's Thornton Lacey, but first he turns his attention to Mr Rushworth's Sotherton Court. Rushworth is full of the subject since staying with a friend who has employed Humphry Repton, the real-life landscape gardener, to refashion his grounds.

Repton was the foremost garden designer of the period. He remodelled dozens of the greatest gardens in England, including Adlestrop, the Gloucestershire home of Jane Austen's Leigh relations. The fees he charged the Leighs rather amusingly (but accurately) find their way into *Mansfield Park*, where the characters debate whether to employ him. Repton was the successor to the famous Lancelot 'Capability' Brown, who had swept away the straight lines, symmetrical parterres, canals and avenues of old-style English gardens and replaced them with undulating lawns, serpentine expanses of water reflecting the house, and clumps of trees on the horizon. Repton developed this style by retaining the fluid, natural look but adding more variety and colour. He introduced many features, such as the ballustraded terrace, the conservatory and the trellis-covered walk, which eased the transition between house and garden. Regency people demanded comfort as well as show from their surroundings.

In *Mansfield Park*, Sotherton has escaped the Brown treatment and now seems dreadfully old-fashioned; Mr Rushworth wants to give it a modern look. Despite the likely sacrifice of a fine old avenue of oak, which distresses Fanny (Fanny hates change of any kind), even Edmund thinks Mr Rushworth is right to modernise. Sotherton and Everingham are great estates, but the owners of quite small properties shared the itch for improvements. Mary tells of her uncle buying a summer cottage on the Thames, which 'being excessively pretty, it was soon found necessary to be improved; and for three months we were all dirt and confusion, without a gravel walk to step on or a bench fit for use.' The Grants have improved the grounds of Mansfield Parsonage, converting a rough hedgerow boundary into a shrubbery – principally evergreen – with a walk and benches to give opportunities for exercise and rest to ladies.

While gentlemen seemed most to care about the impression their property makes – the grand design – ladies were more concerned with amenities – the details that give comfort and pleasure. Lady Bertram's only advice to Mr Rushworth is to have a shrubbery: 'one likes to get out into a shrubbery in fine weather.' Mary Crawford stipulates for any property in the country 'shrubberies and flower gardens and rustic seats innumerable.' Lady Bertram also has her flower garden at Mansfield Park, complete with shady alcove in which she can sit and watch others labour. Flower gardens were fashionable again, after the Brown years of interminable lawn, an innovation encouraged by the exotic species being brought back by explorers from all parts of the globe. Mrs Grant grows tender plants and, in *Persuasion*, the flower garden at Kellynch Hall is considered the province of the lady of the house, Elizabeth Elliot.

'While Fanny cut the roses'.

Jane Austen herself loved flowers and mentions collecting seeds from friends and choosing flowering shrubs to plant. The lack of a garden had been one of the depressing features of her Bath life, but in Southampton and then Chawton she could revel in growing flowers again. At Chawton too, the Austen ladies enjoyed similar amenities to those at Mansfield Parsonage, thanks to brother Edward's generosity. The cottage had formerly been lived in by his steward, but in 1809 improvements were made to suit the social status and gender of the new occupants, and the grounds were 'arranged as best might be, for ladies' occupation.' In *My Aunt Jane Austen*, niece Caroline Austen tells us that 'a high wooden fence shut out the road … all the length of the little domain, and trees were planted inside to form a shrubbery walk – which carried round the enclosure, gave a very sufficient space for exercise.'

(On the death of the last family occupant, Cassandra Austen, in 1845, the cottage, which had housed four inmates plus their servants, was 'divided into habitations for the poor, and made to accommodate several families.' In fact the cottage was sliced vertically into three separate dwellings. Among the changes out of doors, 'Trees were cut down' and 'all that could be termed pleasure ground … reverted again to more ordinary purposes.' Shrubbery walks were strictly for the genteel!)

Another improvement made by Edward to increase the cottage's privacy for his mother and sisters was to block up the sitting-room window facing the road, and cut a new window looking out onto the garden. This window is in quite a different architectural style from the rest of the house, having playful gothic glazing bars which were highly fashionable in 1809. In *Mansfield Park*, it is very likely that Admiral Crawford's summer cottage at Twickenham was also improved in this style, since it particularly suited such buildings. It was used a lot at the seaside (Sidmouth in Devon is rich in examples) but even more pertinent is that it was at Twickenham that the

Mr Yates felt it acutely.

gothic style was first employed in domestic building – by Horace Walpole at his famous Strawberry Hill extravaganza.

The use of gothic and other ornamental features – balconies, verandas, gables and barley-sugar chimneys – was a reaction to the severe classical style that had held sway in domestic architecture through most of the eighteenth century. As such, it parallels the movement in garden design from the plain and pure to the intricate and detailed. But only a few of the buildings Jane Austen knew would have been so up-to-date, and when one is singled out in her novels she tends to make a little fun of it for trying too hard – Uppercross Cottage in *Persuasion,* for example, which she describes catching the traveller's eye 'with its veranda, French windows and other prettinesses.' Uppercross Cottage, in fact, has been 'elevated' from a farm-house for the young squire's occupation on his marriage – rather like Chawton Cottage itself, made fit for gentry living in the early nineteenth century.

Another small property that has been 'improved' by French windows is Mansfield Parsonage, where the sitting room window has been 'cut down to the ground, and opening on a little lawn' – so that the ladies can easily step outside. For the most part, however, Jane Austen is sparing on architectural descriptions, and we must imagine most of the houses occupied by her characters to be classical (or Palladian – the terms are more or less interchangeable) in design, with flat fronts and a symmetrical arrangement of sash windows. This blueprint for a well-proportioned building served for best part of a century, whether for terraces of town houses in London and Bath, or great country mansions, or medium-sized rectories and houses.

Mansfield Park itself is characterised only as 'a spacious, modern-built house.' The word 'modern' refers to the Palladian style; the house is old enough to require being completely refurnished if Mary Crawford were to become its mistress! The house is 'so well placed and well screened as to deserve to be in any collection of engravings of gentlemen's seats in the kingdom', which implies both considerable size and a building date some time in the middle of the eighteenth century when positioning a house to command views over its park was usual. Sotherton is different. Not only are the grounds unimproved, but the building itself – which Edmund tells us is Elizabethan, and of brick – is ill-placed in one of the lowest spots of the park. From its windows its owners cannot survey the extent of their grounds. In *Emma,* Jane Austen was to describe Donwell Abbey, converted to a home after the Reformation, as having been sited 'with all the old neglect of prospect', but in both cases she seems rather to admire the lack of pretension which goes with a very old building.

At Thornton Lacey, Edmund simply intends to move the farmyard to some less conspicuous location, which will give his house 'the air of a gentleman's residence.' Henry has more ambitious ideas, way beyond the proper level for a clergyman, changes which would require work 'for five summers at least.' However, even he concedes that it is a good house already, not 'a scrambling collection of low single rooms, with as many roofs as chimneys' –

anathema to the Georgians. Like many parsonage houses, it has evidently been rebuilt in Palladian style for some eighteenth-century occupant, using family money.

Jane Austen's own birthplace and beloved home, Steventon Rectory, which had rather low ceilings and a damp cellar, was pulled down and rebuilt by her brother Edward, with a complete lack of sentiment, to fit it for one of his own sons in 1823. As Mary Crawford says, 'every generation has its improvements.' In *Mansfield Park*, Jane Austen shows herself aware of new movements in religion as in building and gardening; and seems to suggest that the best of the new can be accommodated along with what is worth keeping of the old.

Geographical Settings
Caroline Sanderson

During the two-year period when she was working on *Mansfield Park*, Jane Austen wrote a letter to her sister Cassandra which shows us just how meticulous she was in her geographical research for her novels. 'If you could discover whether Northamptonshire is a Country of Hedgerows, I should be glad' she wrote in January 1813. Jane also applied to her brother Henry for information: he is known to have made business trips to Northampton-shire. Perhaps someone confirmed that there were indeed hedgerows there, for in Chapter 22 of the finished novel, as they are taking a walk in the gardens of Mansfield Parsonage, Fanny Price remarks to Mary Crawford: 'Every time I come into this shrubbery, I am more struck with its growth and beauty. Three years ago, this was nothing but a rough hedgerow along the upper side of the field.'

Why Jane chose to set 'Mansfield Park' in Northamptonshire is not known: it was not a place she knew personally. Today, as in Jane Austen's time, Northamptonshire is a county of attractive villages, many of which boast tall church spires. There are numerous fine country houses, set in undulating green countryside, which may have inspired Jane to place the mansion of Mansfield there. The county town of Northampton lies some seventy miles north of London and it is there that Mrs Norris goes to meet 10-year-old Fanny Price when she comes to live at Mansfield Park for the first time. For the remaining four-mile journey to her new home, her aunt ' ... talks to her the whole way of her wonderful good fortune and the extraordinary degree of gratitude and good behaviour which it ought to produce,' thus setting the tone for her hectoring behaviour towards Fanny during the years that follow.

Unlike Jane Austen, poor Fanny does not have a good grasp of geography. Her cousins, Maria and Julia Bertram, are astounded at her ignorance. 'Do you know, we asked her last night which way she would go to get to Ireland; and she said, she should cross to the Isle of Wight. She thinks of nothing

"Oh, this is beautiful, indeed!"

but the Isle of Wight, and she calls it *the Island* as if there were no other island in the world.' Fanny has grown up in Portsmouth, from which the Isle of Wight is clearly visible across the stretch of water known as The Solent.

Lady Bertram is the former Miss Maria Ward from the neighbouring county of Huntingdon who 'with only seven thousand pounds, had the good luck to captivate Sir Thomas Bertam.' 'All Huntingdon exclaimed on the greatness of the match,' we are told. In consequence of 'a little ill-health and a great deal of indolence,' Lady Bertram gives up the family house in London and spends her time wholly in the country in contrast to almost all the other characters in the novel whose departures to places at home and abroad punctuate the novel. Nowhere else in Jane Austen's work do her characters travel so frequently or so far afield, and rarely is the contrast between town and country life so sharply under the spotlight.

The frequent comings and goings in the novel begin with the arrival of Fanny's brother William, who spends a week with his sister shortly after she is established at Mansfield Park before he goes away to sea. Some years later, after the death of Mr Norris, Dr and Mrs Grant come to live at Mansfield Parsonage, half a mile from the Park. Some months later, Sir Thomas Bertram, who has recently suffered losses on his West India Estate, finds it 'expedient to go to Antigua for the better arrangement of his affairs.' Many wealthy English families had plantations in the West Indies at that time, their profitability dependent on slave labour. In 1807, following years of campaigning by William Wilberforce and other members of the Anti-Slavery Committee, Parliament passed a bill abolishing the slave trade in British territories abroad, with obvious financial repercussions for anyone with land and investments in the West Indies. As Mrs Norris remarks, 'Sir Thomas' means will be rather straitened, if the Antigua estate is to make such poor returns.'

Sir Thomas Bertram takes Tom, his wayward eldest son, with him to Antigua, 'in the hope of detaching him from some bad connections at home,' and expects to be away for the best part of a year. In fact it is two years before Sir Thomas returns, and in the meantime, Maria Bertram becomes engaged to wealthy Mr Rushworth who has lately succeeded to 'one of the largest estates and finest places in the country,' Sotherton Court, which lies ten miles from Mansfield. Shortly afterwards, Mary Crawford and her brother Henry arrive at Mansfield Parsonage to stay with their half-sister, Mrs Grant. Henry has a good estate in Everingham in Norfolk but is rarely there for any length of time. 'To any thing like a permanence of abode, or limitation of society, Henry Crawford had, unluckily, a great dislike.' Mary has 'mostly been used to London' having lived for much of her life with an uncle and aunt in Hill Street, in the central and fashionable district of Mayfair. The effect that this town upbringing has had on Mary's character and disposition later becomes clear.

Like Henry Crawford, Fanny's eldest cousin Tom Bertram is constantly on the move, his trips being made purely in the pursuit of pleasure. On his return from the West Indies, a year ahead of his father, he makes directly

Montpellier Pump Room, Cheltenham, one of Thomas Hulley's Six Views of Cheltenham, *1813.*

for Ramsgate, the most fashionable resort on the Kent coast at that time to stay with his friends the Sneyds for a week. Not long after the Crawfords' arrival at Mansfield, he sets off again for the races and to enjoy the sea air at Weymouth, another smart resort of the day. When he has gone, Mary Crawford decides to try and capture the heart of his younger brother Edmund instead. After flirting outrageously with Maria Bertram during a visit to the home of her fiancé Mr Rushworth at Sotherton Court, Henry Crawford departs to spend two weeks at his Norfolk estate, 'a fortnight of such dullness to the Miss Bertrams as ought to have put them both on their guard.' Tom Bertram returns home and is soon joined at Mansfield by Hon. John Yates, a new acquaintance he has made at Weymouth. Mr Yates has lately been a guest at Ecclesford, a large country house in Cornwall where, to his great disappointment, a theatrical party has broken up unexpectedly early. The idea of putting on a play – *Lovers' Vows* – at Mansfield Park instead is soon adopted, much to Fanny's chagrin.

The theatricals are brought to an abrupt end however when Sir Thomas Bertram finally returns from Antigua. Fanny, greatly relieved, loves to hear her uncle talk of the West Indies: 'I could listen to him for an hour together. It entertains *me* more than many other things have done – but then I am unlike other people I dare say.' Fanny also questions her uncle about the slave trade, one of the most controversial issues of the time. Henry Crawford, ever restless, disappears to join his uncle at Bath promising, in Maria Bertram's earshot, to return if there is any prospect of a renewal of *Lovers' Vows*. 'From Bath, Norfolk, London, York – wherever I may be … I will attend you from any place in England, at an hour's notice.' Mary Crawford remains at Mansfield, spending her first autumn in the country since she was little. Accustomed as Mary is to the amusements of watering-holes such as Tunbridge and Cheltenham, Mrs Grant becomes anxious for her half-sister 'not finding Mansfield dull as winter comes on.'

'Poor Fanny!' cried William
(Hugh Thomson).

Maria and Mr Rushworth are married and take a house for a few weeks in the fashionable Sussex seaside resort of Brighton, which is 'almost as gay in winter as in summer.' When 'the novelty of amusement' there is over, Mr and Mrs Rushworth, accompanied by Julia, move on to London for the winter season. Fanny and Mary Crawford are thrown increasingly together at Mansfield, since Mary, despondent at the lack of amusement 'in the gloom and dirt' of November in the country, is glad of Fanny's company. Since Mary 'has never spent so happy a summer' as the past one at Mansfield, she tells Fanny that she can 'even suppose it pleasant to spend *half* the year in the country, under certain circumstances.' Before long however she betrays her true feelings about the tedium of life away from the town by remarking to Mrs Grant: 'The sweets of house-keeping in a country village! Commend me to the nurseryman and the poulterer,' implying that she would much rather live in town where food is produced and supplied by others. This remark is further evidence of how ill-suited Mary Crawford is to life as a country parson's wife.

Fanny receives news of her brother William, whose ship, *HMS Antwerp*, has sailed up the Channel and into Portsmouth. It drops anchor at Spithead, a safe anchorage just off Portsmouth, and William is soon on his way to spend his leave at Mansfield Park with his sister. William Price has been seven years at sea on active service in both the Mediterranean and the West Indies, during which time he has 'known every variety of danger, which sea and war together could offer.'

Jane Austen knew a great deal about the dangers of being a sailor, since two of her brothers, Frank and Charles, were in the Navy during the Revolutionary and Napoleonic Wars. Home to the Royal Naval dockyard, Portsmouth was Britain's biggest seaport at that time, with a harbour deep enough to take the largest ships. During the war with France, it was from Portsmouth that the ships of the nation's fleet set sail to do battle. There was also a military garrison in the town to protect it from land or sea invasion. Both of Jane Austen's sailor brothers attended the Royal Naval Academy at Portsmouth, and from 1806 to 1809 Jane Austen herself lived only twenty miles away in the neighbouring port town of Southampton with her mother and sister. Having left Bath after the death of Mr Austen in 1805, the Austen women found a home with Jane's brother Frank and his wife Mary who was no doubt glad of their company during her husband's long absences at sea. Jane almost certainly visited Portsmouth during that time and would have been able to use her observations in the writing of *Mansfield Park* a few years later.

Fanny's filial devotion to William provokes strong feelings in her new admirer, Henry Crawford, who has now returned from Bath and Norfolk, and determines on making Fanny fall in love with him. William, who is a midshipman, is desperate to receive an officer's commission and be made a lieutenant, but he needs a recommendation. Henry Crawford, keen to get into Fanny's good books, secures William a meeting in London with his uncle who is an Admiral. The two men leave the day after the ball at Mansfield Park, which Sir Thomas Bertram throws in Fanny and William's honour, and Edmund leaves shortly afterwards for the cathedral city of Peterborough where he is to be ordained.

Henry Crawford returns from London and continues to pay court to Fanny, telling his sister that when they are married he 'will not take her from Northamptonshire. I shall let Everingham and rent a place in this neighbourhood.' When Henry Crawford finally proposes to Fanny, however, her refusal is made even more traumatic by Sir Thomas Bertram's disappointment at her having turned down so advantageous a match. With her unwelcome suitor on the point of leaving again, this time for London with his sister, Fanny hopes and believes that the distractions of London will cool his ardour. 'In London he would soon learn to wonder at his infatuation, and be thankful for the right reason in her, which had saved him from its evil consequences.' Little does Fanny realise how right she will turn out to be about the effect of the big city on Mr Crawford.

With the Crawfords in London, the next visitor at Mansfield is Fanny's brother William, now, thanks to Admiral Crawford's recommendation, second lieutenant of the sloop HMS *Thrush*, currently docked at Portsmouth. Sir Thomas Bertram decides that Fanny should accompany William back to Portsmouth when he goes to rejoin his ship, to spend a little time with her family whom she has not seen for eight or nine years. He hopes that 'a little abstinence from the elegancies and luxuries of Mansfield Park would bring her mind into a sober state, and incline her to a juster estimate of the value of greater permanence, and equal comfort, of which she had the offer.'

Fanny and William's journey to Portsmouth takes two days by post-chaise, travelling via Oxford and Newbury where they stay overnight. On arrival in Portsmouth, the carriage has to cross over the moat which once surrounded town on its landward side. 'They passed the drawbridge, and entered the town; and the light was only beginning to fail, as, guided by William's powerful voice, they were rattled into a narrow street, leading from the high street, and drawn up before the door of a small house now inhabited by Mr Price.' The house is indeed modest by comparison with the grandeurs of Mansfield Park. 'She was taken into a parlour, so small that her first conviction was of its being only a passage-room to something better.' William goes to rejoin his ship, and Fanny is left to reacquaint herself with her family, 'anxious to be useful, and not to appear above her home, or in any ways disqualified or disinclined, by her foreign education, from contributing to help to its comforts.' She soon finds she now has little in common with either of her parents however, and is made quite miserable by living in 'incessant noise.' 'The smallness of the house and thinness of the walls brought everything so close to her that, added to … all her recent agitation, she hardly knew how to bear it.' Soon she is forced to conclude that 'though Mansfield Park might have some pains, Portsmouth could have no pleasures.'

Portsmouth today is very different from the place it was in Jane Austen's time. Though still a busy port, many of its old buildings were destroyed during Second World War bombing raids, and few eighteenth-century houses remain in the area of the town where Jane Austen places the Price family. The town's old fortifications, which still existed in Jane Austen's time, have gone, although the ramparts, dockyard and the Garrison Chapel, which Fanny visits later on during her stay in Portsmouth, remain. The dockyard is now home both to HMS *Victory*, Admiral Lord Nelson's flagship from the Battle of Trafalgar in 1805, and the wreck of the *Mary Rose*, a Tudor warship from the time of King Henry VIII which was salvaged from the Solent during the 1980s.

Fanny has been in Portsmouth for about a month when Henry Crawford pays her an unexpected and not altogether welcome visit. Nevertheless, Fanny and her sister Susan show him around the town and dockyard and on Sunday he accompanies the family to church at the Garrison Chapel. Later they take a walk on the ramparts as Mrs Price is wont to do every Sunday throughout the year. 'It was her public place; there she met her acquaintance, heard a little news, talked over the badness of the Portsmouth servants, and wound up her spirits for the six days ensuing.' Fanny walks holding onto Henry Crawford's arm. It is a lovely day; 'everything looked so beautiful under the influence of such a sky, the effects of the shadows pursuing each other, on the ships at Spithead and the island beyond with the ever-varying hues of the sea now at high water, dancing in its glee and dashing against the ramparts with so fine a sound, produced altogether such a combination of charms for Fanny, as made her gradually almost careless of the circumstances under which she felt them.' Henry Crawford is such pleasant company that Fanny's attitude towards him softens somewhat, and she even finds herself regretting his departure a little when he takes his leave for London. His absence makes her miss Mansfield Park all the more, and she frets over what will happen when Edmund goes to London and sees Mary Crawford again.

Edmund spends three weeks in London in the hope of asking Mary to marry him, but finds her manner towards him greatly altered. Upset he returns to Mansfield, but within days he is on his way to Newmarket to fetch home his brother Tom, who has been taken seriously ill after a neglected fall and bouts of heavy drinking whilst attending the races there. Fanny longs to be there so she can be of comfort to Lady Bertram and realises that Mansfield Park has become the place she regards as home. She laments the fact that during the three months she has been in Portsmouth she has lost all the pleasures of spring in the country. 'She had not known before what pleasures she *had* to lose in passing March and April in a town ... to have confinement, bad air, bad smells, substituted for liberty, freshness, and verdure.' Fanny's love of the countryside is deliberately contrasted with Mary Crawford's obvious enjoyment of the pleasures of town life. The fact that Tom Bertram's sisters are so unwilling to leave London to be at their mother's side during their brother's illness is also attributed by Fanny to the evils of town life: 'Fanny was disposed to think the influence of London very much at war with all respectable attachments.' Such feelings are only increased when she receives a letter from Mary, in which her glee at the dangerous illness that might possibly lead to the death of Mansfield's eldest son and heir is only thinly disguised.

All Fanny's instincts are shown to be correct when Mrs Rushworth leaves her husband for Henry Crawford, and Julia Bertram elopes with Mr Yates. With Mr Rushworth away in Bath, visiting his mother, Maria had left their house in Wimpole Street in central London to spend the Easter holidays with friends in Twickenham, a village on the River Thames to the west of London. Henry Crawford was staying close by in Richmond, in the same neighbourhood. Thrown together once again, they are unable to resist temptation, and an unhappy end to their scandalous affair is inevitable.

Mansfield Park ends with a number of permanent departures from Northamptonshire on the one hand, and some happy homecomings on the other. As Maria can no longer be received either at Mansfield Park or in polite society, Mrs Norris leaves Mansfield to devote herself to her disgraced niece. They go to live 'in another country – remote and private, where, shut up together with little society … it may be reasonably supposed that their tempers became their mutual punishment.' 'After what had passed to wound and alienate the two families,' Dr and Mrs Grant move out of Mansfield Parsonage and return to London. Mary Crawford finds a home there with them, but husbands who can 'satisfy the better taste she had acquired at Mansfield' prove difficult to find.

Fanny returns to Mansfield Park for good, to the great relief and delight of Sir Thomas and Lady Bertram. In due course, Edmund 'ceases to care about Miss Crawford' and becomes 'as anxious to marry Fanny, as Fanny herself could desire.' When the living becomes vacant on the death of Dr Grant, Edmund and Fanny come to live at Mansfield Parsonage. And Fanny's place by Lady Bertram's side at Mansfield Park is taken by a one final arrival in Northamptonshire in the shape of Fanny's sister Susan.

No, no, no!, she cried, hiding her face.

A Modern Perspective
Josephine Ross

'I suppose I am graver than other people.'

Fanny Price, *Mansfield Park*, Chapter 21

There are some readers today who regard *Mansfield Park* as Jane Austen's least successful, and least enjoyable, novel. For those who relish the wit and spirit of Lizzy Bennet in *Pride and Prejudice*, Fanny Price, with her meekness and timidity, may seem to lack vitality as a heroine. Upright, honourable clergyman Edmund Bertram has none of the dash and glamour of fellow-heroes such as gorgeous Mr Darcy, or charming Henry Tilney in *Northanger Abbey*, while the overall moral tone of the novel can seem bleak, and even oppressive.

Looked at him for a moment in speechless admiration.

Cruel Mrs Norris (to whom Fanny constantly submits) is no match in comic terms for the immortal Lady Catherine de Bourgh, whose attempted bullying Lizzy Bennet cheerfully resists, and the young, smiling villains of the piece, Henry and Mary Crawford, have at times succeeded in seducing readers' interest, and sympathies, away from the virtuous hero and heroine. 'I suppose I am graver than other people,' Fanny Price wistfully admits; and as a successor to irresistible Elizabeth Bennet, whose declaration 'I dearly love a laugh' is the keynote of the 'light, and bright, and sparkling' *Pride and Prejudice*, she could scarcely present a greater contrast.

And yet, to many more of Jane Austen's admirers, *Mansfield Park* is a *tour de force*, its very differences of approach and outlook from those of her earlier novels a fresh proof of her extraordinary scope and brilliance.

It should be borne in mind that Lizzy's credo, 'I dearly love a laugh,' is followed by the caution; 'but I hope I never ridicule what is wise, or good.' *Pride and Prejudice* is a novel illuminated by laughter; in *Mansfield Park* Jane Austen consciously turns to a darker, more complex examination of what is wise or good – or otherwise – in human nature. Discussing Fanny Price's attractions, in Chapter 24, Mary Crawford observes, '[She has] a sort of beauty that grows on one.' Many readers, past and present, would agree that the power and beauty of *Mansfield Park* never cease to grow on them.

Though *Mansfield Park* was completed in July 1813, only six months after the publication of *Pride and Prejudice*, the two novels were conceived at very different stages in the author's career, and under very different circumstances. When she began work on the latter (then entitled *First Impressions*) in 1796, Jane Austen was 20 years old, still living in some style with her sister and brothers at their father's rectory at Steventon, in Hampshire, where the family kept a carriage, employed servants, and could afford many of life's luxuries, including fashionable clothes, seaside holidays and a full social life for their daughters. By the time this early work came to be revised and retitled for publication, the author's lifestyle and prospects had changed radically. With her widowed mother and unmarried sister she was living on a combined income of some £500 a year, in a cottage lent to them by her brother who had inherited property, including a grand country mansion, Godmersham Park – not unlike the fictional *Mansfield Park*, though in Kent, rather than Northamptonshire. Times had changed for Jane Austen; and so had her approach to her fiction.

Once settled at Chawton cottage, now a single woman in her 30s, she determined to become, at last, a professional writer. Several past attempts at getting her works published had come to nothing; the original version of *Pride and Prejudice* had been rejected, by return of post; *Northanger Abbey*, though purchased by a London 'bookseller' for £10, had never appeared in print. At last, in 1811, she began to fulfil her ambitions. *Sense and Sensibility* (a reworking of a novel-in-letters begun in the 1790s as *Elinor and Marianne*) came out in October of that year, to be followed, in January 1813, by the revised and retitled *Pride and Prejudice*. In the meantime, she had begun work

on an entirely new novel: the first of this mature major writing phase –
Mansfield Park. That it should have been so different in tone and atmosphere
from its predecessors was surely understandable.

The buoyant young woman of the 1790s, who loved dancing, dresses and
joking with her sister and friends about 'admirers', was now a maiden aunt
in her mid-30s, chiefly occupied with caring for her mother, attending to a
growing brood of nephews and nieces, and keeping house on a small budget.
Her choice of a patient, emotionally-repressed and intellectually-isolated
young woman, rather than a merry Lizzy Bennet or carefree Catherine
Morland, as the heroine of her first new novel was scarcely surprising.

The charge that gentle, unassuming Fanny Price is 'insipid' is one that
has been levelled at this heroine ever since the novel came out in May
1814. It was, indeed, a criticism made by Jane Austen's own mother, as
the author noted with amusement, in a list of 'Opinions of Mansfield Park'
that she drew up at the time. Readers' reactions to 'M.P.' varied almost as
widely then as now. While some of the Austen family and their friends
and acquaintances were 'very much pleased with it,' praising everything
from the character of Mrs Norris, and 'Mr Rushworth's stupidity,' to 'the
scene at Portsmouth,' and 'all the humorous parts,' others had reservations,
chiefly regarding the character and conduct of Fanny; and many 'preferred
P.&P.' Among the novel's admirers, however, a Scottish reader named Lady
Robert Kerr showed unusual perception in her response: declaring herself
wholly 'delighted with it,' she added that 'M.P.' was 'universally admired in
Edinburgh, by all the *wise ones.*'

The 'wise ones,' then and now, were right: far from being inferior to Jane
Austen's other works, Mansfield Park is in many regards the most dramatic,
ambitious and profound of all her novels. The pivotal character of Fanny
Price – cool-headed, clear-sighted and dependent upon her own inner
strengths for her moral survival – may well be seen as a feminist prototype,
as she struggles to retain her principles, and dreams, under constant
emotional blackmail in the name of family, duty and marriage. The novel's
central themes are not merely striking, but challenging and even provoc-
ative – ranging as they do from adultery, betrayal and greed to the slave
trade, with a glancing mention at sexual perversion on the way. 'Let other
pens dwell on guilt and misery,' Jane Austen wrote in the closing chapter;
but as ever, she was being ironic. Without being overly dwelt on, 'guilt and
misery' play a greater part in *Mansfield Park* than in any of her other works.

The dramatic situation established at the outset is in itself disturbing,
however familiar it might have been to Regency readers. Shy little Fanny
Price, whose parents have more children than they can afford, is sent away
from home to be brought up by her mother's rich relations – with the dual
purpose of relieving her father's purse and bettering her own chances in
life. Such unofficial, unsupervised adoptions – even among the 'educated'
or 'officer classes' – were by no means unusual at the time, and are a notable
feature of Jane Austen's fiction, as of her life. The brother who provided her

mother, sister and her with Chawton cottage had himself been 'adopted' as a boy by a rich, childless couple; through this event he had been enabled to enjoy a splendid lifestyle himself, and provide for his female dependents as they aged. However happy the outcome, his experience evidently haunted his younger sister; and she returns to it more than once in her novels. In *Emma*, an important plot-line involves the handing-over of Mr Weston's motherless son Frank to the wealthy Churchills, whose surname he takes; in *Mansfield Park* the whole story revolves around the plight of bewildered little Fanny Price, sent to live in a grand country house where she will be, in effect, a displaced person – supposedly of her cousins' world, but not sharing its rights and privileges, estranged from her own down-at-heel family at Portsmouth, and yet not belonging to the segregated underclass of servants, who must wait on her, while pitying or patronising her.

Her rich, but emotionally-inhibited, uncle, Sir Thomas Bertram, is quick to flare up on Fanny's behalf where his own family pride is concerned, but as he comes, remorsefully, to acknowledge, he has done nothing to show her affection, or secure her self-esteem, while she was growing up. Cinderella-like, she is left to the neglect of her beautiful, selfish cousins and their circle, and the spiteful bullying of her other aunt, Mrs Norris, who flatters and spunges off the Bertrams, and bolsters her own inferior position in the household by exploiting Fanny as she does the servants. In this sad, half-lit world, Fanny's only true friend and solace (apart from her books) is her younger male cousin, Edmund Bertram, for whom she cherishes a secret passion which she knows can never be fulfilled. As the novel progresses, she has to watch, powerlessly, as he is drawn in by his own, less worthy, sexual desire for another woman – cynical, worldly Mary Crawford – who seeks not merely to ensnare Edmund as her husband, but to deter him from his calling to become a clergyman.

There is a widespread misconception that Jane Austen intended *Mansfield Park's* main theme to be 'ordination.' This is based on a misreading of a letter written in January 1813 by the author while at work on 'M.P.'; having mentioned 'S.&S.,' and the newly-published 'P.&P.,' she goes on, 'Now I will try to write of something else, and it shall be a complete change of subject – ordination – I am glad to find your enquiries have ended so well.' Meticulous as always, she had evidently asked Cassandra (whose late fiancé was an army chaplain) to do some background research for her. Religion, and the role of the clergy, certainly figure strongly in *Mansfield Park*; but it is worldly corruption, rather than the spiritual process of ordination, which dominates the narrative.

For all the shortcomings of her treatment there, Mansfield Park itself will come to represent, in Fanny's eyes, a place of 'elegance, propriety, regularity, harmony,' where 'peace and tranquillity' are the order of the day, and life at its best 'proceeded in a regular course of cheerful orderliness.' This model of a stately rural Eden is, however, disrupted by the arrival of two deceptively charming, engaging newcomers who arrive from London, bringing with them all the taints of immorality and corruption supposedly associated, in the contemporary imagination, with the sprawling, anonymous, licentious capital.

'Here I am … in this scene of dissipation and vice, and I begin already to find my morals corrupted,' Jane Austen had written teasingly to her sister in 1796, on arriving in London for a visit. Brother and sister Henry and Mary Crawford, both devotees of London, and in his case, educated there, at Westminster School, have indeed left a scene of 'dissipation and vice': their uncle, Admiral Crawford, with whom they have been living, has taken a mistress 'under his roof' thus obliging his unmarried niece, for form's sake, to find accommodation elsewhere; in this case, with her sister, Mrs Grant, at the Mansfield parsonage. Outwardly, the Crawfords are an addition to the neighbourhood, being good-looking, obliging, beautifully-mannered and highly eligible as guests (or indeed, marriage partners). But as the Bertrams are increasingly 'drawn in' by them, Fanny alone sees the dark realities beneath their surface attractions. 'Varnish and gilding hide many stains,' Mary Crawford asserts, in justifying London society's tolerance of misconduct among the rich and well-connected. There is no deceiving Fanny, however.

Fanny was obliged to introduce him.

With the arrival of the Crawfords, the staid propriety of Mansfield Park is rapidly disrupted by disorder and disharmony, and its atmosphere becomes increasingly sexually-charged. Sir Thomas is away, overseeing his properties in the distant West Indies; in his absence, flirtations, jealousies and rivalries break out, as Maria and Julia Bertram vie for the attentions of fascinating Henry Crawford – whose interest in the elder sister begins to threaten her mercenary, but outwardly-respectable, engagement, to rich, foolish Mr Rushworth. Most alarmingly, the young Bertrams and their friends succumb to a fashionable country-house craze for amateur theatricals – deciding to put on the play *Lovers' Vows*, which Fanny, to her horror, finds includes scenes 'totally improper for home representation'. Her female cousins' roles will, she knows, appal her strait-laced uncle on his return – 'the situation of one and the language of the other so unfit to be expressed by any woman of modesty'. In her refusal to become involved, Fanny is initially supported by her beloved, like-minded cousin Edmund; but as matters progress, even he succumbs to the others' peer-pressure – largely, as Fanny is painfully aware, on account of his ever-deepening feelings towards Miss Crawford.

The 'extremely pretty' Mary Crawford is the embodiment of dangerous, subtle, seductive temptation. To Edmund's delight she plays the harp – evoking images of a pretty woman drawing her fingers across the strings of a large, lyre-like instrument settled upright between her legs, slightly drawing up her clinging muslin gown. Under Edmund's tuition she takes to riding a horse with a physical aptitude, and eager appetite, for the sport which Fanny can only envy, watching from a distance as the man she loves guides her rival's hand on the reins, or lifts her, laughing, in his arms 'as she sprang down with his help' from the saddle. 'Lord … How you did tremble when Sir Thomas first had you put on,' the fatherly old coachman reminds Fanny, observing with admiration how Miss Crawford, by contrast 'active and fearless', only longs to go faster.

'*She found herself the next moment conducted by Mr Crawford to the top of the room*' (Hugh Thomson).

It is Mary Crawford, naturally, who makes the only mildly salacious joke to appear in any of Jane Austen's novels. This has been much misunderstood by commentators in recent times, and requires clarification, for the author's sake as well as the reader's. When Miss Crawford, referring to life in her uncle's London household, mentions the Admirals she met there, adding 'Of *Rears*, and *Vices*, I saw enough – now, do not be suspecting me of a pun, I entreat you,' she is not – emphatically – referring to sodomy in the Navy, as some have assumed. Homosexual anal intercourse was an act punishable by the death penalty in Jane Austen's day, and would not under any circumstances have been even hinted at by her in a work of light fiction aimed principally at a young, female readership. (Returning a novel by Mme. de Genlis to the library after reading only 20 pages, in 1807, Jane Austen wrote indignantly, 'We were disgusted … It has indelicacies which disgrace a pen hitherto so pure.') Mary Crawford's saucy innuendo relates merely to the prevalent Regency fashion for whipping: '*le vice anglais*' – wholly unfit as a topic for a lady's conversation, but legal, widespread, and familiar to any schoolgirl who might glance in a print shop window at the political cartoons of Rowlandson, or Gillray, in which birches and buttocks featured regularly.

To compound Fanny Price's miseries, she has to face what, to her, is tantamount to an assault, in the form of an honourable – even eligible, and in worldly terms, desirable – marriage proposal from Henry Crawford. It is now that the strengths of this sensitive heroine are tested to the full, as she battles to retain her integrity under pressures of every kind. Marrying the rich, attractive, devoted Mr Crawford would not only give her 'consequence,' and an 'establishment' of her own, but enable her to do good to others, from improving the lot of her husband's tenants, and the promotion prospects of her beloved sailor brother, William, to assisting her improvident family at Portsmouth. Her uncle Sir Thomas, at whose expense she will live until she marries, calls her ungrateful and selfish for refusing such an offer; even Edmund, on whose judgement she so often relies, urges her to accept. There is certainly nothing 'insipid' about a heroine who can remain true to her principles in such a situation.

The darker, sadder side of life is constantly in evidence in *Mansfield Park*. Fanny Price's disillusionment on returning to her long-missed family home in Portsmouth, only to find it a place of noise, chaos and mismanagement, is exquisitely – almost cinematically – evoked, as Fanny finds her nostalgic fantasies of a loving family environment replaced by all the horrors of mess, shouting, bad manners, disgusting food and a prevailing lack of concern for others, in an ill-run house governed by a foul-mouthed father and slapdash mother, attended by resentful serving-girls. Faced with such a miserable alternative to her already-beleaguered existence at Mansfield Park, Fanny's determination not to take the escape route offered by Mr Crawford's proposal of marriage is the more impressive.

Grimmest of all the elements which overshadow this novel is the awareness of what Sir Thomas Bertram's ownership of property in the West Indies must surely involve. On her uncle's return from Antigua, Fanny's attempts to enquire about his experiences, and the situation there, are greeted with 'a dead silence': the only appropriate response, in a work of light fiction, to the enormities of the slave trade. Though the trade itself had been abolished in Britain seven years before *Mansfield Park* appeared, the use of slave labour in the colonies remained legal – a source of ineradicable guilt to its perpetrators and misery to its victims. Actual slavery was not abolished in the British Empire until 1833.

The joyful consent which met Edmund's application.

And yet, alongside its tragic, and darkly-troubled, strands, *Mansfield Park* contains some of the most beautiful descriptive passages Jane Austen ever wrote. Contrasting with the cramped gloom of her parents' house, Fanny's visits to the dockyard are exquisitely evocative, as she gazes out at the glorious, tall-masted ships lying at anchor off Spithead, and revels in the freshness and beauty of the sea, 'dancing in its glee and dashing against the ramparts.' The scene in which Fanny looks up at the night sky, during a party at Mansfield, and yearns to go down onto the lawn for 'some stargazing' with Edmund, lingers in the mind – as does the brilliantly-symbolic scene of the Bertrams' visit to Mr Rushworth's mansion, during which several of the group find themselves confined behind a high, locked, iron gate. While deluded Mr Rushworth goes for the key, Henry Crawford murmurs, with serpentine allure to Maria Bertram, 'I think you might with little difficulty pass round the edge of the gate here, with my assistance …' It is of course the eventual adultery of this couple – Henry's flagrant, unpardonable act, in which she is eagerly complicit – in helping Maria to 'pass round' the iron gates of social and sexual propriety, which will bring about the novel's happy outcome, freeing Edmund and Fanny from the Crawfords' malign influences, and clearing the path to their marriage.

Opinions of *Mansfield Park* have varied widely down the centuries, and no doubt the novel will continue to spark debate and discussion in future years. But among Jane Austen's readers, all over the world, there are many 'wise ones' who will agree with 'Mr J. Plumptre,' friend and admirer of her favourite niece, Fanny Knight, who (the author recorded with satisfaction) declared, 'I never read a novel which interested me so very much throughout.'

Principal Characters

Fanny Price is the eldest daughter of Mrs Price who, having eight other children, is thankful to have Fanny brought up in the family of her brother-in-law Sir Thomas Bertram at Mansfield Park. Her mother defied her family and married a poor lieutenant of the marines for love. Fanny is sensitive and shy, and her status at Mansfield Park as a dependent, poor relation only intensifies these traits. The bulk of the novel takes place when she is between fifteen and seventeen.

Sir Thomas Bertram is the husband of Fanny's aunt, Lady Bertram, and a Member of Parliament. He owns the Mansfield Park estate in Northamptonshire, and an estate in Antigua. He is stern and correct; 'with all the cost and care of an anxious and expensive education he had brought up his daughters without their understanding their first duties.' He welcomes Fanny as the ideal daughter he never had.

Lady Bertram is the sister of Fanny Price's mother and is married to the wealthy Sir Thomas Bertram. 'A woman of very languid feelings, and a temper remarkably easy and indolent.'

Tom Bertram is the elder son of Sir Thomas and Lady Bertram. Tom is principally interested in carousing in London society and enjoying the pleasures of the theatre with his friend Mr Yates. Tom incurs large debts, forcing Sir Thomas to sell the church position that was to have gone to Edmund, Tom's younger brother. One celebratory journey leaves Tom with a fever, and in his suffering he learns to become what he ought to be – useful to his father, steady and quiet and no longer living for himself.

Edmund Bertram is the younger son of Sir Thomas and Lady Bertram. He plans to be a clergyman. He alone among his family has any consideration for Fanny's feelings. As her protector and friend, he has great influence over her and helps to form her character. Edmund becomes attracted to Miss Crawford, but her callous and irreligious nature disillusions him. He is consoled by Fanny.

Maria Bertram is the elder daughter of Sir Thomas and Lady Bertram. She becomes engaged to Mr Rushworth, but then becomes attached to Henry Crawford. She is eventually relegated, by her father, to a remote house with her nagging aunt.

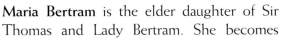

Mrs Norris is the officious widowed elder sister of Lady Bertram and Fanny Price's mother, who lives near Mansfield Park. Her late husband, Mr Norris,

was the previous parson at Mansfield Park. She is of a managing, uncharitable and miserly disposition. She dislikes Fanny, whose life she makes a misery.

Henry Crawford is the brother of Mrs Grant and Miss Mary Crawford. A charming and eligible bachelor who shows interest in Maria, Julia and, later, Fanny, he was brought up by his dissolute uncle Admiral Crawford.

Mary Crawford is the pretty, dark-haired, witty and charming sister of Mr Crawford and Mrs Grant, who takes a keen interest in Edmund Bertram in spite of his being a second son. Though she loses her power over Edmund Bertram, the charm of his sincerity, steadiness and integrity makes her dissatisfied with her frivolous life.

Mr Rushworth is 'A heavy young man, with not more than common sense'. He is the wealthy owner of Sotherton Court who becomes engaged to Maria Bertram.

Julia Bertram is the younger daughter of Sir Thomas and Lady Bertram. She has strong feelings towards Mr Crawford, but soon learns that he prefers her sister Maria, despite, or because of, her sister's engagement. She then begins a flirtation with Mr Yates.

Mrs Grant is the wife – later widow – of the current parson at the Mansfield Park parsonage, and half-sister to Mr Henry Crawford and Miss Mary Crawford.

Mrs Price is Fanny's mother and Lady Bertram's sister who married Lieutenant Price of the marines. A 'partial, ill-judging parent. A dawdle, a slattern who neither taught nor restrained her children, whose house was the scene of mismanagement and discomfort from beginning to end.' Mrs Price's alcoholic husband was disabled and released from the service on half pay, and she had to settle for a life far less comfortable than that of her sisters.

John Yates, a good friend of Tom Bertram, had 'not much to recommend him beyond habits of fashion and expense'. Tom and Yates carouse in London society and bring their love of the theatre to Mansfield Park. Yates also expresses interest in Julia Bertram.

William Price is Fanny's favourite brother. At first a midshipman in the Royal Navy, he is promoted to Lieutenant.

Susan Price is Fanny's younger sister, with whom Fanny first becomes close on a visit home.

Emma

Modern Interpretations
John Wiltshire

Austen's *Emma*, gladsome, clever, and rich, seems to unite the comedy of *Pride and Prejudice* with the complexity of *Mansfield Park*, and has been read for nearly two centuries with very few to dispute its place as its author's greatest achievement. It was the second work to be completed in Jane Austen's Chawton period, which saw her living in a village, perhaps not unlike the Highbury of the novel, surrounded and supported by a family of unattached ladies. It is in fact the depth and complexity of Emma's rendering of a compact, rather isolated community, and its combining of this tight focus with immense narrative ingenuity, that has provided readers with great amusement, endless opportunities for explication, and faced film-makers with insuperable challenges.

Emma Woodhouse, with her delight in schemes and scheming of all kinds and her pleasure in contradiction for its own sake, is the motor force of the novel, a character whose energy and imaginative gusto runs headlong into the cramped and routine ways of a world only as large as the village, and always threatening to shrink to the size of her invalid father's drawing room. *Emma* is told from the point of view of its heroine, though slyly enough managing to suggest that she sees with the eyes of prejudice, and even occasionally delighting to trick the reader by blending its own narrative 'voice' with her own inner thoughts. Full of references to deceptions and games, and itself gaily teasing the reader, the novel is also at times surprisingly touching and even painful. Reginald Farrer wrote as far back as 1917 that even 'twelve readings' of *Emma* would give pleasure 'not repeated only, but squared and squared again with each perusal,' indicating that, on each re-reading, one finds more and more to enjoy and discover. So it is no surprise to find that critics – who usually offer, perforce, only one 'reading' of the novel – offer diverse interpretations that often complement rather than oppose each other. And the criticism of *Emma*, more than any other of the novels, tends towards delighted appreciation, and increasingly towards wonderment at its technical skill and artifice.

The most discussed technical achievement of *Emma* has been its employment of 'free indirect speech'. This is the mode (or trope) by which the thoughts of the character through whom the reader receives most of his or her information, Emma herself, are simultaneously represented and critiqued. 'When free indirect style mimics Emma's thoughts and feelings, it simultaneously inflects them into keener observations of its own; for our benefit, if never for hers, it identifies, ridicules, corrects all the secret vanities and self-deceptions of which Emma, pleased as Punch, remains comically unconscious' (D. A. Miller offers a penetrating discussion in *Jane Austen and the Secret of Style*, 2003). Earlier critics used this as a cue for the sternly moral-

Cloakroom of the Clifton Assembly Rooms, *painted by Rolins Sharples (opposite)*.

He was very sure there must be a lady in the case.

istic view that Emma's character faults are continually being exposed. Thus Marilyn Butler in *Jane Austen and the War of Ideas* (1975) argued that 'The novel's attitude to the workings of Emma's consciousness is steadily critical. Although so much of the action takes place in the inner life, the theme of the novel is scepticism about the qualities that make it up – intuition, imagination, original insight.' Free indirect speech, in A. Walton Litz's words, made certain 'that we would understand and criticize every aspect of Emma's self-deception by establishing a context of ironic qualifications and explicit judgements' (*Jane Austen: A Study of her Artistic Development*, 1965). Later critics have argued rather that 'the authorial relation to character in free indirect speech' mitigates against just such judgements – such a 'composite narrative' connecting the reader with the character, not detaching us from her. In Frances Ferguson's words, 'the novel is hard on Emma to exactly the same extent that it is committed to her' (Jane Austen, *Emma*, and the Impact of Form,' *Modern Language Quarterly*, March 2000).

If, according to the earlier criticism, the novel exposed Emma's self-deceptions, Mr Knightley embodied the standard by which they were to be measured. 'The reader always knows when [Emma] is wrong, because the novel's other style ['manly and direct'] has given him the unmistakable note of simplicity and sincerity,' Butler claimed, a point re-fashioned in Roger Gard's *Jane Austen's Novels: the Art of Clarity* (1992) so that it applies to Emma and Knightley when they act in concert: 'This clear-headed efficiency is a kind of moral pointer. Clear speech is always indicative in Jane Austen.' 'Knightley is established early as completely reliable,' declared Wayne Booth in his influential *The Rhetoric of Fiction* of 1961. Many interpretations of the novel in the later twentieth century therefore considered Knightley a version of the 'mentor-lover,' familiar to readers of eighteenth-century fiction in such incarnations as Sir Charles Grandison, Lord Orville (in Frances Burney's *Evelina*) or even Mr Darcy. This is the male who is at one and the same time both the heroine's love interest, and in a position to teach her the truth about herself and the world she lives in. Such readings considered the book to be about the dangers of Emma's erring imagination, and focused on the progression of incidents in the novel that educate and eventually, perhaps, reform her. Though there is something very unfashionable about this approach, which Eve Sedgwick famously labelled 'the spectacle of a girl being taught a lesson' in her essay 'Jane Austen and the Masturbating Girl' (*Tendencies*, 1993), it points to an important aspect of the novel's narrative structure. Its comedy does turn on the fact that Emma is first egregiously mistaken about Mr Elton's intentions, then about Frank Churchill and Jane Fairfax, then (whilst thinking she won't commit the same error again) about Harriet and Frank – and that the reader must at least half suspect this. What Sedgwick derided as a lesson is largely inseparable from the reader enjoying the joke.

Mr Knightley's position as custodian of good sense, though, can certainly be questioned and qualified. In *Jane Austen and the Fiction of her Time* (1999) Mary Waldron re-reads one of the novel's most famous set-pieces, the first big quarrel between Emma and Knightley over Harriet's refusal of Robert Martin's proposal. Waldron argues that Knightley is 'complacent' and 'smug' in his advocacy of Robert Martin's courtship, joining with his socially inferior 'friend' in 'a male conspiracy to trap Harriet before she has time to protest'. She suggests that Knightley's arguments are partisan, and when challenged by Emma, contradictory. Waldron's Emma, on the other hand, is 'rational' and 'cogent.' Knightley's arguments 'are a mass of ill-thought notions, which he is quite prepared to reverse in the interests of getting his own way.' It is interesting when a critic starts to sound like Emma herself, and useful to be reminded that Knightley is not always right, and that Emma does scent a male conspiracy. But is he really smug? 'I praised the fair lady too, and altogether sent [Martin] away very happy. If he had not esteemed my opinion before, he would have thought highly of me then; and, I dare say, left the house thinking me the best friend and counsellor man ever had.' His attitude is one of irony at his own role; and the phrase 'fair lady,' which Waldron finds 'diminishes' Harriet, typifies his benevolent amusement at the whole transaction. 'The problem with such arguments,' as Terry Castle remarks in her 'Introduction' to the Oxford World's Classics edition of the novel (1998), 'is how deeply they betray the experience of reading.' A first reader of *Emma* will probably, following Austen's clues, side with Mr Knightley, and events in the novel certainly prove him to be usually correct. Another reading though, might produce another version – perhaps one in which the reader finds both participants in this quarrel making sweeping generalisations and assertions as they set to in a confrontation that provides the reader with the enjoyable spectacle of two very intelligent people crossing swords and losing their heads. And this is a variety of several different scenes between them that in Castle's words 'fairly buzz with sexual tension.'

Criticism of *Emma*, though continuing to focus on the Emma/Knightley relationship, has increasingly acknowledged the importance of the matrix of village life, and its network of relationships and dependencies in which they live. 'The predicted responses of dull Highbury are not just a comic background for the main protagonists' lives,' comments Roger Gard, 'They are interactive with those lives, and each depends intimately on each.' Gard shows, for example, how a moment in which Mr Knightley's love for Emma is hinted at occurs in the midst of the neighbourly conspiracy to chide Jane Fairfax for walking in the rain; and how Miss Bates's long speeches during the ball at the Crown are full of amusing information hinting at Frank Churchill's constant attendance on Jane. So that Miss Bates's chatter is important to what Castle calls 'the illusion of being included in a palpably human world.' 'We feel ourselves profoundly involved in Emma's destiny and that of the little community in which she lives and moves.' Miss Bates's ramblings, besides conveying important clues to the hidden romantic plot, give us – with their familiar references to figures who never appear in the novel, like Patty, John Saunders, Mrs Wallis at the bakery, William Larkins, Mr Perry – a feeling of depth and intricacy, the pulse of a living community formed by gifts, charity, neighbourliness and gossip. 'Her talk is a constant validation of others, concern for others, and applause for others' concern for her,' Isobel Grundy writes; 'Miss Bates's talk weaves a web of interdependence, of reciprocity.' ('Why do they talk so much? How can we stand it?' in *The Talk in Jane Austen*, 2002).

Miss Bates is invited to all the festivities of the gentry, but she also pays charity visits to her father's old groom, gossips to Patty, and is familiar with Larkins, Mr Knightley's agent. The apothecary Mr Perry calls her his 'very old friend.' The word friend is ubiquitous in this novel, just as the notion of friendship is essential to its ethical world. The generalised benevolence that is characteristic of Highbury means different things between different people, but, as William Deresiewitz argues, this 'old style of Highbury friendship create[s] the conditions of its own transcendence', when the word 'friend' assumes a potent meaning between John Knightley and Jane Fairfax, and, ultimately between Emma and Frank Churchill (*Jane Austen and the Romantic Poets*, 2004). It is also a pivotal word in the later encounters between Emma and Knightley. From this point of view *Emma* presents an apparently classless society, in which neighbourliness and benevolence can seem to override and subsume the still salient distinctions of wealth and status.

More recently, critics have understood *Emma* as a contribution to national consciousness in the closing year of the Napoleonic Wars. Roger Sales, in his chapter on the novel in *Jane Austen and Representations of Regency England* (1994), argues that 'the differences between English and French values,' are a recurrent motif of the text, and that they are 'embodied respectively by the village and the watering place' (Frank Churchill is associated with Weymouth, Mrs Elton with Bath). However, Sales suggests, Mr Knightley's 'Francophobia' is not necessarily shared by the novel. Others have disagreed. Claudia Johnson's 'Remaking English Manhood in *Emma*,' in her *Equivocal Beings* (1995), argues that the novel creates a new plain style of manliness which 'is a matter of national import.' *Emma* 'persistently asks how a man should behave and what he ought to do.' It 'works … to redefine masculinity.' Mr Knightley's manliness is contrasted both with Mr Woodhouse's old-fashioned courtesy and sentimentality, and Frank Churchill's modern gallantry. Situating the novel after Burkean sentiment had had its day Johnson argues that *Emma* seeks 'to recover a native tradition of gentry liberty, which valued its manly independence from tyrannical rule, where that rule is figured as courtly, feminine, and feminizing … – a tradition which the French Revolution made dangerous by fulfilling.' In valuing the 'manly' it also valued the 'manliness' in women like Emma herself, so that the concept is both re-invented and cleansed of its sexist implications.

Mr Knightley's contrast of the amiable, 'the true English style,' which is sincere and direct, with the 'aimable,' gallant and dissembling, French version, is important too in Brian Southam's 'Emma: England, Peace and Patriotism' in *Jane Austen and the Navy* (2000). Southam's point is that *Emma* 'is the only novel in which Jane Austen examines the ideas of Englishness and patriotism', and where 'the traditional enmity of England and France

Fashionable full dress, Le Beau Monde, *November 1806.*

is played out in the antipathy between George Knightley, a gentle-manly John Bull, and the Frenchified Frank Churchill.' Frank's 'patriotism,' exercised in purchasing gloves at Ford's shop, is the 'refuge of a scoundrel' (to use Samuel Johnson's John Bullish phrase): whilst the Donwell Abbey estate, home of the Knightleys for centuries, is celebrated as both ancient and functional, and 'identified as being quintessentially English.' Thus this apparently parochial novel, with its very confined setting, reverberates with political and historical implications.

Modern criticism of the novel, then, has progressed from a focus on Emma and Mr Knightley, to an interest in the community in which their relationship is set, and thence outwards further, to England in 1815. This recognition that the novel is a deep and intricate work of art, and a contribution to national culture, is hardly reflected in the two films released in 1996. The British film directed by Dairmuid Lawrence (1997) reminds the viewer of the class society that accords Emma and Knightley their privileges, but fails to capture the depth of the local community. The Hollywood film, written and directed by Douglas McGrath (1996), is more interested in comedy than romance, and in creating a nostalgic world, to carry any of the import of the novel. In both films the role of Miss Bates, such a key to the novel's own world, is only focused on at the Box Hill picnic.

The British *Emma*, with script by Andrew Davies, does try to place Emma's story within a social setting. But rather than the tightly-knit, and seemingly classless community of the novel (in which Miss Bates interacts with everyone in the village) it presents a Marxist sense of this as a class society. (David Monaghan in *Jane Austen on Screen* (2003) however, gives a cogent account of the film as a demonstration of the conservative 'Burke's organicist social theories.') The labour of servants is as conspicuous here as it is inconspicuous in the novel. Those scenes in *Emma* which suggest so amusingly and at the same time so gratifyingly how deeply runs the notion of kindness in Highbury (as Deresiewitz notes) are omitted. The film replaces the novel's sense of a functional, integrated community with a hierarchical one. The invented final scene, in which Emma and Knightley address the labourers and servants, and Emma shakes hands with Robert Martin, seeks to present a reconciliation, to make a final comedic resolution of these divisions, but the effect is really to underscore the hierarchy, rather than to dissolve it.

The Miramax film is a star vehicle for Gwyneth Paltrow, which alludes to the 1940 *Pride and Prejudice*. Both begin with a credit sequence that empha-sises the distance of its action from the contemporary world. 'It happened in Old England' in the earlier film is now 'A time when one's town was one's world' and both title sequences are accompanied by drawings of villages and great houses. Though the film credits state that it was filmed 'on location in Dorset and London,' the effect is consciously to imitate the artificial studio-world of the forties film. In *Emma*, the cycle of the seasons – beginning with approaching winter, moving through spring to mid-summer – is integral to its realism, but in this film there is no sense of seasonal development; instead there is a wildly pastoral effect, as Paltrow, always hatless and clad in flimsy

She left the sofa.

Grecian-style gowns, meets Frank Churchill outdoors in February. The curious tent under which Emma and Harriet exchange confidences reproduces a similar one in *Pride and Prejudice*, with the same quaintly period touch. And the archery scene between Garson and Olivier (itself derived from the nineteenth-century illustrated editions of Austen) is archly recreated in an exchange of barbs between Paltrow and Jeremy Northam's Mr Knightley. The film includes moments of latter-day screwball comedy, with a clumsy Harriet dropping her basket, and running jokes – such as Emma's attempts to get away from Mr Elton's attentions -- that turn Austen's comedy into farce. The gardens over-bloom fantastically, the settings are grandiose and Victorian (rather than modest and Regency) and filmed in syrupy amber light. This film is not about Old England, it is about Old Hollywood.

Both movies try to reproduce the novel's illusion of delightful intimacy with the imaginative inner life of Emma Woodhouse. The McGrath film intermittently uses the voice-over and has Emma confiding her thoughts to her 'Dear Diary'(!) or praying aloud in a chapel. These are deliberately old-fashioned strategies, but there is some clever modern editing through which Emma's inward thoughts segue into her spoken words. The Davies script uses fantasy or dream-sequences, in the manner of the older British *Northanger Abbey*, to represent Emma's imagination. Some of these are plausible visual parallels to Emma's thoughts in the novel (such as her idea that Jane Fairfax was rescued from drowning by Mr Dixon), others are more interventionist. Emma looks at a portrait of Frank Churchill and he, amazingly, steps forward and kisses her hand. But the film does at least attempt to reproduce the comic play between Emma's inner life and the actuality that surrrounds her.

Neither version has the secure artistic purpose of *Clueless* (1995), the relatively modest teen comedy that captures more of *Emma*'s warmth and appeal than either. But *Clueless* imitates only the first third of the novel closely, and is a fantasy, whereas Jane Austen's *Emma*, whilst presenting a wholly enjoyable experience, and employing techniques of consummate artistry, somehow, as so many critics agree, convinces the reader that the world it presents is real.

Regency Life
Maggie Lane

Food and Farming

Jane Austen grew up in a household that was virtually self-sufficient in food. Her father, besides being a clergyman, was a gentleman farmer, renting a 200-acre farm and employing a bailiff to oversee its working. It was a mixed farm, producing cereal crops and meat. The surplus not required by the household – and it was a large household, comprising not only the seven children but the servants and a number of boarding pupils – was sold for profit. Farming talk – the state of the harvest, the effect of the weather, prices at market – was familiar to Jane from an early age.

Her mother looked after the poultry yard, dairy, beehives and kitchen garden, as well as overseeing the cookery and planning of menus. Only citrus fruits, spices, tea, coffee and sugar had to be purchased, and these commodities were valued accordingly.

Jane and her sister Cassandra were trained by their mother in all the arts of housekeeping, for even having a number of servants left the mistress of the house with the task of directing them in their work. Jane's letters are full of remarks about the provision of food and drink. Interestingly, however, she gives her heroines very little concern with such matters. In *Pride and Prejudice*, Mrs Bennet remarks indignantly that *her* daughters have nothing to do in the kitchen; it is fortunate indeed that Jane and Elizabeth both marry wealthy husbands. How the untrained, feckless Lydia will run her house is another matter – probably with as much lack of method and comfort as the slatternly Mrs Price in *Mansfield Park*. Mrs Bennet has done her daughters – and her putative grandchildren – no favours.

It is in the novel *Emma* that food production and consumption are most conspicuous. This is partly because Emma Woodhouse herself is already mistress of a household, keeping house for her father even before her marriage, and partly because the hero is a gentleman farmer who takes an active interest in the cultivation of his land. Food, which most frequently appears in the guise of a gift from one person who has plenty to others who are without, runs through *Emma* like a metaphor for the spiritual nourishment and interdependence of a community. In this sense, it is the novel most rooted in the fundamentals of life. Tied firmly to the seasons, there is a solidity about the world of *Emma* that generations of readers have found deeply satisfying.

Not that Emma herself ever thinks or talks about food in the sense of a meal anticipated or enjoyed. None of the heroines is allowed to have the natural relish for food that Jane Austen's own letters evince. In fiction, she regards preoccupation with food as vulgar, shallow or greedy, and only the most unworthy characters are guilty of it. No, Emma's relationship with food is that of the lady bountiful. Suiting her own notions of herself as principal lady in the community, she takes pride in providing exquisite dishes for her guests and charity to her neighbours. Housekeeping comes easily to Emma, she has been doing it since she was sixteen, and the comfortable income of her father supports a housekeeper and a cook as well as numerous under-servants at Hartfield. All Emma has to do is give orders.

Emma's gifts of food range from soup for poor cottagers, through a hind-quarter of pork for the impoverished but still genteel Mrs and Miss Bates (widow and spinster daughter of a former vicar of Highbury, in rather similar circumstances to Jane, Cassandra and their mother) and the offer, not taken up, of arrowroot for the sick Jane Fairfax. As a hostess, Emma provides delicacies like fricassee of sweetbreads, minced chicken and scalloped oysters to the old ladies who play cards with her father and who, having dined unfashionably early, appreciate a good supper at the end of the evening. These dishes, we

'With a slice of Mrs Weston's wedding-cake'
(Hugh Thomson).

understand, are more refined than their own humble kitchens can produce, and eating such food at Hartfield comprises one of the pleasures that make turning out on a cold winter evening worthwhile.

The joke is that Emma's father, though full of benevolence and courtesy to his old neighbours, is so frightened of indigestion that he discourages them from eating what Emma has provided. 'His own stomach could bear nothing rich, and he could never believe other people to be different from himself. What was unwholesome to him, he regarded as unfit for anybody.' His attitude to food is the opposite of life-enhancing, as he tries to stop everybody eating anything good, including the wedding-cake that joyously makes the rounds of the village at the beginning of the story – and even worse, as he tries to force on everybody his own favourite 'basin of gruel, thin but not too thin.' There is no more comic scene in Jane Austen than that in which, 'while the ladies were comfortably clearing the nicer things,' Mr Woodhouse gently harangues them: 'Mrs Bates, let me propose your venturing on one of these eggs. An egg boiled very soft is not unwholesome. Serle understands boiling an egg better than anybody. I would not recommend an egg boiled by anybody else – but you need not be afraid – they are very small, you see – one of our small eggs will not hurt you,' and so on.

Emma is not the only food-giver in the neighbourhood of Highbury. Mr Knightley gives the last of his apples to the Bates household, and invites all his friends to pick and eat his strawberries in season. The tenant farmer Robert Martin's courtship of Harriet Smith includes gathering walnuts for her, going three miles out of his way. His mother, Mrs Martin, sends Harriet back to Mrs Goddard's school, where she is a parlour-boarder, with a goose, 'a beautiful goose, the finest goose Mrs Goddard had ever seen.' Mrs Goddard then shares this treat with her employees; she 'had dressed it on a Sunday and asked all three teachers, Miss Nash, Miss Prince and Miss Richardson, to sup with her.' The net result is a picture of a community where food is abundant and where the producers of food – Mr Knightley and the Martins on their respective farms, and the Woodhouses who evidently keep pigs ('our Hartfield pork') and hens ('one of our small eggs') make sure the fruits of the soil are shared fairly with those whose lack of land mean they cannot produce food for themselves.

The good management of his farm is the all-absorbing interest in Mr Knightley's life, coupled with doing right by his neighbours and – despite her faults – falling in love with Emma. He eagerly discusses with his brother the disposition of various fields for wheat, turnips or spring corn, and even when entertaining guests at Donwell keeps an eye on the clover to see if it is ready for cutting. Mr Knightley farms the Donwell Abbey home farm with the help of a bailiff, William Larkins, and rents out his other farm, Abbey Mill, to Robert Martin. As men engaged in the same business, though of different social standing, Mr Knightley and Mr Martin hold each other in high esteem personally and professionally. 'I never hear better sense from anyone than Robert Martin,' says Mr Knightley, while his contentment in William Larkins' company is a standing joke in the novel.

Even the pleasure-grounds at Donwell Abbey are characterised not by elegant improvements, as in some of Jane Austen's other great houses, but by productive orchards, strawberry beds and 'the old Abbey fish-ponds.' From here too can be viewed the 'rich pastures' and 'spreading flocks' of Abbey Mill Farm: what Jane Austen calls its 'appendages of prosperity and beauty.' For her, the English landscape is never more beautiful than when it is also productive, and kept in good trim. The prosperity of Abbey Mill Farm is the achievement of Robert Martin, a new breed of tenant farmer, better educated than his forbears, reading the *Agricultural Reports* to keep up with the latest ideas in farming.

This was the age of agricultural reform. Large farms were more economical. The old system of open fields cultivated in strips by peasant proprietors, with everyone having rights to common and waste land, had almost disappeared in favour of the kind of fields we know today, bordered by hedges and in the ownership of a few individuals. Enclosure of this kind, which required individual Acts of Parliament, and which had far-reaching effects on the population, turning the majority into agricultural labourers rather than their own masters, but producing enough food to sustain a rising population, including those in the burgeoning towns, had been taking place for a century and was now almost complete, the wars with Revolutionary and Napoleonic France providing the final impetus. The appearance of the countryside was transformed into the lovely patchwork we think of as quintessentially English. Other reforms included crop rotation, so that no field need lie fallow, the cultivation of turnips as cattle-fodder, enabling them to be over-wintered, and the invention of machinery such as seed-drills and threshing machines. All these modern methods are followed by Mr Knightley.

The success of Britain's farming community in adopting new ways is measured by the fact that by 1800 wool and mutton output had doubled compared with a century earlier, and grain production had kept pace with a population increase of some seventy per cent. It is this success, and the obligation to make sure everybody shares in it, that *Emma* celebrates.

The Role of Women

One person in Highbury who is *not* sustained by the abundance of food on offer is Jane Fairfax who, in her illness and secret misery, cannot be coaxed to eat: in her aunt's words, 'Jane would hardly eat anything; Mr Perry recommended nourishing food; but everything they could command (and never had anybody such good neighbours) was distasteful.' Jane Fairfax is one of three young women in Jane Austen's novels who, powerless and at the mercy of men, seek relief in one aspect of their lives that they *can* control, their personal consumption of food.

The other two are Marianne Dashwood in *Sense and Sensibility*, and Fanny Price in the Portsmouth scenes in *Mansfield Park*. Though their stories are

very different, all three are unfortunate in being desired and trifled with by young men of independent means who have been accustomed all their lives to having their own way. While these men come and go at will, Marianne, Fanny and Jane are immobile, constrained not only by an almost total lack of money that they can call their own, but by the type of behaviour their society authorises in respectable young women.

That Jane Austen was deeply and imaginatively engaged by the place of women in society, their constraints and their options, their advantages and their drawbacks, is indisputable. She is never strident on the subject of women's wrongs, and in general she shies away from advocating change, but there are plenty of comments in her letters and novels to show she was aware of imbalance between the sexes.

'Poor Woman! I shall support her as long as I can, because she *is* a Woman, & I hate her Husband,' she wrote of the suffering, though hardly admirable, Caroline, Princess of Wales, in a letter to a friend. In *Mansfield Park*, she questions the double standard that wreaks social ostracism on a female adulterer but lets her male co-offender off scot-free. In *Persuasion*, Anne Elliot, usually the mildest of heroines, protests that men have had the advantage in telling their own side of the story: 'Education has been theirs in so much higher a degree; the pen has been in their hands.' Anne acknowledges that women lead sheltered, protected lives in comparison to men, who often have hardships and dangers to contend with. But even that is not always in women's favour: 'we live at home, quiet, confined, and our feelings prey upon us,' while men always have some business or occupation to take them out into the world.

In the early novels, Jane Austen touches for the most part obliquely on the lack of opportunities for women; the heroines are concerned to marry the men they love, but are not concerned about what will happen to them if they do not marry at all. In *Pride and Prejudice* there is an insouciance about Elizabeth Bennet on this subject that probably reflects the youthful optimism of her creator. Mrs Bennet's famous obsession with finding husbands for her five daughters is mocked rather than applauded as proper maternal care for their futures. It is left to Charlotte Lucas to voice the fact that matrimony is 'the only honourable provision' for an educated woman of small fortune, and because she accepts the odious Mr Collins on that basis, her views, however realistic, are accorded no moral weight.

By the time she came to write *Emma*, however, Jane Austen was approaching forty years old. Her own youthful flirtations had come to nothing, and the one proposal of marriage she had received, at the age of twenty-seven, had come from a man she did not care for enough to marry. She had settled into a fairly contented early middle age (her niece thought she put on the garb of middle age unnecessarily early), sustained by her family relationships and rich creative life. Her novels were her 'darling' children, in some ways preferable to the real children who would almost certainly have followed marriage. 'Poor animal, she will be worn out before she is thirty,' she wrote of a niece who was producing a baby a year. Three of her sisters-in-law died in childbirth, two after giving birth to eleven children, another at the age of twenty-four leaving three tiny girls motherless.

Nevertheless, the passing years had taught her how financially precarious was the situation of most women of her class if they did not marry. Though a gentlewoman lost caste if she was known to do anything for money, Jane Austen rejoiced in her own modest (and anonymous) earnings in the last few years of her life. It irked her that she, her sister and their widowed mother had to rely on the charity of brothers. Had nothing been forthcoming from that quarter – and all the brothers had their own families or their own financial difficulties to contend with – how would Jane and her sister have lived? There were two answers, both of which she explores in *Emma*.

Like Miss Bates, she might have found herself devoting her middle years to the care of an elderly mother and the endeavour to make a small income go as far as possible. The Austen women must have been reduced to lodging in a cramped set of rooms (as they had in Bath, for some year and a half, before other arrangements were provided by the brothers). In depicting the Bates household, Jane Austen trains her clear vision on a situation perilously close to her own. 'A single woman, with a very narrow income, must be a ridiculous, disagreeable old maid!' thinks Emma herself. Another novelist of mature years might have made Miss Bates's predicament the focus of her novel. But Jane Austen is writing firmly within the courtship genre, and Miss Bates is presented as a comic character, albeit with some sympathy. The difference with her creator is one of intellect, not circumstance. Miss Bates 'had no intellectual superiority to make atonement to herself, or frighten those who might hate her, into outward respect.' It is not hard to read this remark of Jane Austen's autobiographically, and to guess at the moments of social pain that underlie it.

He stopt to look in.

The other path open to educated women without fortune was governessing, about which *Emma* has much to say. Jane Fairfax, destined to be a governess, makes the comparison with slavery: 'widely different certainly as to the guilt of those who carry it on; but as to the greater misery of the victims, I do not know where it lies.' Jane Austen pitied the life of even a well-treated governess. She cultivated a friendship with Anne Sharp, the woman employed by her rich brother Edward to teach his large brood, and corresponded with her long after she had left his employment. (We do not know what Edward's wife thought of her sister-in-law treating a member of the household staff as an equal.) In *Emma* Miss Taylor has been almost one of the family at Hartfield, but it is not to be compared with having a home of her own.

Alternatively women could teach in a school, which avoids the servant stigma but brings its own difficulties. Mrs Goddard, the *proprietor* of a school, is mistress of her own fate and enjoys the rewards of her labours, but her three assistants, though presumably not unkindly treated, seem to have no possibility of life outside the school. They are included in none of the social activities of Highbury. Nobody thinks to invite them to the ball

at the Crown. Their only connection with the village seems to be mooning through the windows at passing men . 'I would rather do anything than be teacher at a school,' says a character in Jane Austen's unfinished fragment 'The Watsons.' 'I have been to school, and know what a life they lead.' Jane Austen too had been to school.

And while the working matrons, Mrs Wallis the baker, Mrs Stokes the landlady and Mrs Ford the draper (we do not know whether they have husbands, or are widows, or have adopted the honorary title Mrs), like Mrs Goddard, are accorded the respect due to them in the community, all in all, earning one's own living does not seem particularly desirable in *Emma*. Miss Taylor and Miss Fairfax escape that fate with a relief that is shared by all their true friends; and while Miss Smith's unknown father supplies enough money to keep her in board and lodging, with nothing to occupy her time, there is no suggestion that she would be a better woman, or have a more fulfilled life, if she went out to work. Marriage is her only resource; and as she is pretty, she 'is a girl who will marry somebody or other,' in Mr Knightley's words.

Towards the end of the book, as Emma is learning to be more sympathetic to others, she sits 'musing on the difference of woman's destiny', struck by the contrast between the rich and capricious Mrs Churchill's 'importance in the world,' and Jane Fairfax's: 'one was everything, the other nothing.' Emma herself is an unusual heroine in that she possesses a comfortable home and fortune even without marriage, and consequently thinks that she has none of women's usual inducements to marry. The passage in which she explains this to Harriet is unique in Jane Austen's fiction, for Emma projects ahead as to what her life as a single woman of mature years might be – and while we are meant to smile at Emma's self-satisfaction and perhaps delusion, the actual picture she paints is not a bad one, thanks to a sufficiency of money.

But despite her advantages, Emma is not really free; she cannot walk far without a companion, has never fulfilled her wish to see the sea, and is as tied to her father as many a wife to her husband. Money makes a big difference to the women in Jane Austen's world, but even the comfortably-off have to accommodate their desires to the realities of a patriarchal society.

Geographical Settings
Caroline Sanderson

The English county of Surrey is the setting for Jane Austen's fourth published novel, *Emma*, a book featuring that heroine of whom Jane Austen once remarked 'no-one but myself will much like.' It is the most confined of her novels; all the action in the main narrative takes place within seven miles of the fictional village of Highbury. This localised setting reflects the fact that Emma herself has lived a relatively charmed life within comfortable surroundings and has never ventured far from them. She has thus remained blithely blind to the ways of the wider world; Highbury is her domain and she has reigned over it since she was a child.

Jane Austen stayed in Surrey on several occasions and regularly passed through the county on her way to and from the homes of her brothers Henry and Edward in London and Kent. A plausible model for Highbury, which is described as a 'large and populous village almost amounting to a town' is Great Bookham near Leatherhead, which was home to her mother's cousin, Cassandra and her husband, the Revd Samuel Cooke, who was also Jane's godfather. Cooke was vicar at Great Bookham for more than 50 years, from 1769 until his death in 1820. It seems that Jane may not have been keen on staying with the Cookes. In a letter of January 1799 she remarks to Cassandra: 'I can assure You (*sic*) that I dread the idea of going to Bookham as much as you can do.' Jane's godfather, however, was an admirer of her work, particularly *Mansfield Park*. According to Jane, in another of her letters, he proclaimed it 'the most sensible Novel he ever read, and the manner in which I treat the Clergy, delights them very much.' *Emma* was written between January 1814 and March 1815, and as Jane is known to have stayed with the Cookes in 1814, it is possible that her visit provided her with much useful geographical material for her novel.

Half an hour shut up with my housekeeper.

Great Bookham has another interesting literary association. Between 1793 and 1797 it was the home of the novelist Fanny Burney, and her husband General d'Arblay, a French aristocrat in exile. The d'Arblays encountered the Cookes on many occasions, but it is not known if they ever met Jane Austen. That Jane admired and learned from Fanny Burney's work is undeniable. Take the following amusing description from one of her letters of an acquaintance she met in Kent in 1796: 'Miss Fletcher and I were very thick, but I am the thinnest of the two – She wore her purple Muslin, which is pretty enough tho' it does not become her complexion. There are two Traits in her Character which are pleasing; namely, she admires *Camilla* [a novel by Fanny Burney], & drinks no cream in her Tea.' It is believed that Jane took the title *Pride and Prejudice* from the end of another of Burney's novels, *Cecilia*.

From her careful description of its location in the novel, it seems likely that Jane Austen had the area of Surrey around Cobham and Leatherhead in mind for Highbury, although no real town corresponds exactly with the place she pinpoints for us. Highbury is nine miles from Richmond-Upon-Thames, and seven from Box Hill. Kingston-Upon-Thames is also nearby; we are told that Robert Martin rides there every week for the market. The London home of Emma's sister, Isabella Knightley, her husband John and five children is sixteen miles away in Brunswick Square, a newly built residential area on what were then the northern outskirts of London. 'Our part of London is so very superior to most others! … We are so very airy! Isabella remarks to reassure her father who is worried about the effect of living in the city on the family's health, and 'could not be induced to go to London, even for poor Isabella's sake.'

'I see very few pearls
in the room except mine'

Jane Austen's very precise description of Highbury's relative location to other places mentioned in the novel is important because it emphasises the insular, static lives that Emma and her father lead. Because her father refuses to travel even very short distances, Emma has never seen the sea, and has never been to London. We also discover that she has never visited Box Hill, a renowned local beauty spot that lies only seven miles away. Her father's constant indisposition demands that she remains close to Hartfield at all times. She cannot contemplate leaving him even overnight, making a trip to London, for example, impossible. 'You, who know how very, very seldom I am ever two hours from Hartfield,' Emma remarks tellingly at one point to Mr Knightley. Prior to the strawberry-picking expedition, Mr Woodhouse – and presumably Emma too – have not visited Donwell Abbey, the home of Mr Knightley, for two years, despite it being only a mile or so to the south of Highbury.

By contrast, most of the other characters in the book have much wider horizons and are often away from Highbury. Frank Churchill spends much of the novel shuttling between his father, Mr Weston in Highbury, and his wealthy uncle and aunt, Mr and Mrs Churchill, who brought him up. Frank is at the beck and call of Mrs Churchill, whose health is as unpredictable as that of Mr Woodhouse. At first, when recalled to his grandmother's side, Frank must journey to their home in Enscombe, Yorkshire, 190 miles north of London. Later in the novel, the Churchills move south to stay in London, because Mrs Churchill 'takes it into her head' that Yorkshire is too cold for her, though Mr Weston has another theory. 'The fact is, I suppose that she is tired of Enscombe. She has been a longer time stationary there than she ever was before, and she begins to want change. It is a retired place. A fine place, but very retired.' Mr and Mrs Churchill's move south makes it much easier for Frank to visit Highbury. We are told on one occasion that he is even able to ride down for 'a couple of hours.'

No sooner have Mr and Mrs Churchill arrived in London, however, than they are on the move again on account of Mrs Churchill's nerves being 'under continual irritation.' 'It soon appeared that London was not the place for her. She could not endure its noise.' The Churchills remove to Richmond where 'a ready-furnished house in a favourite spot was engaged, and much benefit expected from the change.' Frank is now within easy reach of Highbury, being only nine miles and 'an hour's ride' away. His father is delighted. 'There was no comfort in having him in London; he might as well be at Enscombe; but Richmond was the very distance for easy intercourse.' Though London seems a world away to Mr Weston, Frank Churchill thinks nothing of 'travelling sixteen miles twice over' just to get his hair cut there. 'A sudden freak seemed to have seized him at breakfast, and he had sent for a chaise and set off.' This notable incident is designed to show up Frank's frivolous tendencies against the steady and sensible temperament of Mr Knightley, who would never dream of doing such a thing. Emma's 'very good opinion of Frank Churchill' is 'a little shaken' by the incident: 'there was an air of foppery and nonsense in it which she could not approve.' Frank's apparent restlessness surfaces again during the visit to Donwell Abbey, in the course of which he quarrels with Jane Fairfax. 'I ought to travel. I am tired of doing nothing. I want a change ... I am sick of England and would leave it tomorrow, if I could.'

Another character in *Emma* who often talks of places away from Highbury is Mrs Elton. The erstwhile Miss Augusta Hawkins of Bristol, with ten thousand pounds, whom Mr Elton meets and proposes to in the space of four weeks in Bath is constantly making comparisons – usually unfavourable ones – between Highbury and the home of her sister, Selina, who is married to a Mr Suckling of Maple Grove. 'The rich brother-in-law near Bristol was the pride of the alliance, and his place and his carriages were the pride of him.' Ironically, Mrs Elton is the youngest of two daughters of a Bristol merchant ('Bristol was her home, the very heart of Bristol'), which was little recommendation at the time. Bristol was notorious as a squalid, unsavoury place, full of smoke from its sugar refineries, and other factories, and with strong links to the slave trade. The relatively low-born Mrs Elton's constant lauding of Maple Grove, and her delusions of grandeur, which include referring to her husband as her '*caro sposo*', mark her out as a flashy woman lacking in refinement. However, since her elder sister's fortunate marriage to a wealthy man, she has acquired a taste for the good things in life. When Emma finally marries Mr Knightley at the end of the novel, her wedding is described as being 'very much like other weddings, where the parties have no taste for finery or parade.' Mrs Elton thinks it is all 'extremely shabby' however and 'very inferior to her own ... Selina would stare when she heard of it.'

Though Emma herself has never been to the seaside, several coastal towns receive a mention in the novel. During a visit to Hartfield by Emma's sister, Isabella Knightley and her family, the relative merits of various English seaside resorts are discussed. Isabella takes after her father in her preoccupation with her own health. She laments the inability of the cook she hired during their recent holiday by the sea in Southend to make 'a basin of nice smooth gruel.' Mr Woodhouse is appalled. 'Ah! there is no end to the sad consequences of your going to South End. It does not bear talking of ... moreover, if you must to the sea, it had better not have been to South End. South End is an unhealthy place.' Mr Woodhouse has had Cromer in Norfolk recommended to him ('very pure air'), but when John Knightley protests that it is a hundred miles away from their home in London (Southend is only forty), Mr Woodhouse counters with, 'Better not move at all, better stay in London altogether than travel forty miles to get into a worse air.'

Frank Churchill and Jane Fairfax first meet at the south coast resort of Weymouth in Dorset. Weymouth, which had the distinction of being frequented by King George III in the late eighteenth century, is jokingly described by Jane as 'altogether a shocking place ... without recommendation of any kind' in a letter she wrote in 1804 to her sister Cassandra who had been staying there with their brother Henry and his wife Eliza. Weymouth remained a fashionable resort into the early nineteenth century, and it is therefore plausible that Frank Churchill and Jane Fairfax should

A detail from Weymouth Bay *by John Constable, c.1816.*

*The horror was then
their own portion.*

find themselves staying in the town at the same time, Jane in the company of her friends, Colonel and Mrs Campbell and Mr and Mrs Dixon.

Later, Emma, who has not yet met Frank Churchill but has heard a great deal about him, questions Jane closely as to what he is like. Was he handsome? Was he agreeable? Jane's evasive answers are a great disappointment. 'At a watering-place, or in a common London acquaintance, it was difficult to decide on such points.' Little does Emma guess at the truth, for it is also at Weymouth that Frank and Jane's secret engagement is embarked upon.

These are only short geographical diversions, however, from the main setting of *Emma* in the county of Surrey. In the two hundred years since *Emma* was written, Surrey has witnessed a great deal of development. Small country villages have mushroomed into commuter belt towns, and the northern half of the county now merges indistinguishably with the suburbs of Greater London. In places, however, it is still possible to find pockets of attractive, rural countryside, to remind us of what the whole county was once like; after all, Emma herself remarks to Mrs Elton that 'Surry (*sic*) is full of beauties.' One such place is Box Hill, a steep chalk escarpment in the North Downs near Dorking, which Jane Austen chose as the setting for one of the most memorable and telling episodes in *Emma*.

Now in the care of the National Trust, Box Hill has long been one of the best-known and most popular beauty spots in southern England. At 600 feet, the summit affords spectacular views of the kind of pastoral, green rolling scenery for which England is renowned, and its slopes provide a habitat for a remarkable variety of flora and fauna, as well as the ancient box woodland that gives the hill its name.

Many writers have visited Box Hill. The nineteenth-century novelist and poet George Meredith lived at the bottom in a flint and brick house where he was visited by such literary luminaries of the time as J.M. Barrie, George Gissing, Henry James and Robert Louis Stevenson. And ordinary tourists have been coming to Box Hill in search of recreation for centuries. In *A Tour Through the Whole Island of Great Britain* (1724–26) Daniel Defoe observed that, 'here every Sunday, during the summer season, there used to be a rendez-vous of coaches and horsemen, with abundance of gentleman and ladies from Epsome to take the air, and walk in the box-woods; and in a word, divert, or debauch, or perhaps both, as they thought fit.'

Box Hill is, of course, the scene of the fateful picnic in *Emma*, when Emma is rude to Miss Bates, much to the chagrin of Mr Knightley. When he reprimands her, it suddenly dawns on Emma how much she cares about having his good opinion, and this is the prelude to her realisation that she loves him. Though Emma is keen to visit Box Hill – 'she wished to see what every body found so well worth seeing' – the outing is somewhat ill-starred from the beginning. Emma, seeking as ever to avoid the vulgar Mrs Elton and her *caro sposo*, hopes that it will be done in a 'quiet, unpretending, elegant way, infinitely superior to the bustle and preparation, the regular eating and drinking, and picnic parade of the Eltons and Sucklings.' Mr Weston, however, invites all and sundry, maintaining that, 'One cannot have too large a party. A large party secures its own amusement.'

On the day of the excursion the weather is fine, and 'all other outward circumstances of arrangement, accommodation and punctuality were in favour of a pleasant party.' Despite a 'burst of admiration' on first arriving, however, there is something lacking: 'There was a languor, a want of spirits, a want of union, which could not be got over.' To fill the void Emma flirts outrageously with Frank Churchill, who responds enthusiastically and loudly: 'Let every body on the Hill hear me if they can. Let my accents swell to Mickleham on one side, and Dorking on the other.' In an attempt to rouse the other members of the party Frank proposes a game in which each person must say 'one thing very clever … two things moderately clever … or three things very dull indeed.' When Miss Bates opts for three things Emma cannot help herself: 'Ah! ma'am, but there may be a difficulty. Pardon me, but you will be limited as to number – only three at once.'

Jane Austen's novels contain very few topographical descriptions, and *Emma* is no exception. Even the spectacular view from Box Hill is only alluded to briefly, when Emma, growing 'tired at last of flattery and merriment' walks off alone 'in tranquil observation of the beautiful views beneath her.' The setting is just a backdrop to this pivotal chapter in which all Emma's plans and pretensions start to unravel, and she begins to understand her true feelings and pay proper attention to those of others. Nevertheless, Jane Austen must have chosen this location with care, and Box Hill remains one of the few places where we can still walk with certainty in the footsteps of her characters.

At the end of *Emma*, the characters disperse to begin new lives. Jane Fairfax and Frank Churchill leave Surrey to begin married life together in Yorkshire at Enscombe. Harriet is proposed to by Robert Martin whilst she is staying in London with the John Knightleys, and once married, goes to live at Abbey Mill Farm on Mr Knightley's Donwell Abbey estate.

And for a time anyway, it seems as if Emma may finally get to see the sea! She and Mr Knightley lay plans for their marriage to take place whilst John and Isabella are staying at Hartfield, 'to allow them the fortnight's absence in a tour to the sea-side.' But Mr Woodhouse has such difficulty in reconciling himself to the idea of his daughter being married, that in the end, Emma decides she cannot proceed with the honeymoon. So she remains at Hartfield after the wedding, and Mr Knightley takes up residence there with her. As we take our leave of the newly-weds, it seems that Emma's horizons are destined to remain confined to the small area of Surrey in and around Highbury.

And yet, perhaps not. In his 'Memoir of Jane Austen' published in 1870, Jane's nephew, J.E. Austen-Leigh reveals that his aunt 'would if asked, tell us many particulars about the subsequent careers of some of her people.' In this way, he learnt that 'Mr Woodhouse survived his daughter's marriage, and kept her and Mr Knightley from settling at Donwell, about two years.' So we can imagine Emma finally becoming mistress of Donwell Abbey and

I shall be sure to say three dull things as soon as ever I open my mouth, shan't I?

gazing on its 'sweet view – sweet to the eye and the mind. English verdure, English culture, English comfort, seen under a sun bright without being offensive.' And perhaps even tearing herself away from it for the occasional trip to London, or that long-awaited holiday by the sea.

A Modern Perspective

Josephine Ross

'The proportions must be preserved, you know'

Mr Elton, Emma, Chapter 6

In the summer of 1814, a remarkable exchange of letters on the subject of writing fiction took place between Jane Austen and her eldest niece – lively, artistic Anna Austen, then aged just 21. Anna had embarked on a novel of her own, and naturally turned for advice and assistance to her literary aunt – the author of three modestly-successful published works: *Sense and Sensibility*, *Pride and Prejudice* and *Mansfield Park*. The correspondence that ensued would throw extraordinary light on Jane Austen's approach to the creative process. As successive instalments of Anna's manuscript were sent and returned, her Aunt Jane responded with detailed assessments, mixing praise and encouragement with constructive criticism and suggestions – whilst stressing, with fond concern for a would-be fellow-author's feelings, 'If *you* think differently, however, you need not mind me.'

Among the points raised – the need for strict social accuracy, the importance of realistic characterisation and dialogue, the hazards of too much descriptive detail – one comment in particular would stand out: after warning Anna not to venture into settings where she was not 'quite at home' (such as the world of Irish society) 'Aunt Jane' wrote approvingly, 'You are now collecting your People ... into such a spot as is the delight of my life; 3 or 4 Families in a Country Village is the very thing to work on.' What was not mentioned, in any surviving letter from this historic exchange, was the fact that, while assisting her niece with the never-to-be-published *Enthusiasm*, or *Which is the Man?* Jane Austen was herself at work on one of the greatest novels in the English language, *Emma*.

When she began to write *Emma*, in late January 1814, she was entering her thirty-ninth year. Settled contentedly, if modestly, at Chawton cottage in Hampshire, with her unmarried sister and widowed mother, she had achieved a certain critical reputation with her three previous novels, all published anonymously, by the middle-ranking London firm of T. Egerton; but her career to date had yet to earn her more than a few hundred pounds in profit; and as she confided in November of that year, 'Tho' I like praise ... I like what Edward calls *Pewter* too.' Beneath the teasing reference to her schoolboy nephew's Regency slang lay a painful truth: approaching middle age, as a single woman with almost no inherited wealth, Jane Austen was more than ever aware of the role played by 'Pewter' in defining social status, and ensuring domestic comfort – for women in particular. With this fourth novel, in which financial security (or the lack of it) in women's lives would be a central theme, she was determined to achieve commercial, as well as artistic, success. Once completed, *Emma* – the only one of her six novels to feature an independently-rich heroine – would be offered, not to Egerton, whose sales of her earlier works had proved so financially unrewarding, but to the most famous and fashionable 'Bookseller' of the day – John Murray of Albemarle Street, friend, patron and highly-lucrative publisher of bestselling authors from Lord Byron to Walter Scott.

'Mr Murray's letter is come. He is a rogue, of course, but a civil one,' Jane Austen reported to her sister Cassandra with mingled delight and deprecation, on 17 October 1815. She added, 'He sends more praise, however, than I expected.' The deal was eventually struck (handled somewhat ineptly by her businessman brother Henry) but brought no immediate remuneration. Having turned down an initial outright offer of £450 for *Emma*, to include the copyrights of *Mansfield Park* and *Sense and Sensibility*, she settled that *Emma* and a new edition of *Mansfield Park* should be published at her own expense, with 10% commission to Murray. It was a sign of her faith in *Emma*'s sales prospects that she opted for such a potentially risky arrangement; as matters turned out, it was an unwise decision. Nonetheless, becoming a John Murray author was in itself a mark of literary success, which could be expected to bring other benefits, from high production standards to favourable notices in the press through Murray's influence.

When *Emma* eventually appeared, at the end of December 1815, it was handsomely printed in an edition of 2,000 three-volume copies, costing 21 shillings a set, and early sales were encouraging. What Jane Austen fortunately did not know was that, for all his civility and praise, John Murray had no great opinion of this latest novel by an obscure country gentlewoman. Sending a review copy to his friend (and most successful author) Walter Scott, he wrote cautiously 'Have you a fancy to dash off an article on *Emma*?,' adding 'It wants incident and romance, does it not?' Scott's response – a now-famous essay in the Murray-owned literary journal *The Quarterly Review* – would be eloquent in its praise for 'the Authoress's's' merits, but the great Mr Murray himself had fallen into an all-too-familiar trap where Jane Austen's fiction is concerned: that of mistaking subtlety, delicacy and outward restraint for a lack of passion, drama and depth.

Certainly *Emma* can be read, on one level, as a mere light, enjoyable comedy of manners involving '3 or 4 Families in a Country Village' and the mishaps and misconceptions that befall them, written with a due attention to all the points of style and technique that the author had endeavoured to impress upon her protégée niece Anna. As Scott was one of the first to realise, however, it is also a masterpiece.

Unlike Anna's *Enthusiasm*, with its cast of implausible aristocrats, Jane Austen's *Emma* revolves around the lives of what Scott approvingly called the 'middling classes of society,' and reflects 'characters that the reader cannot fail to recognise,' 'common occurrences' and 'nature as she really exists.' Perhaps

She absolutely refused to allow me.

"He did not know what was come to his master lately."

with Murray's doubting comments in mind, Scott singled out for special praise the shift from 'romance' to 'real life' represented by *Emma*; and he emphasised that, while this novel might offer less 'story' than the writer's previous works, it had no lack of 'dramatic effect.' *Emma*, he wrote admiringly, was written by an author 'with a knowledge of the human heart.'

Scott compared Jane Austen's technique to the flawless Flemish school of painting; but to many readers in the twenty-first century the resemblance is more immediately to the art of Gainsborough, or Constable, in the delicacy of composition and deeply-felt connection with English pastoral society poised on the threshold of the Industrial Revolution. A telling passage in Chapter 42 of *Emma* evokes, lyrically, the ordered landscape in which this great novel is set: looking out from Donwell Abbey, the hero's ancestral home, across woods, fruitful meadows and a flourishing farm, embraced by the 'close and handsome curve' of a river, the heroine reflects, 'It was a sweet view – sweet to the eye and the mind. English verdure, English culture, English comfort, seen under a sun bright, without being oppressive.'

With the exception of the aristocracy (for whom Jane Austen's letters and novels generally show scant respect), the fictional 'Country Village' of Highbury contains a microcosm of early nineteenth-century rural English society, from the long-established Knightleys, squires of Donwell Abbey and its estate, through the gradations of military family, vicar, doctor, schoolteachers and trades-people, right down to the gypsies who lurk on the outskirts, begging and alarming the more fortunate. It is a social order which – on balance – the heroine learns it is better not to disrupt, even with the best of intentions.

At the top of this village hierarchy are the true gentry headed by the novel's hero Mr Knightley, latest in a long line of benevolent owners of Donwell Abbey and its environs. On almost equal terms with him, by virtue of birth, good breeding and good manners, are the heroine Emma Woodhouse and her family, inheritors of 'elegant,' if less historic, Hartfield. Also part of their old, well-ordered world – though very differently circumstanced – are old Mrs Bates, a clergyman's widow, and her spinster daughter, the grandmother and aunt of beautiful, well-bred but penniless Jane Fairfax, orphaned daughter of an officer who has died fighting in the Napoleonic Wars. To the original Regency readers of *Emma* – published six months after the Battle of Waterloo had freed Europe from Napoleon Bonaparte and his Imperial ambitions – the plight of these impoverished gentlewomen, reduced to living in rented lodgings, and grateful for the kindness (or charity) of their neighbours and local community, would have struck a special chord.

Chief among the newcomers to this society – newly-rich, upwardly-mobile products of the burgeoning worlds of industry and trade – are the Cole family ('only moderately genteel,' but 'very good sort of people'), and more prominently, the young vicar and his bride, the Eltons. Mrs Elton, affected, pretentious daughter of a Bristol merchant, is one of Jane Austen's great comic creations, on a par with – though very different from – Lady

Catherine de Bourgh in *Pride and Prejudice*. Whereas domineering *grande dame* Lady Catherine derives her self-esteem from old birth and the supposed superiority of rank, Mrs Elton (née Miss Augusta Hawkins) bases hers on a recently-acquired fortune of £10,000, a veneer of 'elegance' and accomplishments, and her sister's marriage to a man with a large income, a country mansion ('Maple Grove … A charming place!'), and every modern luxury, including the latest in expensive transport, a 'barouche-landau,' to which she refers at every opportunity.

Writing in an age of fast-expanding consumerism, Jane Austen makes exquisitely artful use in *Emma* of the significance of possessions, carriages in particular. When not bragging of the barouche-landau, Mrs Elton boasts of her own vehicle and its horse-power. 'I believe we drive faster than anybody!' To own a carriage required an income of at least £500; in one subtle plot-line there is talk of the local doctor 'setting up his carriage,' to his patients' gossiping interest. It is typical of down-to-earth, wholly unpretentious Mr Knightley that, for all his wealth and position, he rarely uses his, preferring to walk or ride whenever possible.

Musical instruments – another status symbol – are used to similar dramatic effect. Well-bred, but poor, Jane Fairfax, who is genuinely musical, does not possess a piano (until her secret fiancé, in another plot-twist, sends her one); the Coles, however – who are now in fortune and style of living, second only to the family at Hartfield – own a magnificent, brand-new grand pianoforte, although Mrs Cole cheerfully admits, 'I do not know one note from another.'

The Gallery of Fashion *by Niklaus von Heideloff, July 1796.*

Property is always a guide to character in Jane Austen's fiction, and throughout *Emma* the Regency craze for 'improvements' to houses and grounds mirrors 'improvements' to characters' social status. Mr Knightley's Donwell Abbey, as befitting 'the residence of a family of such true gentility,' is 'rambling and irregular,' its grounds unaffected by 'fashion and extravagance.' The Coles, by contrast, have extended and aggrandised their house; while a strong hint as to Mr Elton's true nature is given early in the novel when his vicarage, 'with no advantage of situation,' is described as 'very much smartened up by the present proprietor.' Naive young Harriet Smith, the pretty, illegitimate schoolgirl whom Emma has taken as her protégée with a view to 'improving' her mind and marriage prospects, is especially struck by Mr Elton's yellow curtains – yellow being a fashionable and expensive feature of much modern Regency decor.

We may infer that there are no smart 'yellow curtains' in the mellow, rustic interiors of Abbey Mill Farm, on the Donwell estate, where Harriet's worthy, decent suitor Robert Martin lives and farms as Mr Knightley's tenant. Harriet's artless accounts of her visits to the family there are deeply touching: she speaks of 'moonlight walks and merry evening games'; of Mr Martin going 'three miles round one day, in order to bring her some walnuts, because she had said how fond she was of them'; of how he had brought his shepherd's son into the parlour one night to sing for her. 'I am going to take a heroine whom no-one but myself will much like,' Jane Austen reportedly told her family, when starting work on *Emma*; and the reader is never closer to detesting Emma and her misplaced, snobbish, bossy meddling than when she pressures Harriet into rejecting Robert Martin and the admirable rural lifestyle he represents, in favour of the sly, superficial pseudo-gentlemanly Mr Elton. 'For shame, Emma!' we want to cry – as her mild, indulgent former governess Mrs Weston does, albeit smilingly, over a less important offence.

And yet, unlike Mrs Elton, Emma is not in any sense hateful; only human. While showing us unsparingly her follies and errors, Jane Austen leaves us in no doubt as to her innate goodness of heart and moral worth, beneath the mistakes of judgement – the result of an over-privileged and indulged upbringing. She is seen taking comfort and food – unpatronisingly – to the local poor. She is not vain about her own beauty. She is endlessly patient with her kindly but self-centred father; she is a devoted sister and aunt; above all, she is stricken with remorse when made aware, finally, of her 'horrible blunders,' from insulting poor, foolish Miss Bates with a silly joke to interfering in others' lives for what she fondly believes is their benefit.

Self-deception is Emma's besetting flaw; and deception, whether of self or (more importantly) of others is at the heart of this sublime novel. The fashionable word-games, riddles and 'charades' with which the characters amuse themselves are echoed by the more serious and dramatic mind-games that they persistently play with one another. Charming Frank Churchill, adopted heir to a fortune, may be a 'gentleman' in rank, but he is wholly 'ungentlemanlike' (a favourite Jane Austen word) in his behaviour towards both Emma and Jane Fairfax, in pretending to pay court to one in order to conceal his secret engagement to the other. Emma deceives her protégée Harriet into believing that she is too good for Robert Martin, and that Mr Elton is courting her; Mr Elton deceives himself into believing that Emma is courting him; Harriet ultimately deceives herself into believing that Mr Knightley is courting her. Only on learning this does Emma, with pain, begin to understand what harm she may have done to herself, as well as others, by attempting to interfere in peoples' lives. As she acknowledges soberly, 'Mr Knightley is the last man in the world who would intentionally give any woman the idea of his feeling more for her than he really does.' It is at this point that she begins 'to understand, thoroughly understand, her own heart.'

Mr Knightley, the constant voice of sense and reason, deceives neither himself nor others. As eminent critics have pointed out, *Emma* is (among other things) a brilliantly-crafted detective novel, which requires at least a second reading for all the scrupulously-planted clues as to the real story that is unfolding to become apparent. Mr Knightley, through cool observation and a judgement unclouded by prejudice or conceit, sees below surfaces. He warns Emma of 'some double-dealing' on the part of Frank Churchill; he tells her of the risks she is taking in seeking to raise Harriet Smith out of her natural sphere, in which she is content; above all, he judges the inhabitants of what is essentially his domain, Highbury, on the basis of individual merit, not class or money. Emma initially declines even to be spoken to by Robert Martin; Mr Knightley says with pleasure, 'I believe he considers me as one of his best friends.'

The apparently stable Georgian world into which Jane Austen was born, in 1775, had set great store by the traditional principles of order, reason and proportion, in life as in art and architecture. (Watching Emma draw Harriet's portrait, Mr Elton observes fervently, 'The proportions must be preserved, you know.') By the time *Emma* appeared, in 1815, the author would seem to have come full circle in her attitude to these 'rules.' In *Pride and Prejudice*, published only two years earlier, the spirited, unconventional heroine Elizabeth Bennet is incensed at the notion that, just because she has some vulgar relations, she is herself unworthy to marry Mr Darcy and become mistress of Pemberley. When his snobbish aunt, Lady Catherine de Bourgh, exclaims indignantly, 'Are the shades of Pemberley to be thus polluted?' the reader responds with an unquestioning 'Yes!' on behalf of defiant, deserving Lizzy. Yet in *Emma* we are expected equally to endorse Emma's views as she reflects, with 'honest pride and complacency' that her sister's marriage to Mr Knightley's brother has 'given them neither men, nor names, nor places that could raise a blush,' by allying them 'unexceptionably,' to 'a family of such true gentility, untainted in blood.' On finding that Harriet Smith is the child, not of a gentleman but a tradesman, of only modest means, we share Emma's relief that 'the stain of illegitimacy, unbleached by nobility or wealth' has not been imposed, through marriage, on any leading Highbury family.

By the time *Emma* was published, the slave trade had been abolished, under British law, for eight years, but the appalling suffering involved was far from ended. Jane Fairfax is scrupulous in separating her plight from that of the physically enslaved; but she is driven to muse, with pain, on the differing degrees of oppression which one human being may inflict on another. Mrs Elton – aware of the suspicions which her father's description as a 'Bristol —merchant' may arouse, bridles that her brother-in-law was always 'rather a friend to the abolition'. There is a subtle ambiguity in that 'rather.' The author's own views on the 'sale … of human flesh,' from the ghastly traffic in slaves abroad to the social and economic oppression of women at home, can, however, be in no doubt.

Jane Austen's hopes that *Emma* might prove to be her own 'preservative from want' in later life were not fulfilled. Though early sales were brisk, the earnings had to be offset against losses on the John Murray reprint of *Mansfield Park*, and by the time she died in 1817, aged only forty-one, Jane Austen's profits from *Emma* were barely £40. In 1821 the last unsold copies were remaindered by Murray, at the bargain price of 2 shillings a set.

Today, a first edition of *Emma* would (if one could be found) cost upwards of £15,000. That she died with not the faintest inkling of the 'praise' and 'pewter' that *Emma* would one day command, as one of the greatest master-pieces in English literature, is perhaps the only one of life's ironies that would have given Jane Austen no amusement.

Principal Characters

Emma Woodhouse, the protagonist of the story, is a pretty, high-spirited, intellectual, and slightly spoiled woman of 21. Though vowing she will never marry, she delights in making matches for others.

Mr Henry Woodhouse is Emma's valetudinarian father. Frequently, his punctilious kindness is at war with invalid caution, and he has a dislike of all kinds of novelty and change.

Mr George Knightley, Emma's brother-in-law, aged about 37, is among the very few people to find any fault with Emma. Knightley is highly respected and considered very much a gentleman, and there is a no-nonsense air about him. He is the standard against which all the men in Emma's life are measured. He is constantly disputing with Mrs Weston about Emma's spoiled upbringing because of his long and deep-seated affection for her.

Mr Frank Churchill is an amiable man who manages to be liked by everyone except for Mr Knightley, who considers him quite immature. Frank thoroughly enjoys dancing and music and likes to live life to the fullest. Frank may be viewed as a less villainous version of characters from other Austen novels, such as Mr Wickham from *Pride and Prejudice* or Willoughby from *Sense and Sensibility*.

Jane Fairfax is an orphan whose only family consists of an aunt, Miss Bates, and a grandmother, Mrs Bates. She is regarded as a very elegant woman with the best of manners and is also very well educated and exceptionally talented in singing and playing the piano; in fact, she is the sole person that Emma envies.

Harriet Smith, a young friend of Emma's, is a very pretty girl who is too easily led by others, especially Emma. The illegitimate daughter of initially unknown parents, Harriet has been educated at a nearby school. Emma takes her under her wing early in the novel, and she becomes the subject of some of Emma's misguided matchmaking attempts. Harriet rebuffs a marriage proposal from farmer Robert Martin because of Emma's belief that he is beneath her, despite Harriet's own humble origins.

Philip Elton is the good-looking and ambitious young vicar. Emma wants him to marry Harriet; he wants to marry Emma. Mr Elton displays his mercenary nature by quickly marrying another woman of means after Emma's rejection.

Mrs Weston, formerly Miss Taylor, was Emma's governess for sixteen years and remains her closest friend and confidante after she marries Mr Weston in the opening chapter. Mrs Weston acts as a surrogate mother to Emma and, occasionally, as a voice of moderation and reason.

Augusta Elton is Mr Elton's monied but abrasive wife. She is portrayed to be a very pretentious woman who always likes to be the centre of attention and is generally disliked by Emma and her circle. She patronises Jane, which earns Jane the sympathy of others.

Mr Weston, formerly a captain of the militia and widower of Miss Churchill, came from a great Yorkshire family. He is a man 'of unexceptional character, easy fortune, suitable age and pleasant manners' who marries Anna Taylor, Emma's companion and friend. Father of Frank Churchill.

Robert Martin is a sensible young man of 24, though somewhat abrupt in manner. He loves Harriet Smith and is refused by her because of Emma's intervention. He is a tenant farmer and is highly regarded by his landlord, Mr Knightley.

Mrs Goddard is the mistress of 'a real, honest, old-fashioned boarding-school … She was a plain, motherly kind of woman who had worked hard in her youth, and now thought herself entitled to the occasional holiday of a tea-visit' at one of which she introduces Harriet Smith to Emma.

Miss Bates is an old maid whose mother is a friend of Mr Woodhouse's. She is slighted by Emma for being ridiculous. Emma is later confronted by Mr Knightley about it and tries to make amends

Northanger Abbey

Modern Interpretations
John Wiltshire

The youthful freshness of *Northanger Abbey* has provided readers with much enjoyment and critics with tough challenges. In many ways, this story of a naïve but very good-hearted young lady who makes a series of simple mistakes is an everywoman narrative: there is nothing special about Catherine, except her honesty. She misunderstands the characters of those she meets, but these characters, too, are not complex. Anyone but Catherine would see that John Thorpe is a stupid braggart and bully in their first conversation, a Regency boy-racer who boasts that his horse 'cannot go less than ten miles an hour'. That General Tilney is a domestic tyrant should be obvious to anyone less naïvely unsuspecting than Catherine. In sharp contrast to a later mature novel like *Mansfield Park*, the psychology of *Northanger Abbey* is transparent. Almost all motives in *Mansfield Park* are mixed, goodness is diluted, badness adulterated, but the reader is rarely in any doubt how to assess the characters in *Northanger Abbey*. Isabella's word is not to be trusted for a moment, and the comedy lies in the obvious contrast between her avowed motives – 'let's give those boys the slip' – and her real ones – 'let's chase after them'. There's nothing difficult or taxing in the reader's response. For this reason Isabella, though capable of meanness towards Catherine, is not a wholly detestable character; like Lydia in *Pride and Prejudice*, she has generated so much uncomplicated comedy for the reader that she is readily forgiven.

If other characters are straightforward, another strand of comedy lies in the interplay between the mind of the savvy narrator and the thinking of the sweet heroine. This is a novel where the author has no scruple about voicing her own opinions and interjecting them into accounts of her heroine's feelings. 'Little as Catherine was in the habit of judging for herself, *and unfixed as were her general notions of what men ought to be,* she could not entirely repress a doubt, as she bore with the effusions of his endless conceit, of his being altogether completely agreeable' (my italics). The banging together of two quite different styles and two quite distinct judgements of Thorpe here sparks amusement, but it does not really diminish Catherine. Rather it entrusts her, as she tentatively begins to make judgements of her own, to the reader's amused kindness.

This transparent quality of *Northanger Abbey* has challenged its critics and commentators. Most, plying their trade, have decided that the best chance for elucidatory industry lies elsewhere. Much criticism has been focused on the relationship of the novel to earlier texts, with the assumption that Jane Austen is alluding to, or paralleling, or satirising other novels, and expects the reader to notice this. One critic, Roger Gard, in *Jane Austen's Novels: the Art of Clarity* (1992), has argued persuasively that the reader does not need to know

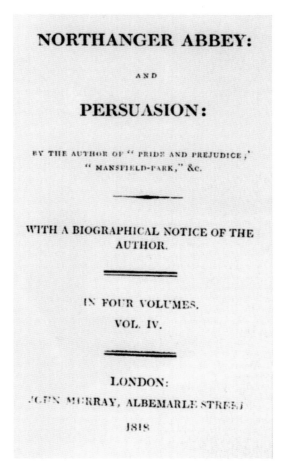

A view of Bath from Claverton Road, from John Claude Nattes' Bath *(opposite).*

anything of the books Catherine and Isabella are reading to grasp the comic aims of the novel. His claim is that the Gothic and sentimental works Jane Austen has in her sights are themselves created sufficiently by the text's references to them – and they are, more or less, the clichés of romantic fiction, now as then. One clear example of this is when Catherine, excited at the prospect of 'Blaize Castle', imagines 'all the happiness which its walls could supply' of being lost in one of the ancient edifice's 'narrow winding vaults', 'or even of having their lamp, their only lamp, extinguished by a sudden gust of wind, and of being left in total darkness' – an anticipation of the pleasing terrors of the funfair. And it is an amusing take on the novel itself that some of the members of Karen Joy Fowler's *The Jane Austen Book Club* (2004) are surprised to learn that Ann Radcliffe's *The Mysteries of Udolpho* – like the other books Isabella recommends to Catherine – is a real novel. On the other hand, a reader's enjoyment would be heightened by knowing, like Austen's first readers, that Blaise Castle was a contemporary 'folly', built in 1766.

"Catherine grows quite a good-looking girl"

The challenge that *Northanger Abbey* presents for the critic is to reconcile the novel's continuous apparent referentiality with its equally apparent freshness – the quality that the nineteenth-century critic George Lewes described as its 'unflagging vivacity'. Certainly *Northanger Abbey* has its affinities with other novels of the time (the 1790s) and is much concerned with their influence on readers. 'It is a novel about novels and novel-readers,' remarked Anne Henry Ehrenpreis in her 'Introduction' to the Penguin edition (1972), an emphasis taken up by Marilyn Butler in her more recent 'Introduction' to the same imprint. 'The pervasiveness of the theme of reading from the first paragraph to the last queries the frequent claim that the novel does not hang together.' Recent accounts, such as Mary Waldron's in *Jane Austen and the Fiction of her Time* (1999), focus on *Northanger Abbey*'s parallels, not so much with Gothic fiction, as with Charlotte Smith's *Emmeline* (1788) and Charlotte Lennox's earlier *The Female Quixote* (1752). (Though Mary Lascelles spotted the novel's relation to *Emmeline* as early as 1934.) Marilyn Butler suggests that Burney's *Camilla*, to which Jane Austen was a subscriber in 1796, is the 'model Jane Austen most wants her reader to keep in mind'. More obvious parallels might also be found in Burney's *Evelina*, since both novels are concerned with a naïve young lady brought up in the country, and introduced into 'the world' under the guidance of an inadequate chaperone. 'The world' in *Evelina* is fashionable London, in *Northanger Abbey*, fashionable Bath. Just as *Evelina* introduces the heroine into the various new venues and entertainments of the gentry, so *Northanger Abbey* introduces Catherine into the rooms and streets of Bath, assumed to be familiar to the novel's readers. Both Evelina and Catherine fall into a series of mistakes: Evelina because she does not know the rules of etiquette, Catherine because she accepts everyone at face value. Both get into embarrassing scrapes as a result, and have to extricate themselves. And Isabella Thorpe is plainly modelled on Evelina's cousins, the Brangton sisters, with the same social ambitions, the same pursuit of 'beaux'. But *Northanger Abbey*'s sprightly vivacity is all its own.

In her *Romantic Austen* (2002), Clara Tuite offers a more productive and interesting suggestion about the novel's relation to the Gothic texts of the 1790s. She argues that the characteristic 'female Gothic' of Ann Radcliffe introduced the notion of interiority into the novel, since its focus was not so much on horrific or spine-chilling events, as on the female protagonist's responses to them. Radcliffe developed that mode of 'free indirect speech' – the technique by which the private thoughts of the character are represented – which was to be so essential to Austen's own form of the novel. Tuite goes on to suggest that Austen's relation to Radcliffe is not in any simple sense parodic, if this means standing outside the narrative, but from within an immersed, saturated relationship. Her parody is thus distinct from those of male writers such as Eaton Stannard Barratt, whose burlesque *The Heroine, or Adventures of a Fair Romance Reader* (1813), is often cited. Austen's relationship with this precursor is both amused and a kind of bonding. In *The Business of Common Life* (1995), David Kaufman notes another kind of continuity and possible indeptedness: 'that certain women authors of the gothic,' like Radcliffe, 'take up the pen to naturalise the genre's extravagance and subdue it,' and that this 'demystificatory impulse is further explored in *Northanger Abbey*'.

She felt the awkwardness of having no party to join.

The novel certainly contrasts the world of the Gothic with everyday life, but one recurrent critical issue has raised the question of whether, whilst discrediting the Gothic's invitation to hectic imaginings, it nevertheless 'prohibits us from trusting too unsuspiciously in "common life"' as Claudia L. Johnson argues in *Jane Austen: Women, Politics and the Novel* (1988). Johnson's reading is a distinctively feminist one. In particular, she focuses on the treatment of women in *Northanger Abbey* – a domination by men from which the hero, Henry Tilney, in her view is by no means exempt. She argues he is not 'essentially' different from John Thorpe or General Tilney, only exercising his power over Catherine and his sister more subtly. (His qualities of kindness and intelligence are presumably not essential differences.) This is a notably unamused reading in which Catherine's 'failure to appreciate Henry's humor is another instance of the wisdom she unwittingly articulates throughout the novel.' Marilyn Butler counters such arguments as these by suggesting that Henry is clearly distinguished from the 'men's men', the representatives of patriarchy, in the novel. 'Henry is a mysterious, almost allegorical figure, who stands for androgynous ideas, youthful play, the comic spirit, romance.' He doubles for Jane Austen, 'by representing, in his inventiveness and playfulness, the voice and creative role of the author.'

Critics have argued in other ways that this book, far from being a repudiation of the Gothic novel, is a kind of sequel. It was a brief remark of Lionel Trilling's in his famous essay on *Mansfield Park* (1957) that laid the foundations for many modern interpretations of *Northanger Abbey*. 'We are quick, too quick, to understand that [the novel] invites us into a snug conspiracy to disabuse the little heroine of the errors of her corrupted fancy – Catherine Morland, having become addicted to novels of terror, has accepted their inadmissible premise, she believes that life is violent and unpredictable.' But, argued Trilling, 'that is exactly what life is shown to be by the events of the story: it is we who must be disabused of our belief that life is sane and orderly.' Tony Tanner's essay in *Jane Austen* (1986) went a step further: not only does the novel ask the reader to revise their convictions, it demonstrates that real life may be actually worse than the horrors imagined by the writers of Gothic fiction. Writing of General Tilney he declares, 'It is this irrational ruthless unfeeling anger in the Abbey which Catherine has to encounter – arguably more sinister and frightening than anything in the Gothic novels which so engaged her imagination. For this is the real thing: the utter egotism, hardness and insensitivity of the human heart, and the frightening power of the enraged figure of parental authority.' Tilney's action in sending

Always arm-in-arm when they walked.

Catherine away from his house is, in his view, an 'atrocity'. More temperately, Rachel Brownstein in *Becoming a Heroine* (revised edition, 1994) writes, 'A selfish, materialistic, rude, inconsiderate man, General Tilney is prosaically rather than exotically evil.' Butler emphasises that the General is the incarnation of a progressive or Whig view of society, disregarding social responsibility in favour of consumerism, display and the pursuit of control.

In such accounts as Tanner's, Henry Tilney's speech rebuking Catherine for her Gothic-inspired fantasies about his father must be intended ironically by the author. And, in fact, many modern critics find it impossible to take his defence of contemporary English manners and culture seriously. 'Dear Miss Morland, consider the dreadful nature of the suspicions you have entertained. What have you been judging from? Remember the country and the age in which we live. Remember we are English, that we are Christians … Does our education prepare us for such atrocities? Do our laws connive at them? Could they be perpetrated without being known, in a country like this … where every man is surrounded by a neighbourhood of voluntary spies … ?' If such readers as Tanner are right, Henry is deluded, himself fantasising, seeking to 'evoke an England which is a kind of phantasm of peaceful life from which the possibility of horror and violence has been eradicated.' But this is historically quite false, he argues, citing Warren Roberts in *Jane Austen and the French Revolution* (1979) who states that 'Austen was referring to actual spies who were serving or trying to serve Pitt and the government, and whose purpose was to crush the various agents of radicalism and subversion'.

The employment of spies in the 1790s is a well-established fact, but this is not what Jane Austen is saying. Unlike Tanner and Roberts she uses language exactly, and she writes not of 'actual' but of 'voluntary' spies. She is referring to neighbourhood gossip of the kind Mr Bennet comments on: 'For what do we live but to make sport of our neighbours and to be laughed at in our turn?' The phrase has many parallels in Samuel Johnson who, in *Idler* (*1758–1760*) 78 for example, declares that at a spa 'each visitor is known to be a spy upon the rest'. 'What has it been but a system of hypocrisy and deceit, espionage and treachery?' cries Emma Woodhouse. 'Espionage' is certainly a French word, but the 'system' she is indignantly referring to merely is Frank Churchill's plan to pull the wool over everyone's eyes. And the crucial point of Tilney's speech is Dr Johnson's, the moralist who was at the height of his influence during the decade that Austen was writing this novel. Catherine's ideas are a 'dangerous prevalence of imagination', in the famous phrase from *Rasselas* (1752). 'Dear Miss Morland, what ideas have you been admitting?' Tilney cries. Abashed by his rebuke, Catherine thinks that her folly 'seemed even criminal'. The fact that the novel goes on to show that General Henry Tilney is a brutal man does not wipe out the general truth of Tilney's statements, nor, more importantly, the novelist's moral urgency at this point.

These accounts of *Northanger Abbey* in effect subvert the text's burlesque of Gothic horrors by reintroducing them in another form and by making Henry Tilney, teasing, ironic and by the end of the novel in love with Catherine's innocence, merely a cipher for patriarchal domination. By insisting on the blackness of General Tilney they come close to turning a fresh and comic novel into a melodrama. Their interpretations are taken a step further in the only film released to date of *Northanger Abbey*, a BBC movie (1987) directed by Giles Foster, with script by Maggie Wadey. More ambitious and more expensively produced than previous BBC adaptations, this attempts a wholesale rethinking or reworking of the novel in visual terms. It inaugurates a new freedom of adaptation, which licences the script and director to depart radically from the novel that is their source.

The film opens with a crude illustration of a man carrying the helpless body of a girl, a picture which becomes a vivid shot of a monstrous older male with a female victim in his arms. Accompanied by wailing female voices on the soundtrack, this opening leaves no doubt that this is a scene of abduction and possible rape. We cut to a young Catherine's eyes lifted from her book, and glistening with sexual arousal. Soon, Catherine, *en route* to Bath, imagines a similar scene of abduction, this time with two young men tugging at each of her arms. The eerie high-pitched music continues throughout the opening sequence, in which many scenes are set in darkness. 'It makes very good sense for a modern cinematic adaptation of a novel about a young girl who is looking for love and adventure to show her indulging in erotic fantasies,' writes Sue Parrill in *Jane Austen on Film and Television* (2002). Perhaps, but one of Jane Austen's points about Catherine is that she is completely (comically and engagingly) innocent; she is shocked when she happens to overhear a flirtatious conversation between Isabella and Captain Tilney. And these visual representations of Catherine's imaginative life are in fact drawn from the erotic fantasies of the male, not the female, Gothic. Their source is in the pictures of Henry Fuseli, Lewis's *The Monk* (the only Gothic novel John Thorpe has any time for!) or the much later *Dracula* (1897) of Bram Stoker.

Mr John Thorpe

The film's world is a modernist Gothic fantasy, in which every opportunity is taken to 'make it strange'. General Tilney, an overbearingly sinister figure, carries a hawk on his shoulder, an emblem of his vicious nature. He is accompanied by a female character, the Marchioness (who has no referent in the novel) plastered with white make-up and dressed entirely in black. Perhaps the intention is to remind the viewer that the period of the novel is contemporary with the French Revolution, and thus to add another element of danger or horror to the mix. The Marchioness is accompanied by a little negro page-boy wearing a powdered white wig – another addition presumably authorised by historical authenticity, but as presented in the film only invoking the unmotivated and strange. In one scene he leads Catherine outside and performs cartwheels for her. The effect of these additions is to make the whole *mise-en-scéne* even more bizarre, and their presence owes more to the then-fashionable cinematic Gothic fantasy of Federico Fellini and Ken Russell than to any persuasive historicising intention. From exaggerated costuming, to overacting, to the insistent sound-track, the effect, intentional or not, is unsettling. Still more odd and unsettling is the fact that the actors playing Henry Tilney and John Thorpe, both red-haired, look strangely alike. Is this an accident, or is the film making Claudia Johnson's point that Tilney is just another version of the patriarchal male? By making Northanger Abbey not a modern house but a real medieval castle, Catherine's Gothic imaginings are validated, not satirised.

In other words, the film performs a re-Gothicising of Austen's anti-Gothic, and anti-romantic, text. Later adaptations have used the freedom to alter the original that this version of *Northanger Abbey* initiated, as when Thompson's *Sense and Sensibility* introduces the character of Margaret Dashwood or (more controversially) Tom Wright's Bennets become a happy rather than a dysfunctional family. Patricia Rozema's *Mansfield Park*

(1999) has clear affinities with this film in its preference for the exotic, the bizarre and the sexually explicit. But Rozema's film, like this one, is not a success, choosing to ignore the source novel's own specific qualities in pursuit of its own agenda. Though encouraged in its revision by tendencies in contemporary criticism, this version of *Northanger Abbey* is not a renovation of Austen's novel but a repudiation of it.

Regency Life
Maggie Lane

Fashion

During the four decades of Jane Austen's life, fashion underwent considerable and continual change. At the time of her birth in 1775, for the richest in society at least, gowns were heavy and full, made of rich brocades, silks and satins, hooped and looped over underskirts and stomachers, with three-quarter-length sleeves finished with lace ruffles. Men wore equally richly coloured or embroidered suits of coat, waistcoat and knee breeches, with buckled shoes and stockings, and a powdered wig. More ordinary country people, like Jane Austen's own parents, would have worn a toned-down version of all this. Clothes were very much a reflection of one's social status. Only the most immobile people could cope with the weight of such clothes, and only the wealthiest could afford the expensive materials of which they were made.

But as Jane was growing up in the 1780s and 1790s, clothes were becoming less heavy and elaborate. Because cleanliness was increasingly valued, lightweight, washable fabrics such as cambric and muslin were now the fashion and colours were paler, valued precisely because they showed up any *lack* of cleanliness. Having servants and money enough to keep clean was the new mark of gentility.

In women's dress the waist was gradually rising, emphasised by a broad sash in a contrasting shade, above which a crossover style of bodice and ruched neckerchief gave the 'pouter pigeon' look so characteristic of this age. Men too were moving towards plain-coloured coats and buff pantaloons tucked into their boots or shoes. Women's hair now tumbled onto the shoulders in curls, in the evening often ornamented by a headband and tall feathers, such as Catherine Morland observes at her first Bath ball, while out of doors a broad-brimmed hat, tied under the chin with ribbon, completed the picture. This was the look to which Jane Austen herself would have aspired as a fashion-conscious young lady making her entrance into local society, and which she must have had in mind for the heroines of the three novels composed in the 1790s: *Sense and Sensibility, Pride and Prejudice* and *Northanger Abbey*. The 1995 film of *Sense and Sensibility*, starring Emma Thompson and Kate Winslet, gives the best filmic impression of this late eighteenth-century look.

The first decade of the nineteenth century saw a dramatic development as what is known as the Empire Style crossed the Channel from Napoleon's

The boldness of his riding

France. The waist now rose to be right under the bust, with a tiny bodice and short sleeves, the rest of the dress taking a narrow, columnar shape, often trailing on the floor, in imitation of the antique drapery. Diaphanous, clinging fabrics such as gauze and muslin, usually in white, were worn with minimal underwear to avoid spoiling the line. This could not have been an easy style to wear for any but the youngest and slenderest of women, and hardly suited the British climate. As it happens, none of Jane Austen's novels was conceived in this rather extreme decade for fashion, though *Northanger Abbey* was slightly revised about 1802–03 while Jane Austen was living in Bath and therefore on the spot to observe the latest trends.

The question of whether a woman should wear white seems to have been quite contentious. Jane Austen herself evidently admired it, as several remarks in her letters attest, and in *Northanger Abbey* Eleanor Tilney, the model of propriety and elegance, always wears white. However, Jane Austen's aunt, Mrs Leigh Perrot, thought that white was an absurd pretension in Bath – with its dirty pavements – but she was of the older generation less adaptable to change. As late as 1813, when she was writing *Mansfield Park*, Jane Austen has her hero say, 'A woman can never be too fine [that is, too showy] while she is all in white,' and in the same novel another older woman, Mrs Norris, is pleased with a housekeeper who has turned away two housemaids for wearing white gowns – evidently aping their betters!

Difficult-to-wear styles could not hold out long against a growing desire for practicality and variety. Filmy white dress continued to be fashionable in the evenings, but the second decade of the century saw medium-weight cottons and poplins in colours and prints for daytime wear, with widening skirts, often trimmed or flounced at the hem. Balanced by more ornamentation at bodice, sleeve and hem, here was much more scope for self-expression and ingenuity. This is the true Regency period to which the final three novels belong, and which is usually chosen by film and television adaptations as illustrative of Jane Austen's world.

Women's hair in these decades was worn in Grecian style, either short and curled (if necessary, twisted into papers while one slept) or swept up, with escaping tendrils, and held in place with encircling bands. Jane Austen talks about her own long hair being plaited up out of sight, and her short (front) hair curling naturally, as can be seen in the only authentic portrait we have of her, by Cassandra in about 1810. In this she wears a muslin cap, as most older women did indoors – what their nieces later called 'the garb of middle age', which the sisters adopted unnecessarily early. It saved a lot of trouble with hairdressing and always looked fresh and clean, which seems to have been Jane's principal concern, but it also signified that one no longer expected a marriage proposal! Out of doors women of all ages wore bonnets, of straw in summer or fabric in winter, with funnel sides and a variety of trimmings. Shopping in Bath in 1799, Jane Austen debated between fruit or flowers as a trimming, and Isabella Thorpe talks about green or coquelicot (poppy red) ribbon on hats.

Kensington Gardens dress, Le Beau Monde,
June 1808.

For additional warmth, women might wear a shawl indoors, or a cloak, spencer or pelisse out of doors. The spencer was a short coat cut on the lines of the bodice, finishing under the bust, in some heavier material than the gown, while the pelisse was similarly shaped but with a long skirt like the gown itself. Both garments might be fastened with tiny buttons or decorative frogging, and had long sleeves, sometimes extending to the knuckles. In 1811 Jane Austen and her sister had pelisses made by a London dressmaker at a total cost of seventeen shillings each, including buttons that she thought very expensive and eight shillings for the making up.

'I wish such things were to be bought ready made,' she had written, in 1798, about giving instructions for a new gown. Garments were either made at home by ladies or their servants, or made by a professional dressmaker to the lady's specification. Either way, the lady had virtually to design the various elements of the gown herself, and all she had to go on were what other people wore, or fashion plates if she was lucky enough to see any publications containing them. This is why Catherine Morland and Mrs Allen, up from the country, spend the first few days of their Bath holiday learning what is chiefly worn, before venturing into public. Isabella Thorpe, seeking admiration for her ball gown, boasts that 'the sleeves were entirely my own thought'. Even the wealthy Eleanor Tilney makes some of her own elegant white gowns at home, perhaps with the help of her maid, since her brother talks of her beginning with a length of muslin and 'cutting it into pieces'.

When Jane Austen writes in her letters of buying a gown, she means a length of fabric sufficient to make a gown – seven yards for her sister and her mother, seven and a half for herself since she is taller. Although she was a fine needlewoman – examples of her work are on show at the Jane Austen House Museum in Chawton, Hampshire – she and her sister seem to have had all their gowns and outer garments made for them. But they spent much time and ingenuity trimming and altering over the years, to extend the lives of their clothes, as the dress allowance on which they had to look acceptable in society was always small. Only decorative needlework was supposed to be on show when visitors might call; Mrs Austen embarrassed her daughters by doing plain mending in front of callers. She was a particularly thrifty woman (perhaps she had to be), cutting down the scarlet wool riding habit in which she had 'gone away' after her marriage in 1764, and worn out of doors ever since, to make her *fifth* son's first suit of clothes.

Men's clothes continued to look more and more sober and understated – the ideal was to look like an English country gentleman of private means with no need for excessive display. Powdering and wigs were now confined to the older generation of men, the younger ones having their hair cut short. Jane's youngest brother, Charles, had 'a crop' as early as 1799, but the considerably older James and Edward, set in the ways of their youth, were still purchasing wigs in 1814.

For outdoor wear men had the comfort of a great coat, a heavy garment with one or more capes – falling collars – to add bulk and warmth. This male garment is mentioned twice in *Northanger Abbey*. In Catherine's eyes the 'innumerable capes' of Henry Tilney's greatcoat, worn on the journey from Bath to Northanger, look 'so becomingly important'. The innocent sexual attraction she feels for him is thus subtly conveyed.

Although in her letters Jane Austen demonstrates a lively interest in clothes, in her fiction preoccupation with dress is the sure sign of a shallow-minded or vain woman. *Northanger Abbey* contains two such characters, staid Mrs Allen who is old enough to know better, but whose intellectual resources are so few that her sole topic of interest is clothes, and flighty Isabella Thorpe, who dresses to attract male attention. As a consequence, *Northanger Abbey* has rather more about fashion in its pages than any of Jane Austen's other novels, highly suitable for a story set in such a fashionable centre as Bath.

The novel also contains the only heroine to lie awake for ten minutes at night wondering what to wear to meet the hero next day, a rather endearing episode which enables Jane Austen to poke mild fun at her very human and youthful heroine, with a tongue-in-cheek diatribe against the snares of dress such as the conduct books of the period were full of, and a lesson on the indifference of men to the minutiae of female fashion.

As poor Mrs Allen laments, she has never been able to get her husband to know one of her gowns from another.

Travel

When appealed to by an alarmed Catherine Morland for her views on the propriety of driving out with a young man, Mrs Allen, who is supposed to be guarding her young protégé's reputation, has no advice to offer but that 'Open carriages are nasty things. A clean gown is not five minutes' wear in them. You are splashed getting in and getting out; and the wind takes your hair and your bonnet in every direction.'

The open carriage in question is the gig of John Thorpe. Both gigs and curricles were lightweight, and hence speedy vehicles, much favoured by the single young men in Jane Austen's novels. With just two wheels, there was a seat for the owner-driver and one passenger side by side. Thorpe's model is a gig, but is what he calls 'curricle-hung', with 'seat, trunk, sword-case, splashing-board, lamps and silver moulding', and it cost him fifty guineas (£52.50). Henry Tilney's vehicle is the slightly superior curricle, drawn by two horses and therefore faster, though Henry, unlike Thorpe, makes no boast on that score. These owner-driven vehicles gave great scope for showing off, or otherwise, to a lady passenger, which Jane Austen uses to great effect in *Northanger Abbey*, where it becomes one means of Catherine's learning to discriminate between her suitors.

General Tilney travels by chaise, drawn by four horses. The chaise, the coach and the chariot were all enclosed, four-wheeled vehicles driven by a servant coachman. The coach was the largest vehicle, with two seats facing one another, holding a maximum of six, ideal for larger families. The chaise

"Pray, pray stop, Mr Thorpe"

Post-chaises from Payne's Microcosm, *1806.*

and chariot seated two passengers facing the horses, with an occasional let-down seat for a third. When the Tilneys and Catherine make the stately journey from Bath to Northanger, the middle seat is not drawn out, though Eleanor, Catherine and the former's maid are all to travel in it. This is to make room for all the parcels the maid has loaded in. Most of the considerable luggage for the two ladies and two gentlemen would have been packed in trunks strapped on the back of the carriage. Even so, Catherine has to share her seat with a linen package containing her things for the first evening, before the trunks are unpacked.

Whereas the driver of a chaise was mounted on one of the horses, the chariot had the addition of a coach-box for his use. Chariots had an especially staid image, associated with elderly ladies such as the dowager Mrs Rushworth in *Mansfield Park.*

Closed carriages had sufficed when travel was just a matter of getting, with as much comfort as possible, from a to b. But in the Regency period, with the increasing fashion for 'exploring' and viewing the countryside, a new class of vehicles was designed to combine the advantages of both open and closed carriages. The landau was like a coach in its seating arrangements, with the additional refinement that the roof opened from the middle for use in fine weather. The landaulet resembled the chaise with a one-piece hood that opened from the front and was folded down to the back. The barouche and barouche-landau, like the chariot, had a box in front, which could hold the driver and one other. Henry Crawford in *Mansfield Park* famously drives a barouche, and there is great competition between the Bertram sisters as to who shall accompany him on the box, the 'seat of seats'. In *Emma*, Mrs Elton boasts about her brother-in-law's barouche-landau, and at the end of *Persuasion*, Captain Wentworth buys his new wife 'a very pretty landaulette'. Choice of these vehicles is a mark of modernity and fashion in these last three novels of Jane Austen, where they are identified with the younger generation.

All carriages were being improved during the span of Jane Austen's life – improved in terms of comfort, insulation, ventilation and most importantly, springing. Mr Elton remarks on the wonders of modern carriages in *Emma*. Along with improvements in the roads themselves, this made for a golden age of coach travel. The turnpike system financed the improvements in roads by the charge on travellers of tolls. Some great engineers applied their brains to road improvement. John Metcalf developed firm foundations with good systems of drainage and John McAdam revolutionised the road surface itself with crushed stone and tar, while Thomas Telford perfected the art of bridge-building.

The city of Bath itself would hardly have flourished as it did without good roads to convey not only its myriad of visitors, but the array of consumer goods which made its shops such a draw. As Mrs Allen says, 'Here one can step out of doors and get a thing in five minutes.'

Seven miles an hour seems to have been the norm at the time Jane Austen was writing her novels. The Thorpes and Morlands have to give up on their first attempt to get from Bath to Clifton and back – a total of some 26 miles – on a February day. In *Persuasion*, the seventeen miles each way from Uppercross to Lyme Regis, particularly hilly ground, has to be spread over two days in the dark month of November. Jane told her niece Anna, who was writing a novel, that her characters should be *two* days getting from Bath to Dawlish in Devon: they are a hundred miles apart.

Carriages were lit by flaring lamps, but long journeys at night were avoided wherever possible; the short journeys of social life, to local balls and dinners, were arranged for moonlit nights for preference. Even in daylight, accidents could happen, although Jane Austen makes fun of the possibility in the opening pages of *Northanger Abbey*, when she talks about no 'lucky overturn' to introduce the travelling Catherine to a hero. But her own cousin, Jane Williams, as a young married woman, was killed outright when the private vehicle she was travelling in overturned.

The most prestigious way to travel was in the family's own carriage, but for journeys above twenty miles, only the first stage could be accomplished with the family's own horses, after which fresh ones had to be hired at posting inns along the route. The alternative was to give the horses a two-hour rest and feed – 'baiting the horses' – as General Tilney does at the Petty France Inn between Bath and Northanger.

It was calculated by commentators at the time that in order to be able to afford to run a carriage, the family income had to be at least £800 per annum – £1,000 was more comfortable. Mr Austen set up a carriage for his family for a while in the 1790s, but gave it up because finances were too tight. Costs involved included stabling, the wages of a groom-cum-coachman, blacksmith services and hay for the horse (which took between 4 and 8 acres of land). In *Emma*, the rising apothecary Mr Perry is contemplating the great step of setting up his carriage.

If the family did not possess its own carriage, it was possible to hire what was known as a hack chaise. Because of the difficulty of getting it back a long distance to its owner, usually the hired vehicle, as well as the horses, would be changed at each posting inn, involving frequent removals of luggage, with attendant dangers of one's possessions being transferred to the wrong vehicle, as Jane Austen herself once experienced when her portable writing desk was found to be missing. The hack chaise might be driven by the family manservant, if they had one, or by a series of drivers hired along with the vehicle. This is the method by which Catherine Morland, ejected peremptorily from Northanger Abbey and travelling quite alone, is obliged to get home, a journey of eleven hours requiring her to keep her wits about her.

At least she is spared the indignity of the public stagecoach, the lowliest form of travel in Jane Austen's era. Acceptable for men travelling alone, it was rarely resorted to by ladies, though Jane Austen herself did travel that way at least once, from Chawton to London. To pack in as many paying passengers as possible, seats were provided at a lower fare on top, completely exposed to the weather (but avoiding the stuffiness and crowding within!).

A Hackney coach.

Hackney Coach.

When the Steele sisters in *Sense and Sensibility* travel from Devon to London they let it be known that it was 'not in the stage'. In *Mansfield Park* the stagecoach is thought good enough for getting the child Fanny Price from Portsmouth to Northampton, under the care of a tradeswoman or two.

Later in the same novel, both William Price and Edmund Bertram, separately, take a lift on the mail coach. In every way, whether by public transport or by owning their own vehicle, men have the advantage of mobility and independence. Jane Austen herself was often obliged to wait on the convenience of a brother to escort her when she needed to get about.

Had she equalled her sister and most of her brothers in longevity, she would have lived into the age of steam. Only 20 or so years after her death, the golden age of coach travel was over.

Geographical Settings
Caroline Sanderson

'Oh, who can ever be tired of Bath?' Catherine Morland famously remarks in *Northanger Abbey*. A 'cheerful, open' Wiltshire girl of seventeen, she arrives to stay in that famous Georgian town in the company of good-hearted local squire Mr Allen and his wife. Mr Allen has been 'ordered to Bath for the benefit of a gouty constitution,' and Mrs Allen who is fond of Catherine, thinks to broaden her horizons by asking her to accompany them, 'aware that if adventures will not befall a young lady in her own village, she must seek them abroad.'

Until she thus embarks on 'all the difficulties and dangers of a six weeks' residence in Bath', Catherine's entire life has been spent in the village of Fullerton – some eight or nine miles from Salisbury – where she lives with her clergyman father, her mother and nine brothers and sisters and 'likes nothing so well in the world as rolling down the green slope at the back of the house'. Though her journey to Bath, which lies in the next county, is a short one, its sophisticated pleasures and social whirl could not be further from the simple delights of her chaotic but happy rural childhood.

On arrival in Bath, the ingénue Catherine is enchanted with what she sees. 'Catherine was all eager delight; – her eyes were here, there, every where, as they approached its fine and striking environs, and afterwards drove through those streets which conducted them to the hotel. She was come to be happy, and she felt happy already.'

The Allens' comfortable lodgings are in Pulteney Street, a long, broad, elegant avenue in what was then a new and highly fashionable district of eighteenth-century Bath. Built on Sir William Pulteney's former Bathwick estate, this part of Bath lies on the far side of the city's famous, and nowadays much photographed, Pulteney Bridge which spans the River Avon. Designed by Robert Adam, a friend of Sir William's, it was

A famous good thing this marrying scheme!

completed in 1774. A scheme by Thomas Baldwin, incorporating wide new avenues and crescents, and elegant side streets, was eventually adopted for the new district on the eastern side of the Avon. Work began in 1788, but before long the turmoil and financial panic that followed the revolutionary events of 1789 in France led to the collapse of the bank that had provided the funds for the development. Baldwin went bankrupt and building work ground to a halt, leaving many streets unfinished.

Incomplete though it may be, this is still one of the most beautiful and impressive parts of Georgian Bath. Great Pulteney Street, which leads from Pulteney Bridge to Sydney Gardens at its eastern end, is 1,000 feet long and more than 100 feet wide, a magnificent and stately thoroughfare unrivalled in grandeur anywhere else in the city. Some of Bath's most distinguished visitors and residents have resided here, including Admiral Earl Howe, Prince Louis-Napoleon (later Emperor Napoleon III), William Wilberforce and Hannah More, another notable opponent of the slave trade; their former presence nowadays recorded by a succession of blue plaques. Despite the parked cars that now permanently line both sides of the road, the period elegance of Pulteney Street survives, and it is easy to imagine Mr and Mrs Allen and their young friend emerging from between the Corinthian columns of a house here.

As soon as they are settled into their lodgings, Mrs Allen, who is 'admirably fitted to introduce a young lady into public, being as fond of going everywhere and seeing every thing herself as any young lady could be', takes charge of Catherine's first appearance in Bath society. Preparations take several days, since Catherine's 'entrée into life could not take place till after three or four days had been spent in learning what was mostly worn', and until she is 'provided with a dress of the newest fashion'. On the day of the auspicious event itself her hair is 'cut and dressed by the best hand, her clothes put on with care, and Mrs Allen and her maid declared she looked quite as she should do'. Only then does Mrs Allen usher Catherine into her first Bath assembly at the Upper Rooms.

Still sitting with Captain Tilney.

According to a definition of 1751, an assembly was 'a stated and general meeting of the polite persons of both sexes, for the sake of conversation, gallantry, news and play'. Opened in 1771, the Assembly Rooms as they are now called were known in Jane Austen's time as the New Rooms or the Upper Rooms. This was to distinguish them from the Lower Rooms, another venue for assemblies, which once stood between Bath Abbey and the river. Built much earlier, in around 1708, it is at the Lower Rooms that

New Pump Room, c. 1790, by John Nixon.

Catherine Morland is first introduced to Henry Tilney, 'a clergyman ... of a very respectable family in Gloucestershire,' by Mr King, the Master of Ceremonies, a man who actually existed in real life.

By the late eighteenth century, Bath had expanded from its former medieval heart up onto the lower slopes of the Mendip Hills to the north. The newest and thus most desirable addresses, such as Camden Place, The Crescent and The Circle were established in the upper part of town. Because these lofty locations were a very long way home by sedan chair from the Lower Rooms, this venue lost much of its former glamour when the magnificent, and very much closer new Upper Rooms were opened in 1771. Designed by John Wood the Younger, the Upper Rooms were purpose-built for assemblies at a cost of £14,000, raised by shareholders. The spectacular Ballroom with its five enormous crystal chandeliers has a richly stuccoed ceiling and measures almost 107 feet long by 44 feet wide. This huge room, the venue for Catherine's first ball, could accommodate up to 1,000 guests at the twice weekly balls and frequent concerts which took place in Jane Austen's time.

When the Allens arrive at the Upper Rooms, the ballroom is very crowded, and Catherine and Mrs Allen have to squeeze in as best they can, while Mr Allen repairs directly to the card-room, leaving them to 'enjoy a mob by themselves'. The ladies push their way through the crowd to the top of the room, hoping to find seats from which they can watch the dancing, but the throng is still such that they see 'nothing of the dancers but the high feathers of some of the ladies' (head dresses with tall feathers were then all the rage). Mrs Allen fails to meet up with a single acquaintance during the course of the evening, so Catherine is unable to dance, but she cheers up when she hears two gentlemen pronounce her to be a 'pretty girl'.

Before long, Catherine is fully immersed in every aspect of a Bath social life: 'Every morning now brought its regular duties; – shops were to be visited; some new part of the town to be looked at and the Pump-room to be attended, where they paraded up and down for an hour, looking at every body and speaking to no one.' The day after she has been introduced to Mr Tilney at the Lower Rooms, Catherine and Mrs Allen return to the Pump-room, where Catherine looks in vain for her new gentleman acquaintance.

Lying at the very centre of what was Roman Bath, and adjacent to the most important of the city's three thermal springs, the first Pump-room was built in 1706, and later remodelled and enlarged, first by Thomas Baldwin and then, after he went bankrupt, by John Palmer. Like the Upper and Lower Rooms, the Pump-room was a place to be and to be seen. Patrons were able to take a glass of Bath water and peruse the arrivals book, where the names and places of abode of recent arrivals in Bath were inscribed. It is here that Catherine is able to check at which house in Milsom Street the Tilneys have their lodgings.

Though Catherine fails to meet Mr Tilney again, it is at the Pump-room that she is introduced to Isabella Thorpe. Mrs Thorpe, Isabella's mother, proves to be an old schoolfriend of Mrs Allen, and her eldest son, John, an Oxford friend of Catherine's brother, James. Though Miss Thorpe's shortcomings as a bosom pal are soon made deliciously apparent to the reader, Catherine, delighted to have made a friend, pronounces the Pump-room to be 'so favourable for the … completion of female intimacy, so admirably adapted for secret discourses and unlimited confidence'.

At their next meeting in the Pump-room, Isabella Thorpe admonishes Catherine for being merely on time for their rendezvous: 'My dearest creature, what can have made you so late? I have been waiting for you at least this age.' After gossiping over hats (Isabella has seen the 'prettiest one' in a Milsom Street shop window, 'very like yours, only with coquelicot ribbons instead of green'), and the horrors of the latest Gothic novels, Isabella spots two 'odious men who have been staring at me this half hour' and drags Catherine off in hot pursuit when the gentlemen leave the Pump-room.

Having lost sight of Isabella's quarry, the two friends set off towards Milsom Street to shop for hats instead, walking across the Pump Yard to the archway opposite Union-passage, where they attempt to cross Cheap Street. Though a relatively quiet shopping street today, at that time Cheap Street was much busier; 'a street of so impertinent a nature, so unfortunately connected with the great London and Oxford Roads', as Jane Austen puts it. Catherine and Isabella are prevented from crossing by the fast approach of a gig, which on closer inspection proves to contain their respective brothers, James Morland and the boorish 'rattle' John Thorpe, who have just arrived in Bath from Oxford via Tetbury in Gloucestershire. Thorpe boasts at length about the speed and prowess of his poor horses ('nothing ruins horses so much as rest'), in exactly the same way as certain men are wont to drone on about their cars today. 'It is now half after one; we drove out of the inn-yard at Tetbury as the town-clock struck eleven; and I defy any man in England to make my horse go less than ten miles an hour in harness.'

After an unsatisfactory evening at the Upper Rooms during which Catherine meets Mr Tilney again, but fails to dance with him owing to the rather unwelcome attentions of John Thorpe, the Morlands and the Thorpes take a drive up Claverton Down, a steeply wooded area in the hills to the south-east of Bath. Catherine accompanies John Thorpe in his much-lauded gig and has to listen to seemingly endless stories of horses, hunting and shooting, at the end of which 'it was clear to her, that the drive had by no means been very pleasant and that John Thorpe himself was quite disagreeable'. Her unsatisfactory day is compounded on her return when she learns that during the course of 'a turn in the Crescent', Mrs Allen has had a very pleasant walk and talk with Mr Tilney, and his sister, Miss Tilney, who is also now staying in Bath.

The Royal Crescent, one of Bath's most famous landmarks, was begun in 1775, the year of Jane Austen's birth, and known on completion simply as The Crescent. During the Bath season this was the place to parade on a Sunday morning after church, particularly in fine weather. In *Northanger Abbey* we are told that 'a fine Sunday in Bath empties every house of its inhab-

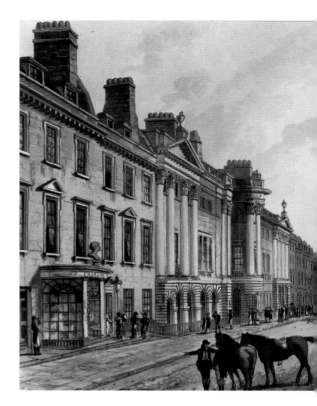

Milsom Street, Bath detail) by John Claude Nattes, 1806

"*Can you stand such a ceremony as this!*"

itants, and all the world appears on such an occasion to walk about and tell their acquaintance what a charming day it is'. On another occasion, having found 'not a genteel face to be seen' in the crowded Pump-room, the Thorpes and the Allens 'hasten away to the Crescent to breath the fresh air of better company'. Jane Austen came here too, though she seemed less fortified by the experience. In a letter of 8 April 1805 she wrote: 'We did not walk long in the Crescent yesterday, it was hot and not crouded enough.'

Catherine is finally introduced to Mr Tilney's sister, Eleanor the following day at the Pump-room, and then, at a cotillion ball at the Upper Rooms, she dances again with Henry. The two have a light-hearted and amusing conversation about matrimony, and then about Bath and the merits of town and country life. Catherine finds Bath very agreeable: 'I do not think I should be tired, if I were to stay here six months.' Mr Tilney is less enthusiastic: 'For six weeks I allow Bath is pleasant enough; but beyond *that* it is the most tiresome place in the world.'

Catherine is delighted when a country walk with Mr and Miss Tilney is arranged for the following day, but the next morning brings wet weather, and whilst she is dithering about whether the outing is likely to go ahead, her brother and the Thorpes arrive, ready to spirit her off on a trip to Blaize Castle in Bristol, via Clifton and Kingsweston. Catherine resists at first, pleading her prior engagement. But her head is full of thrillingly ghoulish notions taken from the Gothic novels she loves, that she is eventually unable to resist the prospect of seeing a castle with 'towers and long galleries', pronounced the 'oldest in the kingdom' by John Thorpe. This is Jane Austen having a bit of fun at her heroine's expense, for Blaize Castle is in fact a folly built in 1766 by Thomas Farr, a Bristol merchant who made a fortune in sugar and became mayor of the city.

Catherine's visit to Blaize Castle is not to be however. The party only make it as far as Keynsham, mid-way between Bath and Bristol, before turning back due to time being too short for their ambitious day's excursion. Everyone is out of humour and Catherine is particularly upset at John Thorpe's having deceived her into thinking that the Tilneys themselves had gone off on an outing 'up the Lansdown Road', when in fact they had called on Catherine shortly after she went out.

Happily, a few days later Catherine does take the much-anticipated walk with the Tilneys. They ascend Beechen Cliff, a steep hill on the southern side of Bath, which affords wonderful views right across the city. Here on this 'noble hill, whose beautiful verdure and hanging coppice render it so striking an object from almost every opening in Bath', a lengthy discussion ensues about whether the view qualifies as 'picturesque' (it does not). Catherine, ashamed of her ignorance of such matters, is all ears: 'Catherine was so hopeful a scholar that when they gained the top of Beechen Cliff, she voluntarily rejected the whole city of Bath, as unworthy to make part of a landscape.' Again, Jane Austen is poking fun, this time at the rigid contemporary notions of the picturesque. 'It seemed that a fine view were no longer to be taken from the top of an (sic) high hill, and that a clear blue sky was no longer proof of a fine day.' Picturesque or not, Beechen Cliff still affords twenty-first-century walkers one of the best vantage points over the city of Bath.

When she returns from her walk, Catherine learns that Isabella Thorpe, her sister Maria and brother John have been on an excursion to the spa town of Clifton in Bristol, where they ate soup at the York Hotel, visited the Pump-room, tasted the waters and ate ice-cream at a pastry-cook's before returning to Bath after a hurried dinner. Clifton, now an upmarket residential suburb of Bristol, complete with elegant Regency terraces and villas, was a mini version of Bath in the eighteenth century. Jane Austen herself visited Clifton, shortly after leaving Bath for good in 1806. The spa there was fed by the same underground source as the hot springs of Bath, but its popularity waned when fears were raised that the hot wells might have been contaminated by Bristol's sewage.

"It was my mother's favourite walk."

The day after the trip to Clifton, James Morland and Isabella announce their engagement. James hastens back home to Fullerton to inform his family and seek his father's consent, and John Thorpe sets off for London. Not long afterwards, Catherine receives an invitation from the Tilneys to stay with them at their home, Northanger Abbey in Gloucestershire. Catherine is in raptures at the prospect: 'Her passion for ancient edifices was next in degree to her passion for Henry Tilney – and castles and abbeys made usually the charm of those reveries which his image did not fill.'

And so to the place which gives this delightful early Jane Austen novel its title. Northanger Abbey, we are told, having been a convent at the time of the Reformation, had passed to an ancestor of the Tilneys on its dissolution. It stands 'low in a valley, sheltered from the north and east by rising woods of oak'. As to its location, there are a few faint clues. Northanger lies thirty miles from Bath, and the journey there is divided into two equal stages, a stop being made at Petty France to give the horses a rest: 'The tediousness of a two-hour wait at Petty France, in which there was nothing to be done except eat without being hungry, and loiter about without anything to see, next followed.' Petty France is a real hamlet on the A46 in Gloucester-shire, around fifteen miles north of Bath and is home to a former coaching inn called Bodkin House. An attractive seventeenth-century building, it features a portrait of Jane Austen on its roadside sign.

Northanger Abbey lies some fifteen miles further on. There are plenty of old Cotswold houses which one could point to as possible models for Northanger Abbey, but there is no evidence that Jane Austen visited any of them. We do know that in 1806, following their stay in Clifton, the Austen women went to stay with a cousin of Jane's mother, the Reverend Thomas Leigh, who was the incumbent at Adlestrop in Gloucestershire, a small village near Stow-on-the-Wold. But although this visit would have allowed Jane Austen to familiarise herself with the Cotswold countryside, *Northanger Abbey* – then called 'Susan' and written between 1798 and 1799 and revised in 1803 whilst Jane was living in Bath – had already been completed.

During the last leg of the journey to Northanger Abbey from Bath, there is a delightfully satirical passage in which Henry Tilney teases Catherine into the even greater expectation of a creepy, Gothic mansion (' … are you prepared to encounter all the horrors that a building such as "what one reads about" may produce? – Have you a stout heart? – Nerves fit for sliding panels and tapestry?'). But when they finally arrive at Northanger, Catherine enters the house 'without feeling one awful foreboding of future misery to herself, or one moment's suspicion of any past scenes of horrors being acted within the solemn edifice'. Northanger Abbey is, in fact, a light, bright, welcoming house. General Tilney, whom she suspects of murdering his wife, or at least of keeping her concealed somewhere about the house, is in reality a snob and a domestic tyrant, and it is this cold reality, rather than any sinister or supernatural goings-on, which lead to Catherine's unceremonious expulsion from Northanger.

But it all ends happily of course. At their first meeting, in the Lower Rooms, Henry Tilney remarks to Catherine that 'nothing in the world advances intimacy so much' as teasing. So it proves, for Tilney and Catherine Morland are married 'within a twelvemonth of the first day of their meeting', and Catherine comes to live at Henry's home, Woodston Parsonage, some twenty miles from Northanger Abbey. Despite General Tilney's dismissal of it as a 'mere Personage', Catherine has, by the end of *Northanger Abbey*, left her Gothic fantasies behind for good, and is surely delighted therefore to be mistress of a 'new-built substantial stone house with a semi-circular sweep and green gates'.

A Modern Perspective
Josephine Ross

'An Abbey! Yes, it was delightful to be really in an Abbey!'
Catherine Morland, *Northanger Abbey*, Chapter 20

To Jane Austen's readers today, it is a touching irony that, by the time she died in 1817, she herself had come to regard her first-completed novel, *Northanger Abbey*, as something of a period piece. Revising the manuscript for its eventual publication, shortly before her death, she decided to include a brief preface, explaining that, though now appearing in print for the first time, 'this little work' had in fact been written long before, and might now seem dated. 'The public are entreated to bear in mind', she warned, 'that thirteen years have passed since it was finished … and that during that period, places, manners, books and opinions have undergone considerable changes.'

Her concerns seemed, initially, to be justified. Published in a joint, 4-volume edition with *Persuasion*, *Northanger Abbey* made no great impression on the Regency public; and in 1821 the last unsold copies were remaindered by John Murray, for just 3s.1d per set. It would be several decades before this enchanting comedy of manners, about a young girl's voyage of self-discovery through life, love and (in particular) literature, would find its rightful place in the canon of English fiction, as the timeless classic that it is.

Today, readers throughout the world revere and relish *Northanger Abbey* — not least, as a uniquely enjoyable historical novel, which brings to life, through the eyes of Jane Austen herself, the 'places, manners, books and opinions' of the late-Georgian era in which she had grown up, and in which it is set. Fiction — it must always be stressed — is not autobiography, but a product of the imagination. Nonetheless, any creative writer will inevitably draw on his or her own first-hand observations of people and situations, and there is much in *Northanger Abbey* that echoes its author's own early life. Like her heroine, naïve, sweet-natured, young Catherine Morland, Jane Austen was a clergyman's daughter, brought up by a scholarly father and down-to-earth mother in a country vicarage, where — like Catherine Morland — she enjoyed, with her sister and brothers, indoor games and outdoor sports of all kinds, 'from cricket, baseball ... and running about the country', to the simple fun of 'rolling down the green slope at the back of the house'. (Steventon Rectory, where Jane Austen was born in 1775, had just such a grassy slope behind it.) And like Catherine Morland, she had the pleasure, in the 1790s, of visiting the great west-country resort of Bath, and sampling the delights of a city as famous for its entertainments and social life, as for the health-giving qualities of its natural spa waters.

It was the air and attitude of a Montoni!

In later years, Jane Austen would come to detest Bath — where, on her father's retirement, she and her family lived, from 1801 to 1806. A countrywoman by upbringing and instinct, with a love of open scenery, fresh air, and long walks, she would write in 1817 of the 'white glare' of its much-vaunted architecture, created on ordered, classically-symmetrical lines from the pale local stone, which would subsequently mellow to a soft honey-gold. The noise, crowds, pollution and tedious round of social obligations came to grate on her nerves — a feeling she would share with the heroine of her subsequent Bath-based novel, *Persuasion*. By the time *Persuasion*, her last-completed work, was written, the city was long past its heyday, the Regency *ton* (or 'polite world') having long moved on to more modish resorts, such as the Prince Regent's beloved Brighton; but in the 1790s it retained just enough of its reputation as a destination for people of taste and fashion to delight a young person in search of amusement, adventure and romance, such as the youthful Jane Austen or Catherine Morland. Far from being a deterrent (as the author feared it would be for her original readers), today the novel's setting against the fascinating backdrop of late-Georgian Bath — with Jane Austen herself, rather than a Barbara Cartland, or even Georgette Heyer, as our narrator, and tour-guide — is integral to *Northanger Abbey*'s lasting appeal.

Describing the 'variety of amusements' enjoyed by her heroine, Jane Austen writes, 'Every morning now brought its regular duties; shops were to be visited, some new part of the town to be looked at, and the Pump-room to be attended. ...' In the celebrated Pump-room, young ladies such as Catherine Morland and her somewhat effusive new friend, Isabella Thorpe, can not only sample the famous waters, but eye the passing crowds, and inspect

"*Good God! How came you up that staircase?*"

the all-important visitors' 'Book', in which the names of new arrivals, and the addresses of their lodgings, are listed. Admiring the local architecture, 'quizzing' the passing faces and fashions of others, watching gentlemen's 'bang-up' curricles clatter by on Milsom Street, or crossing busy Cheap Street 'in quest of pastry, millinery or young men' are among the other daytime activities enjoyed by these lively characters, along with excursions into the surrounding countryside and to nearby tourist sights. By night there are not only concerts, plays, firework-displays and private engagements of all kinds, but – most importantly – the strictly-regulated public balls held weekly in the Upper and Lower Assembly Rooms to attend. There, an official, public Master of Ceremonies, having taken names and assessed guests' eligibility, would make introductions between suitable dancing partners, as the real Mr King did in both Jane Austen's life and her fiction. Master of Ceremonies in Jane Austen's time was no longer Beau Nash, but Mr King. And there Catherine Morland meets the hero of *Northanger Abbey*, the lively, witty, and charming Henry Tilney.

By the time *Northanger Abbey* appeared, as the Regency was drawing to an end, few young ladies would have expected to meet the man of their dreams through a formal introduction in the stuffy and outdated surroundings of a Bath ballroom. But in the novel's beautifully-evoked late-eighteenth-century ambience, the arranged first encounter between Catherine Morland and Henry Tilney, younger son of a rich, imposing, retired General, has all the delicate charm of a Rowlandson drawing, and offers a delightful illustration of the 'manners' and customs of the day. Other examples of soon-to-be-forgotten, now-antiquated codes recur throughout the novel, adding greatly to its appeal for the twenty-first-century reader. The practice of paying – and receiving – formal morning 'calls' gives Catherine Morland an awkward moment when she calls on the hero's delightful sister, Miss Tilney, and is told by the servant at the door ('with a look which did not quite confirm his words') that the lady is not at home', only to see her emerge from the house soon afterwards. Refusing to accept a 'call' – as contemporary readers would have recognised – was a considerable slight. Until her friend explains, apologetically, her reasons, which are based, justifiably, on a prior duty to her father, Catherine can only feel almost 'angry herself, at such angry incivility', whilst wondering if she has inadvertently, in some way, infringed 'the laws of worldly politeness'.

Manners are an infallible guide to character in Jane Austen's fiction; and Miss Tilney's excellent heart, good principles and sympathetic personality are constantly evidenced by her restrained, but considerate and 'elegant' manners – of which Catherine becomes increasingly aware, as she develops in maturity and understanding, in the course of the novel. By contrast (as she also begins to realise) the overheated exuberance of her other female friend – the anti-heroine, Isabella Thorpe – is the sign of affectation and superficiality, not a truly caring nature. Isabella calls Catherine by her Christian name far too early in their acquaintance (a mark of intimacy normally reserved for family members, or friends of long-standing); she flirts outrageously, whilst claiming to have a high regard for the rules of correct behaviour; she exaggerates, manipulates, and tells white lies; above all, she blurs fact and fiction. It is this last, all-important point, around which *Northanger Abbey* principally revolves, and which provides so much of its zest and humour, as well as its insights into human behaviour and enduring truths.

Catherine (again like the author herself) has grown up in a household well-stocked with books; left to browse freely through the family shelves, she has instinctively shown considerable taste in her choice of reading – responding to everything from the plays and poetry of Shakespeare, Pope, Thomson and Gray (favourites of the author herself) to the novels of writers such as Fanny Burney. At the same time, Jane Austen makes it clear, Catherine makes no pretence of enjoying, or excelling in, traditional feminine accomplishments such as drawing and music. Having begged to learn the latter, we learn she 'could not bear it', and was allowed by her easy-going mother 'to leave off' without further ado. Affectation of any kind, but especially where artistic tastes are concerned, is anathema to Jane Austen, and is always roundly condemned in her own great literary works.

At Bath, under the influence of frivolous, shallow Isabella Thorpe, who possesses no true taste or sense, Catherine embarks on a course of intensive reading – this time based entirely on what a pseudo-intellectual character in Jane Austen's last, unfinished novel, *Sanditon*, would dismiss as the 'mere trash of the common Circulating Library', namely, Gothic horror fiction of the most spine-chilling kind. Stimulated by Horace Walpole's celebrated 1760s novel of the supernatural, *The Castle of Otranto*, a cult for such works had emerged during Jane Austen's early life – flowering, in the 1790s, into such massive best-sellers as Mrs Radcliffe's *The Mysteries of Udolpho* and a host of similar 'horrid novels' by the same author and her rivals and imitators. There is nothing wrong with enjoying light fiction, as Jane Austen is at pains to point out. When Catherine Morland shyly mentions *Udolpho* to her clever admirer Henry Tilney, assuming that he would never read a book of that sort, he is quick to contradict her, assuring her that – on the contrary – having borrowed his sister's copy he could not put it down, but finished it in two days: 'My hair standing on end the whole time,' he tells her. With affectionate amusement, he declares, 'The person, be it gentleman or lady, who has not pleasure in a good novel, must be intolerably stupid.'

A voracious reader herself, Jane Austen clearly had pleasure in *Udolpho* and its thrilling fellows, just as she did in what Catherine calls 'better books', meaning more serious prose, plays and poetry of all kinds. The author's impatience with pretentious attitudes towards literature is wonderfully expressed in *Northanger Abbey*, with the famous passage in defence of the novel, in which – at once half-joking and wholly sincere – she dismisses the snobbery and vanity of those who would regard light fiction as inherently inferior to such dull reading as old volumes of *The Spectator* or turgid histories of England. As she engagingly protests on behalf of herself and her fellow novelists, a young lady caught reading a work of fiction, when asked about her book is all too likely to say, 'with affected indifference, or momentary shame' … "Oh! it is

THE

MYSTERIES OF UDOLPHO,

A

ROMANCE;

INTERSPERSED WITH SOME PIECES OF POETRY.

BY

ANN RADCLIFFE,

AUTHOR OF THE ROMANCE OF THE FOREST, ETC.

IN FOUR VOLUMES.

Fate sits on these dark battlements, and frowns,
And, as the portals open to receive me,
Her voice, in sullen echoes through the courts,
Tells of a nameless deed.

VOL. I.

LONDON:
PRINTED FOR G. G. AND J. ROBINSON,
PATERNOSTER-ROW.
1794.

A charming game
with a litter of puppies.

Introduced......as
"Mr Henry Tilney."

only a novel" … in short, only some work in which the greatest powers of the mind are displayed, along with 'the liveliest effusions of wit and humour' … 'conveyed to the world in the best-chosen language.' The passage – a triumph of wit and truthfulness – is another of the 'opinions' expressed in *Northanger Abbey* which remain as apt today as when the work was written.

It was certainly a view that the author was determined to stand by. 'Our family are great Novel-readers, and not ashamed of being so,' Jane Austen wrote stoutly in 1798; in 1813 she complained that two of her and Cassandra's closest friends, the Bigg sisters, ostentatiously displayed in their parlour an array of 'enormous great stupid thick quarto volumes', for the sole purpose of impressing visitors with their intellectual tastes.

As Catherine Morland's friendship with Henry and Eleanor Tilney develops, she is increasingly (though subtly) tutored by them into a more balanced understanding of 'places, manners, books and opinions', with the emphasis on books. While both share her pleasure in novels, their discussions range over literature of many kinds, from the more interesting Histories of scholars such as Hume and Robertson, and the classic *Dictionary* of Dr Johnson, to Gilpin's artistic guides to Picturesque principles in scenery, and even newspaper reporting on current political developments. As ever, Jane Austen is advocating 'extensive reading' as the key to self-education and self-improvement – for women of her era in particular. 'Books of the lighter sort', and 'books of information', equally, have their place in life.

Catherine's discovery, in the course of the narrative, that feeling should always be governed by reason, is enchantingly illustrated by the author's use of burlesque and parody in relating her adventures as she encounters the real world and its ways. Among the numerous jokes involving the conventions of popular fiction, from the ruined abbeys and spectral visions of Gothic horror stories to the swooning beauties and vicious moustachio'd villains of eighteenth-century sentimental romances, one theme in particular would recur, hilariously, in *Northanger Abbey* – the standard device of the hapless heroine's attempted abduction and violation by a heartless (preferably aristocratic) seducer, with the aid of his ruthless henchmen. Jane Austen's own favourite author, throughout her life, was Samuel Richardson, whose classic works *Pamela*, *Clarissa* and *Sir Charles Grandison* specialised in such scenes. She pays laughing homage to Richardson – which modern readers may not recognise – in Chapter 13 of *Northanger Abbey*, when Catherine, eager to run after the Tilneys to explain a misunderstanding, finds her hands grasped on either side by the unpleasant Thorpe brother and sister, as though she were being forcibly pinned down, against her will and despite her protests, to face a dreadful fate. Having set out with a head full of alarming ideas, Catherine will eventually come to realise that she is unlikely to encounter *banditti*, brigands, highwaymen or the sort of 'villains in horsemens' great-coats' by whom she might be 'forced into a travelling chaise and four, which will drive off with incredible speed'. She will, however, meet with a variety of differing real-life characters, both good and bad, and begin to learn through experience how to differentiate between them.

From Bath, Catherine proceeds to the fresh excitements and challenges of a visit to the Tilneys at their ancestral home, Northanger Abbey, and there new revelations await her. Arriving at a real-life abbey, with every hope of finding grim battlements, locked turret rooms, ancient mysteries and spooky, cobwebbed, tapestry-hung bedchambers, Catherine is once again disabused of her imaginings. What she finds at Northanger is a well-to-do, up-to-date, gentleman's residence, containing every comfort and convenience, from elegant china, fresh wallpaper and modern furniture, to the latest in central heating, a 'Rumford stove', (named after its American inventor, Count Rumford). Over the following days (and more importantly, nights) she will come to discover how to separate art from life, and fact from fiction. The old papers found in a chest are merely some abandoned laundry-bills; the family portraits contain no ghastly secrets; and General Tilney, though he walks about with the 'air and attitude of a Montoni' (villain of *Udolpho*), has not murdered or incarcerated his late wife, for all Catherine's fevered imaginings. 'Dearest Miss Morland,' Henry Tilney tenderly admonishes her, 'Consult your own understanding, your own sense of the probable, your own observation of what is passing around you ...' Finally, Jane Austen writes, 'The visions of romance were over. Catherine was completely awakened.'

Mr and Mrs Morland's surprise was considerable.

What this heroine does have to face is not some grisly *exposé*, or attempted abduction, but the prosaic effects of human misconduct. General Tilney, though no theatrical villain, will be guilty of exceedingly bad manners towards an innocent young woman, and a flagrant breach of society's codes, when – finding that Catherine is not, as he thought, a great heiress but an ordinary country vicar's daughter – he turns her unceremoniously out of his house and forces her to find her own way home, unaccompanied.

Sensible as ever, her mother decides that – on balance – the experience has probably done her good, obliging her to show some resourcefulness, and helping her to grow up. With her 'visions of romance' gone, Catherine is better equipped now for real-life romance and the marriage to her hero, with which (of course) the story ends.

By the time *Northanger Abbey* eventually appeared, in 1817, public tastes and perceptions were certainly changing. In the same year, Mary Shelley's classic *Frankenstein* was published, and a new era of science fiction was dawning, to thrill book-lovers and (within a century) cinema-goers everywhere. Yet today the conventions of Gothic fantasy, and 'the old dark house'-style mystery are as familiar, and potent, as when Jane Austen conceived her immortal parody of, and tribute to, the genre, as a vehicle for a profound study of people and ideas. For the modern reader, so far from seeming dated, *Northanger Abbey* has come to represent a rare and satisfying combination of literary pleasures – as a brilliant, burlesque, comic novel; a uniquely appealing historical novel; and above all a 'work in which the greatest powers of the mind' and 'the most thorough knowledge of human nature' are displayed, for all time, by one of the greatest writers who ever lived.

Principal Characters

Catherine Morland is the fourth child and eldest daughter of the Rev. Richard Morley's large family. 'No one who had ever seen Catherine Morland in her infancy would have supposed her born to be a heroine.' She grows from a careless, romping child into a rather pretty girl of seventeen, cheerful and affectionate and 'her mind about as ignorant and uninformed as the female mind at seventeen usually is'. She is taken by her family's neighbours, the Allens, to Bath, where she meets Isabella Thorpe who introduces her to the delightful terrors of horror novels. She sometimes makes the mistake of applying Gothic novels to real life situations, and having convinced herself that General Tilney murdered his wife at his family home, Northanger Abbey, only redeems herself by her real generosity, good principles and open sincerity.

Henry Tilney is the younger son of General Tilney, a clergyman and incumbent of the parish of Woodston, near Northanger Abbey, the Gloucestershire home of the Tilneys. 'He seemed to be about four or five and twenty, was rather tall, had a pleasing countenance, a very intelligent and lively eye, and, if not quite handsome, was very near it.' He is intelligent, well-tempered, and attuned to the motivations and behaviour of those around him. He is very well read, and enjoys novels as much as history books. He has a wry cynical view of human behaviour. He is often amused at the folly of others, but he takes care to gently instruct them properly, if possible, particularly in the case of the naïve Catherine.

Frederick Tilney is Henry's older brother (the presumed heir to the Northanger estate and often referred to simply as 'Captain Tilney'). He is an officer in the army and enjoys pursuing flirtations with pretty girls who are willing to offer him some encouragement.

James Morland is the brother of Catherine and a fellow student of John Thorpe at Oxford University. James is mild-mannered and very caring, like his sister. James falls for Isabella Thorpe and becomes engaged to her, but breaks off the engagement when she begins a flirtation with Frederick Tilney.

Isabella Thorpe is one of Mrs Thorpe's three daughters, and the sister of John Thorpe. She is Catherine's best friend for the first half of the novel. Isabella is attractive and very spirited but, like her mother, she is a gossip and often concerned with superficial things. She enjoys flirting with many young men, and is manipulative and self-serving in her quest to obtain a well-off husband. Ultimately, her nature causes her to lose both James and Frederick Tilney.

John Thorpe is an arrogant and extremely boastful young man. He talks endlessly and rarely listens. 'He was a stout young man, of middling height, who, with a plain face and ungraceful form, seemed fearful of being too handsome unless he wore the dress of a groom.'

Mrs Thorpe is the widowed mother of Isabella and of two other daughters. Like her daughter, she is concerned primarily with gossip, fashion, and money. In conversation with her friend Mrs Allen, she talks mostly about her pride in her children (Mrs Allen has no children) while Mrs Allen talks about her gowns (Mrs Thorpe is not as rich as the Allens).

General Tilney is a stern and rigid retired general with an obsessive nature. He is the sole surviving parent to his three children: Frederick, Henry, and Eleanor. He takes great pride in his home, Northanger Abbey, which he has restored himself. He is preoccupied with both earning money and spending it. He enjoys eating a large dinner and having the best of everything, and he wants his children to marry wealthy people. He has a gruff nature, which makes some, such as Catherine Morland, think poorly of him. 'A very handsome man, of a commanding aspect, past the bloom, but not the vigour of life.'

Mrs Allen is somewhat vacuous but good-humoured. She sees everything in terms of her obsession with clothing and fashion, and has a tendency to utter repetitions of remarks made by others in place of original conversation. 'Mrs Allen was one of that numerous class of females, whose society can raise no other emotion than surprise at there being any man in the world who could like them well enough to marry them. She had neither beauty, genius, accomplishment, nor manner.'

Mr Allen is a kindly man, with some slight resemblance to Mr Bennet of *Pride and Prejudice*.

Mr Morland is Catherine's father, 'a clergyman, without being neglected, or poor, and a very respectable man, though his name was Richard.' He is a generous man.

Mrs Morland, Catherine's mother, 'was a woman of useful, plain sense, with a good temper, and, what is more remarkable, with a good constitution.'

Eleanor Tilney, Henry's sister, is a shy, quiet young woman. 'Miss Tilney had a good figure, a pretty face, and a very agreeable countenance … Her manners showed good sense and good breeding.' She plays little part in Bath, but takes on more importance at Northanger Abbey, and is a convenient chaperone for Catherine and Henry's times together.

Persuasion

Modern Interpretations
John Wiltshire

Over the last few decades *Persuasion* has become recognised as a great as well as a favourite Austen novel. Earlier critics were often content to view this last published of Jane Austen's works as an 'autumnal' text, imagining it, like *The Tempest,* as the artist's farewell to her art. It was read as a work dwelling on time and transience as well as the role of chance and circumstance in human affairs, infused with a melancholy all too easily attributable to the writer's own declining state of health.

The recognition that *Persuasion* was not Jane Austen's final statement, that she was busy with a new novel, *Sanditon*, until illness forced her to give up writing in 1818, has changed all that. It was probably Tony Tanner's chapter on the fragment in his 1986 book, *Jane Austen*, that first brought out the distinctive ambition that makes *Sanditon*, in its fragmentary state (only twelve completed chapters) such a contrast to the work that preceded it. *Sanditon* is the very reverse of melancholy, resigned or contemplative: everything about this high-spirited satire speaks of the writer's energy and resilience. So the idea that *Persuasion* directly reflects its author's own sadness, her own 'declining year', has been superseded.

It has been succeeded by criticism that pinpoints the novel's exciting contemporaneity and its equally compelling artistic energy. This understanding of *Persuasion* has been greatly bolstered by a new recognition of the novel's historical intention. *Persuasion* was begun, according to her sister's memorandum, on 8 August 1815 and put aside, as completed, nine months later in April 1816. More importantly, modern critics make much of the fact that the novel's action takes place precisely during the time of Napoleon's exile on Elba. It begins in the aftermath of Napoleon's surrender in the spring of 1814, and ends in late February 1815, just as Napoleon made his escape. Thus the gradual renewal of the relationship between Anne Elliot and Captain Frederick Wentworth occupies the delusory peace of those nine months. Readers of the book on its publication in 1817 would have known that the happiness with which it concludes was to be overshadowed by the renewal of war. The 'hundred days' of Napoleonic resurgence was put to an end by the battle of Waterloo in June 1815, which also put an end to the ascendancy of the navy as the key arm of national defence. So, as several critics argue, the novel is commemorating an era of naval prestige that has already passed. Perhaps, then, though the period it renders is so recent, this is an historical novel, already aware that the world it depicts is, to all intents and purposes, over, with the conclusion of the decades-long war against the French. 'By pointedly situating the action of *Persuasion* within time, insisting that it matters where we are in history,' Deidre Shauna Lynch writes in an important contribution, 'Austen proposes that large-

The library at Cassiobury Park, Hertfordshire, a late seventeenth-century room redecorated in the Regency style by James Wyatt, c. 1800 (opposite).

scale historical processes help determine how private individuals work out their destinies.'('Introduction' to the Oxford edition of the novel, 2004.)

Persuasion, then, synchronises the events of private life with momentous changes and dramas on the national stage. 'This little history of sorrowful interest,' as the narrator calls Anne's story, implicitly acknowledges the larger history in which this little history resides and is, to a significant extent, controlled by. (It is the peace that has turned the navy men ashore, and enabled them tolook around for potential partners.) The setting of the novel is in a county sparsely populated by gentry, far from the centres of life, an existence of 'sameness and nothingness', and its most significant actions take place in a deserted resort in the off-season, as if to emphasise the distance between the events it relates and the intense world of affairs. These are not simply, though, a 'background' to the action: during the episode in which Mrs Musgrove suddenly remembers the death of her son in the navy, as well as in others, the incursion of the war into private life is clearly signalled. In this scene, Anne is aware, as she observes Captain Wentworth's demeanour, of a cultural domain, a world outside and foreign to the isolated, genteel existence of Somerset landowners. Anne registers the moment of translation, as Wentworth moves from one domain to another, accommodating himself to his gentlemanly role as the confidant of Mrs Musgrove's belated grief. And throughout the novel Wentworth embodies – literally embodies – physical grace, energy and spontaneity. He 'cleared the hedge in a moment' (amazing when you think about it) to persuade the Crofts into giving Anne a lift in their carriage. Eminently a professional navy man, he thus incarnates possibilities of masculine agility and enterprise utterly forbidden to the constricted lives of ladies, who, in Anne's later words, 'sit at home' where their feelings 'prey' upon them.

Certainly, much recent criticism has focused on the novel's depiction of grief and mourning. William Deresiewicz, for example, in *Jane Austen and the Romantic Poets* (2004), stresses the 'psychic arrest' of Anne Elliot's emotional life, and shows how, in the opening chapters of the novel, this is paralleled through the very different stagnation of Sir Walter and Elizabeth. Both, in distinct ways, are locked into destructive and self-destructive attitudes as a result of Lady Elliot's death. In an article in *Partisan Review* (Winter 1995) Elizabeth Dalton explored the nature of Anne Elliot's sadness in these first chapters, where she is depicted as still virtually mourning over her loss of Wentworth. Anne, she argued, maintains a sort of 'phantasmal relationship' with her former fiancé, 'sustaining her love for Wentworth not by marrying him, but by suffering for him.' (And by a kind of self-tormenting interest in the weekly navy list – who, one wonders, takes this in at Kellynch?) Most interestingly, Dalton suggests that the loss of Wentworth is felt so deeply because it revives Anne's feelings at the earlier death of her mother when she was thirteen – an insight especially relevant to the moment at the keyboard in Chapter 6 when the narrative, in a voice which is both Anne's and not Anne's, notices that 'excepting one short period in her life', since that mother's death, her playing has never been appreciated. This earlier devastating loss is thus linked to, and revived by, her later regrets. Such writing might justify the claim made by recent critics for the unexampled subtlety of the means that Austen now uses to explore the depths of her character's psychological history. The emphasis on Anne's fidelity to Wentworth's memory is disputed by Tara Ghoshal Wallace in *Jane Austen and Narrative Authority* (1995) who, through a somewhat tendentious reading of the text, emphasises that 'even while she is painfully attuned to Wentworth, Anne is able to feel and articulate to herself her interest in other men', and suggests that the narrator therefore undermines, and satirises, Anne's conception of her own 'romantic' fidelity.

In her 'Introduction' to the Broadview edition of the novel (1998), Linda Bree comments that Anne's 'continued struggle for self-control, or her repeated need to feel herself useful, slip into something very like masochism, as if she is bent on punishing herself for making the decision that caused her so much grief.' This is a description of Anne Elliot's psychological state that is reiterated in D.A. Miller's *Jane Austen or the Secret of Style* (2003), which challenges the status of a novel he calls 'the sentimental favorite' among Austen's works. Miller claims that Austen's own writing 'corresponds – and hence caters – to Anne's self-mortification'. He argues that the narrative makes no criticism of Anne that Anne has not made of herself, and therefore that the narrator loses the 'cognitive advantage' attained in the other novels through the style of free indirect speech. 'She disables the ironizing inherent in Austen's narration by having already conscripted it as a function of her own scathing self-intimacy.' Instead of finding, as other readers do, that *Persuasion* offers a more subtle inwardness with its main character than earlier novels, as well as a new awareness of lives embedded within European and English history, Miller finds that Persuasion 'amounts to the retraction' of the novelist's 'great world-historical achievement'.

In contrast, Deidre Lynch writes of the novelist's 'glorious assurance', and other recent critics have focused on the novel's powerful intellectual structure – what one might reasonably call the systematic quality of its organisation – and perceive different forms of this. William Deresiewicz argues that the novel has a 'master pattern', a 'logic that underlies, indeed, the entire novel: structurally, imagistically, ethically. It is the logic of nature.' He shows how this 'logic' manifests itself in a multitude of ways in *Persuasion* – from the apparently slight metaphors of 'bloom' and 'blighting', through to its preoccupation with decline and recovery, and even finds it manifest in the novel's depiction of its characters so frequently 'literally descending and ascending, be it hills, stairs or walls'.

Much criticism has focused on Jane Austen's radical re-working of gender issues in this novel. Isabel Grundy, for example, demonstrated (in a volume largely devoted to *Persuasion, Jane Austen's Business,* 1996) that by early nineteenth-century convention, sentiment and resignation were thought to

be the province of women, whilst cheerfulness and resilience were, naturally, the gifts of men. She argued that the novel 'attacks the binary "male humour, female sentiment" in the very bones of its plot. It demonstrates that Anne, a woman, stands to benefit by that mixing in society which men enjoy, that her male lover's emotions are not more transiently felt than hers, and especially that humour is highly congenial to the female mind.' The novel challenges the notion that gender differences are innate, and 'supplies a background of proliferating role-reversal. Throughout this novel men and women repeatedly contradict the stereotypes of what male and female ought to be.' A good example of this is Anne's advice to Benwick about reading where she occupies the 'mentor' role, which in Austen's earlier novels, as in those of her contemporaries, is always given to men – Henry Tilney, for example. In the same volume, Judith Terry showed how the reader is seduced into thinking of Anne as a conventional, submissive heroine, 'overlooked, not just by those in her world, but by us' and how skilfully Jane Austen reverses this in the course of the action, so that the reader is made to revise their notions of gender in the very act of reading the novel. Anne's powerful 'submerged voice' is only revealed through the second or third reading.

The film of *Persuasion* (1995), with script by Nick Dear and directed by Roger Michell, is probably the most successful of the recent Austen adaptations, though it has been poorly received by some Austen critics (see for example the chapters on this film in *Jane Austen on Screen*, 2003). It simplifies the novel, most especially by heightening Anne Elliot's grief and isolation, presenting her as grim, pale-faced, silenced and almost brutally ill-used. (Readers, aware of Anne's intelligence, her intense inner life, as well as her ability to find amusement in the idiosyncrasies of the people about her, learn a different story.) But it succeeds in finding specific cinematic tactics that reproduce some of the novel's distinctive features. 'Gentlemen, the war is over,' Admiral Croft announces at the end of the credit sequence. 'Napoleon has escaped from Elba,' the same character tells the company in the film's invented final scene. Thus the script registers the historical framing of the narrative that modern critics have made so much of. More importantly, this film employs the cinematic means of lighting, *mise-en-scène*, and camera movement to render specific emotional states and communicate the submerged narratives of the spoken text. The moribund isolation of the Elliot family life is captured, for example, in the dark abyss which surrounds the family gathered in the drawing room in the film's opening sequence, with a clock ticking away in the emptiness. The sense of loss is captured in the sequence but shows servants throwing white dustcloths over the pictures and furniture at Kellynch, and in the powerfully desolate scene in which Anne, sitting with Lady Russell among the heavily draped and therefore disguised shapes of tables and chairs, attempts to break the silence that has surrounded the past. The whiteness of the masking is visually associated with Anne's pale face, and the sequence thus registers in visual terms that carapace of mourning which is Anne's psychological state. Even more telling is the brief scene in which Anne, sorting through boxes with a servant in the candle-lit darkness of an attic, comes across the navy list, and nestled within that a folded paper boat. In close-up, the viewer sees that the folded paper is in fact a letter, and makes the connection with Wentworth. (Later Admiral Croft folds paper into a similar little boat for the Musgrove lads, and now it skims down the stream – a tiny indication of Anne's awakening hopes.) These initiations into her intense inner life contrast with the theatrical soliloquy (Anne speaking her thoughts directly to the camera) used to make similar points in the earlier Granada TV version of 1971.

Chiaroscuro dominates these sequences in Dorset. A contrasting scene to the mournful desolation of Kellynch is the occasion of Anne's first dining out at Uppercross in the company of Wentworth. The Musgrove sisters are entertained with his accounts of life at sea, and much gaiety and animation enlivens the table as he tells his stories, teases the young ladies and gets into a friendly argument with his sister. Now the darkness is filled with laughter as the bright and flaring candle flames light up the various faces, all with their differing investments in the talk; Anne silent, but the most involved of them all. This scene is filmed from slightly above, or at an angle to the assembled company, with a roving hand-held camera. The image and therefore the viewer, hovers close, and becomes a part of this animated extended-family party. And the slightly unsteady movement of the camera partakes in the liveliness of the scene, registers Anne's underlying tension, and perhaps even evokes, subliminally, the motion of a ship at sea. The flames of the candles light the faces in ways that convey both intimacy, joyousness and a strange, perhaps even dangerous, excitement.

Another scene of a candle-lit dinner, this time at Lyme, improves on the novel. Once again, the darkness and flames generate intensity. In the novel Anne Elliot's discussions about poetry with Captain Benwick, and her cautions to him about reading too much of it, are merely reported. This seems to be an attempt at a wry form of comedy, in which Anne castigates herself for giving advice she had better administer to herself. Here the exchange is dramatised and transformed. The camera moves down the talkative people at the dinner in the darkened room until it comes to rest on Captain Benwick, at first obscured by Anne's figure opposite him. Their isolation from the main party's festivities is registered by the subduing of other conversation on the soundtrack. Benwick's passion for Byron's poetry allows him, in a moment of intimacy across the table from a sympathetic female listener, to express his own grief at the loss of his fiancée and his bitterness at their decision to postpone their marriage: 'I told her we should wait. For money. Money.' As in the novel, Anne castigates him, but in this creative reworking, she is speaking directly out of her own experience. 'You cannot know the depths of my despair,' he declares; but the melodrama is immediately slaked by Anne's steady, cool response: 'Yes, I can.' This scene allows the film to include, by indirection, the eloquent grief that the narrator of the novel, in one of its own most memorable moments, expresses also by indirection: 'How eloquent could Anne Elliot have been … !' The camera moves to the face of Wentworth, pipe in mouth, contemplative. A movement of his eyes downward registers the implication of her words.

No other sequence in the film but the first party at Uppercross uses a hand-held camera, and in deliberate contrast the indoor scenes set in Bath employ very different filming techniques. In the novel Anne dislikes 'all the white glare of Bath'. White now prevails here as Sir Walter, his daughter and Mrs Clay lounge in their fashionable white-floored apartment, in a light that is bright as Kellynch was dark, but just as barren. The camera has moved as an intimate in earlier sequences but now the Elliot group is filmed with a sweeping, smooth movement around the space, encircling them from a position external to their lives. This camera is detached, disaffected. A smooth-paced swirling shot is repeated in many sequences set in Bath, and its elegant, unimpeded movement, itself a kind of sophisticated technique, mimics (perhaps mocks) fashionable grace and conveys something of the culture of this smart resort.

If the novel is tightly organised through recurrent themes and images, so is the film. Anne's attempt to confide in her friend – 'Lady Russell, I have never – ?,' broken off by Lady Russell's 'Let us not speak of it,' is replicated when, towards the end of the film, Captain Wentworth, catching Anne at an opportune moment, begins, 'Anne, I have never – ?' More importantly, the novel's preoccupation with decline and recovery, descent and ascent, noted by Deresiewitz, is registered in a series of motifs that are barely noticeable, but all the more telling. The opening shot, signalling the end of the war, shows a sailor climbing a ladder out of the boat. As a miserable Anne moves through Kellynch helping to prepare it for rental, a ladder leans against the library shelves, but in the streets of Bath when her hopes are revived, a similar ladder is positioned by a workman to light the street lamp. The 2007 ITV/WGBH film with script by Simon Burke is an interesting comparison. It sometimes seems more influenced by the earlier film than by the novel. Instead of Anne's discovering an old letter enclosed within a volume, she opens a casket and takes out Wentworth's letters tied with ribbon, and thus a scene which conveyed interiority merely becomes a reminder of lost love, and the script reverts to the old-fashioned voice-over to communicate Anne's inner life. The lively candle-lit scene at Uppercross is replaced by one at Lyme, filmed from above, with the camera zooming in on Anne sitting alone at the end of the table. The dialogue with Benwick now borrows from the discussion with Harville at the novel's resolution. In that context, it presents Anne, for the first time in *Persuasion*, as the eloquent and compelling central figure. Displaced, it merely makes her avowals of women's constancy another of the film's frequent reminders of her unavailing love. The substituted climax, with Anne racing along the Crescent at Bath (and then back again) provides one of the few moments of (unintended) comic relief.

This film was advertised as having 'lavish costumes and sumptuous settings'. But the earlier version, with its modest houses, its realistic and unhandsome officers, above all its ensemble acting, is almost uncontaminated by the heritage industry. It is its exquisite use of sound, movement and lighting that gives it glamour.

Regency Life
Maggie Lane

The Navy

Only a few professions were open to men of Jane Austen's class who needed to earn their own living – principally the church, the law, the army and the navy. Medicine was considered rather inferior (Jane Austen's own paternal grandfather had been a physician, but in her novels doctors are the equivalent of tradesmen, and none of her major characters follows this line). Trade itself, except of the most exalted kind, was not compatible with gentry status. Her heroes are landowners, clergymen – and one sailor, Captain Wentworth of *Persuasion*.

Of the two armed services, the army was for men whose families could afford to buy them a commission, and it carried a certain cachet accordingly. Soldiers in Jane Austen's novels are men of good family – Colonel Fitzwilliam, Colonel Brandon, Captain Tilney and General Tilney himself. It was in the Royal Navy that young men without much means could distinguish themselves and make their fortunes chiefly by their own merit, although in the early stages of their careers it was still useful to have friends in positions of influence.

Thus of Jane Austen's own brothers, the two youngest, with no church livings left for them, were destined from an early age for the navy, though there were no naval traditions in the family. Francis and Charles Austen were both enrolled at the Royal Naval Academy in Portsmouth at the tender age of twelve, when they could hardly have known whether they were suited to the life. Horatio Nelson was another son of a clergyman who became a sailor before he was in his teens. In his case, he did not even go to the Academy, but straight to sea.

Fortunately Frank and Charles seemed to enjoy their careers, and both rose eventually to the rank of Admiral. It was in following their endeavours, hardships and successes that Jane conceived an almost romantic attachment to the navy, and a high regard for the general character of the men who served in it. William Price in *Mansfield Park* is her portrait of an eager young officer just starting out on his career, and *Persuasion* depicts a group of naval officers of more mature years, bound together by comradeship and shared experiences. Their warmth and mutual support are bewitching to the heroine, Anne, and are compared favourably with her own family's snobbery and self-centredness.

Her father, Sir Walter Elliot, finds the navy objectionable on two counts – because it spoils the complexion(!) and raises men of humble beginnings to rank and riches. But the general feeling in the country was of gratitude and esteem for the profession which frustrated the ambitions of the enemy, France. The cult of Admiral Nelson, whose death was followed by a spate

Few women could think more of their personal appearance than he did.

Brought home in consequence of a bad fall.

of biographies and the lasting memorial of Trafalgar Square and Nelson's Column, was proof of the nation's pride in its naval supremacy. The battle of Trafalgar in 1805 had been very narrowly missed by Frank Austen, to his lasting regret (the ship he commanded had been sent for supplies) and though he served (incredibly) for another sixty years and rose to be Admiral Sir Francis Austen, by his desire his gravestone merely – but proudly – proclaims him 'one of Nelson's captains'. Charles Austen was serving in North American waters at the time of the great European battle; he was away from home for a seven-year stretch, and when he did return to England it was with a wife and young family gained in Bermuda.

Young naval officers had not much money; when Frank first married he entered into a partnership with his mother and sisters to share household expenses by taking a house to accommodate them all in Southampton. When Charles brought his wife and infant daughters back to England, for the sake of economy they lived for some time on board his ship, just as Mrs Croft has lived, on a total of five ships, with her husband, now Admiral Croft. 'Nothing can exceed the accommodations of a man of war,' she asserts, and her brother, Captain Wentworth, ridicules the company for 'supposing sailors to be living on board without anything to eat, or any cook to dress it if there were, or any servant to wait, or any knife and fork to use'. Jane Austen must have heard her brothers similarly disabusing their acquaintance.

From her brothers Jane absorbed naval expressions, and she uses them to good effect in *Persuasion*. It comes naturally to her sailors to use sea-going metaphors, as when Captain Harville, comfortably talking to Anne, tells Captain Wentworth with a smile, 'I am in very good anchorage here,' or when Admiral Croft expresses the wish that 'Frederick would spread a little more canvas' and do his courting more quickly. Even Mrs Croft says, 'We do not expect to be in smooth water all our days.' She is almost as much a sailor as any of them, and quite as capable, as her carriage-driving skills demonstrate. When the characters get to Bath, Anne delights to see the Crofts walking together in happy independence, 'occasionally forming into a little knot of the navy, Mrs Croft looking as intelligent and keen as any of the officers around them.'

Jane Austen does not, of course, enter into the hardships of the ordinary seaman. Maybe she knew nothing of them. Their diet at this time consisted of salt beef or pork, hard cheese, unleavened bread or biscuit and a gallon of beer a day. There can have been little pleasure in eating such coarse and indigestible fare, but the beer no doubt helped them to drown their sorrows. There was also a ration of rum. Although the efficacy of fresh fruit and vegetables in helping men to recover from scurvy had been noticed as early as the middle of the eighteenth century, it was not until 1795, by which time Frank had been at sea six years, that naval personnel were issued with daily juice of lemons or limes.

Particularly susceptible to scurvy were the pressed men captured for Royal Naval service on their way into home ports from a long voyage on a merchantman. It was horribly cruel to take such men, just as they were looking forward to a spell on land. Although the notorious press gangs did operate on land, rounding up men indiscriminately, the majority of men were obtained afloat, in order to get experienced seamen. Towards the end of the Napoleonic Wars, the ratio of volunteers to pressed men was only one quarter volunteers. And many of those put down as volunteers were really pressed men who chose to take the bounty – a pound or two – when they realised they stood no chance of escape.

The life of such men was held very cheap. During the naval wars of Jane Austen's lifetime, of the hundred thousand sailors who lost their lives, only seven per cent was by enemy action, thirteen per cent by shipwreck, twenty per cent by accident on board, and sixty per cent by disease. As well as scurvy, a major killer was typhus, spread by lice among men living at close quarters. Dysentery was a frequent misery, and flogging was commonplace. Even so, Francis Austen, a strict disciplinarian, was once held to account by the Admiralty for his excessive use of the lash. As a commanding officer, Charles was more like Admiral Nelson himself, loved by his men and obeyed because they revered and trusted him.

Boys first going to sea would attach themselves to a captain – a relation or family friend – and hope, by gaining his good opinion, to secure his help among his brother-officers in looking for promotion. In return he gained the loyalty and effort of his junior officers. Of course, from time to time a captain would be saddled with a hopeless case, as Captain Wentworth is with poor, useless Dick Musgrove, who has only been sent to sea because his parents don't know what else to do with him.

Patronage was essential in gaining the first steps up, from midshipman to lieutenant and from lieutenant to commander. In *Mansfield Park* William Price, who knows nobody, is lucky to be recommended to Admiral Crawford, and Jane's own letters of the 1790s report the strings her father, with no personal acquaintance among the Lords of the Admiralty, had to pull among 'friends of friends' on behalf of his young sons. Further promotion depended on merit and length of service.

Naval rank dictated prize money. The captain would receive one quarter the value of a captured ship, though one third of his prize money went to his Admiral who might be hundreds of miles away, the officers and Warrant Officers another quarter between them, and the ordinary seamen the remainder divided amongst them all. This arrangement did at least give even pressed men the incentive to practise good seamanship and fight for all they were worth. Midshipman Charles Austen spent his first £30 prize money on topaz crosses for his sisters (which may still be seen at the Jane Austen House Museum in Chawton).

In *Persuasion,* Captain Wentworth has made £20,000 in prize money in eight years' warfare. His fortune has all been gained by his own efforts, quite unlike the other heroes of Jane Austen's novels. His situation is unlike theirs, too, in having no inherited home or family rectory to take his bride

In another moment
someone was taking him
from her.

to. He is truly a self-made man, and he and Anne will take their chances together. He can afford to buy her 'a very pretty landaulette,' but where they will live we don't know. *Persuasion* is a tender love story about second chances and enduring attachments, but it is also a paean to the Royal Navy, 'that profession which is, if possible, more distinguished in its domestic virtues than in its national importance.'

Seaside Resorts

Among the beauties of *Persuasion* that have made it a favourite with many of Jane Austen's readers, are the contrasting settings: the autumnal scenes in the country, wintry Bath, and the quaint little seaside resort of Lyme in Dorset. Who, having read *Persuasion*, has not longed to see Lyme for themselves?

Lyme occupies only two chapters in the novel, but they are among the most memorable chapters Jane Austen ever wrote, in terms of both action and feeling. They form a kind of hinge between the long passage in the country, and Anne's permanent (as she thinks) removal to Bath. Several new characters are introduced, including two men who both admire the previously overlooked Anne, and must be regarded as possible suitors for her. Partly as a consequence, Captain Wentworth's feelings for her are reawakened, although this is also the result of the mettle she shows in dealing with Louisa's accident on the Cobb, Anne being the only person to avoid both hysterics and paralysis. Even Captain Wentworth, who must have dealt with many an injured or dying man at sea, is at a loss! The visit to Lyme affects the destinies of several characters, and shows Jane Austen writing at the height of her powers, with all her personages acting in character, yet generating extreme interest in the reader.

Jane Austen herself, with her parents and sister, first visited Lyme in 1803. The family was living in Bath at the time, Mr Austen having retired from his country parish, and each year in the late summer they left the stuffiness of the city for the fresh air and open expanses of the coast, staying in a series of little seaside resorts in Devon and Dorset. They evidently admired Lyme enough to return in 1804, paying a visit of several weeks. *Persuasion* was not written until 1815–16, but the little town and its environs had remained

Lyme Regis, early nineteenth century.

fresh in Jane Austen's memory, and she indulges in what for her is an exceptionally lyrical and heartfelt description of a place.

The Austens were being really quite enterprising in taking these seaside holidays. The fashion was only just spreading to people of limited means, like themselves, and most of the resorts they chose to visit were in their infancy. The major resorts were further east, and more developed. Royal patronage had established Weymouth and Brighton as fashionable resorts for the upper classes, and when Jane Austen mentions them in her fiction they are as scenes of dissipation, idleness and questionable morality. There was an innocence and amateurishness about the smaller, less expensive places that pleased her, and that she celebrates in both *Persuasion* and the fragment left unfinished at her death, *Sanditon*.

The rise of the seaside resort had been greatly assisted by the recommendations of medical men. Dr Russell advised sufferers from everything from leprosy to scurvy to drink a pint of sea water every morning, though how many people could manage this is questionable. Immersion in the sea then became the new cure-all for ills real and imaginary. 'And all, impatient of dry land, agree. With one consent to rush into the sea,' wrote Jane Austen's favourite poet, William Cowper. In the early years, sea-bathing was considered most efficacious if undertaken in cold weather and early in the morning, when the pores were supposed to be open. The novelist Fanny Burney bathed at Brighton in November 1782 at 6am by the light of the moon. Jane Austen's own cousin, the widowed Eliza de Feuillide, spent January and February 1791 at Margate in Kent for the sake of her delicate little son and believed that sea-bathing strengthened both him and herself. Severe weather, frost and snow did not prevent their daily dips. In *Persuasion*, Mary Musgrove, no stoic, bathes in the sea even though it is November.

Bathing machines to protect the privacy of nineteenth-century bathers.

The Gallery of Fashion by *Niklaus von Heideloff, September 1797. Two ladies brave the cliff-top.*

Bathers in Jane Austen's time did not wade into the sea and splash or swim at will. For the sake of modesty, and following the dictates of the medical profession who liked to have everything under their own control, bathers entered and changed in a wheeled bathing machine on the beach, which was then pulled out by a horse or persons to a reasonable depth. Women wore shifts, men were naked from the waist up. One or two burly women (in the case of female bathers) then guided or pushed the bather into the sea and held her under repeatedly. After the first shock, it must have been quite exhilarating.

The season gradually shifted to the warmer months when the quest for health was reinforced by the desire for novelty to while away abundant leisure. The little resorts were soon vying with one another with the provision not only of bathing machines but of shops, libraries, promenades and elegant lodgings. Jane Austen's *Sanditon* takes exactly this as its theme. The opening chapters of this unfinished novel describe the development of a seaside resort, with the two prominent landholders of the place sinking their capital into new buildings and endeavouring to attract tourists. The fragment sparkles with sunshine and sea breezes, while questioning the restlessness and dislocation that such changes can wreak on the old way of life.

Lyme Regis itself had a more significant history than many of the little fishing villages so developed. The 'Regis' – which appears not to have been in use in Jane Austen's day – had been bestowed by Edward I in 1284 and the place was entitled to elect two members of parliament right up until the Reform Act of 1832. The famous arm of the Cobb, which features so prominently in *Persuasion*, was built and rebuilt over the years to shelter ships and protect the land from prevailing westerly storms. Exporting mainly wool and importing Mediterranean commodities such as wine, in 1677 Lyme was the fourteenth largest port in the whole of England, but soon afterwards its trading importance went into a steep decline. For one thing, ships were becoming too big to be accommodated in its harbour, and for another, its communications by road were abysmal. Such was the steepness of its approach, that until as late as 1759, no wheeled traffic could get into Lyme! Nevertheless, it had its moment of fame when, in 1685, the Duke of Monmouth chose to land there and launch his ill-fated attempt on the Crown of England.

A century of decay and disuse followed, in which many of its buildings were allowed to fall down, but in the last quarter of the eighteenth century the fashion for tourism and better roads began to bring new life to the place. One landholder pulled down disused warehouses to build Assembly Rooms modelled on those in Bath. He also tried to fashion a walk round the bay, between the main part of the town and the cluster of cottages at the foot of the Cobb, but this had to be rebuilt many times over the years because the land was (and still is) so unstable. Nevertheless, Jane Austen knew this walk and sends her characters back and forth along it in *Persuasion*. The instability of the land meant there was no scope for constructing the elegant terraces and crescents that were shooting up in other resorts, which is probably what Jane Austen means when she says, 'There is nothing to admire in the buildings themselves.' Lodgers, however genteel, had to be content with small cottages and narrow streets, as the Austens seem to have been themselves (or they would not have returned for a second year), relishing the unpretentiousness of the place and the natural beauty of its setting.

A letter written by Jane Austen from Lyme survives, painting a lively picture of a young woman in her late twenties enjoying her holiday. By day she walks and bathes, staying in longer than she should and so overtiring herself; in the evening she dances at the Assembly Rooms while her parents play cards, Mr Austen departing at nine and walking home with his manservant and a lantern, Mrs Austen and Jane staying a further hour. She describes their lodgings as dirty, without seeming to mind. The month is September, but we know that the previous year the Austens had been in Lyme in November (when a bad fire swept through the town), though no letters survive from that visit.

Part of the charm of the portrait of Lyme in *Persuasion* is that Jane Austen chooses to bring her characters there out of season, and there is a faint air of melancholy mixed with the bracing sea breezes, with the Assembly Rooms shut up and the fashionable visitors gone. The only figures in the landscape are the humble working population of the town, like the boatmen who offer aid to the stricken party on the Cobb; residents like the Captains Harville and Benwick, sailors turned ashore by the peace and seeking an inexpensive cottage to rent; and travellers passing through like Mr Elliot. But to Anne, who has seen so little of her own country, the place is a revelation, not only for the sea itself, but for the hospitality of the Harvilles. Lyme remains in her memory as a source of pleasure, just as it must have remained in Jane Austen's own memory – to be evoked to such good effect in her last completed novel.

Geographical Settings
Caroline Sanderson

The first half of Jane Austen's final novel, *Persuasion*, is set primarily in the English county of Somerset, at Anne Elliot's family home, Kellynch Hall and at Uppercross, the home of her sister Mary and her husband, Charles Musgrove. It is in Somerset that we meet all the principal characters in the novel, and learn the history of Anne's broken engagement to Captain Wentworth. And it is from Uppercross that Anne, Captain Wentworth and the Musgroves set out on their excursion to Lyme Regis. Though their fateful stay in Lyme occupies only two chapters of the novel, they are crucial ones, which set the scene for the second half of the novel, almost all of which takes place in Bath, perhaps the most celebrated and widely-known of the English geographical locations in Jane Austen's novels.

The best preserved Georgian town in England, with its sweeping crescents, and elegant streets of honey-coloured houses, Bath is the quintessential Jane Austen location: in few other places is it quite as easy to imagine ourselves back in Jane's time; nowhere else is it so possible to walk in the footsteps of her characters, tracking their movements by real street names; to stand under the same elegant ceilings and gaze into the same shop windows.

From a small provincial town of 3,000 people, its streets and houses still laid-out along higgledy-piggledy medieval lines, Bath was transformed in a few short decades of the eighteenth century into England's most fashionable watering-hole and a town second only to London in cultural importance. By the end of the century its population had swelled to 30,000 souls. The great attraction was its spa water. Three thermal springs rise through faults in the Mendip Hills and surface in the place where Bath now stands. These springs were already known to the Romans, who built a luxurious health resort around them named *Aquae Sulis*. In medieval times the springs were still in use and the most favoured of the three, closest to Bath Abbey, became known as the 'King's Spring,' after King Henry I. The waters were still famed for their supposed curative powers six centuries later and the eighteenth-century developers of Bath sought to capitalise on their potential to pull in wealthy visitors. 'Many people have come to Bath, tired of taking medicines to no purpose at all,' trumpeted the *Bath Guide* of 1800. 'They have drunk the Bath water with abundance of delight and pleasure, and by the help of a little physic have recovered to admiration.'

A sojourn in Georgian Bath for the genteel eighteenth-century visitor wasn't just about taking the waters, but could also encompass shopping, dancing, promenading, theatre-going, flirting, spouse-hunting and above all people-watching and gossiping. The winter season in Bath was an annual fixture in the calendar of many wealthy English families. For the not so wealthy it could also be a happy hunting ground. It is, after all, in Bath, after a stay of only four weeks, that Mr Elton, the socially ambitious clergyman in *Emma*, bags himself a wife in the enticing shape of Miss Augusta Hawkins with ten thousand a year. Less happily, it is from Bath that Willoughby elopes with Colonel Brandon's ward, Eliza Williams, in *Sense and Sensibility*, and to Bath that Wickham takes himself off 'to enjoy himself' after his all too hasty marriage to Lydia Bennet in *Pride and Prejudice*. The fact that not one of Jane's six major novels is without a mention of Bath is just one indication of its social significance at the time.

Bath was also a place well-known to Jane's family. Her parents were married in the city in 1764, at St Swithin's Church in Walcot Street, which still stands today. Forty years before, an aristocratic forebear of Mrs Austen – James Brydges, the First Duke of Chandos – eager to speculate some of his fortune in the development of Bath, had employed a young stone mason

St Swithin's church in Walcot Street; its spire was completed in August 1790. Jane's father was buried here in 1805.

named John Wood to work for him on some new building projects. Wood's career flourished and he is now remembered as one of the principal architects of Georgian Bath, responsible for such elegant developments as Queen Square, where Jane stayed on an early visit to Bath with her brother Edward in 1799. After several such visits, Jane came to live in Bath in 1801 after her parents took the decision to retire there. The city was to be her home until 1805, and although she wrote very little whilst actually living in Bath, it clearly provided her with plenty of inspiration for her later novels including *Persuasion*. Her intimate knowledge of its streets, shops, grand houses and places of entertainment enabled her to use it as the perfect backdrop for much of the action in this much-loved novel.

Early on in *Persuasion*, we are told that Anne Elliot 'disliked Bath and did not think it agreed with her.' These feelings date from her unhappy teenage years. At the age of fourteen, she had been sent away from Kellynch Hall to school fifty miles away in Bath, following the early death of her mother. Her three years there have left her with a decided aversion for the place. ('She persisted in a very determined, though very silent, disinclination for Bath.') Yet like Jane Austen herself, whose own move to Bath was decided upon by her parents, Anne has no choice but to return there to live, when her father's extravagance forces his family to let out Kellynch and move to a smaller place in town in an attempt to economise.

The Elliot's removal to Bath allows them to preserve face somewhat. In theory they can save money while continuing to live in great style and elegance and move in all the right circles. Early on in the novel, they succeed in renting out Kellynch Hall to Admiral Croft and his wife. Mrs Croft happens to be the sister of Anne's former love, Captain Wentworth, and so, to Anne's great trepidation, her former fiancé re-enters her life. A long let for Kellynch secured,

Sir Walter Elliot and his eldest daughter, the vain and spoilt Elizabeth, soon fix upon one of the smartest addresses in eighteenth-century Bath for their new abode. By the time Anne arrives to join them, catching 'the first dim view of the extensive buildings, smoking in rain, without any wish of seeing them better,' her father and sister have moved into 'a very good house in Camden Place – a lofty distinguished situation, such as becomes a man of consequence; and both he and Elizabeth were settled there, much to their satisfaction.' One wonders how much money was saved! 'Their house was undoubtedly the best in Camden Place; their drawing rooms had many decided advantages over all the others which they had either seen or heard of; and the superiority was not less in the style of the fitting-up, or the taste of the furniture.' Now known as Camden Crescent, the former Camden Place still stands in all its magnificence today: an elegantly curving row of houses which sits at the very top of hilly Georgian Bath. Those who live here enjoy panoramic views of the city and the grandeur of the crescent's distinctive shape is visible from many vantage points below. Perhaps Jane had in mind for the Elliots the grandest house in the crescent, still easily recognisable today by its large decorative pediment.

Jane Austen was adept at choosing locations to suit her characters. This is particularly true of the Bath addresses she selects in *Persuasion*, which has snobbery as one of its prevailing themes. Anne Elliot's old school-friend Mrs Smith, who is crippled with rheumatic fever, lodges in a 'very humble way' in Westgate Buildings, in a deeply unfashionable part of the city, but within carrying distance of the Cross Bath where she has been taking the waters daily. Sir Walter is most put out when he discovers that Anne is deigning to

The Cross Bath by Samuel Hieronymous Grimm, 1789, just after the bath was rebuilt by Thomas Baldwin.

frequent such a place, and to visit a mere Smith at that: 'Westgate Buildings! … and who is a Miss Anne Elliot to be visiting in Westgate Buildings? A Mrs Smith! Westgate Buildings must have been rather surprised by the appearance of a carriage drawn up near its pavement.' On a later visit, Anne Elliot is unable to take advantage of a lift in Lady Russell's carriage, and so must make the long downhill walk from Camden Place to Westgate Buildings. She doesn't mind because it gives her the opportunity to muse on 'high-wrought love and eternal constancy.' The uphill trek back is less pleasant: after a visit to the Musgroves – her sister Mary and her husband Charles, and his sisters Henrietta and Louisa, who are staying in the lower part of town, Anne is faced with 'a toilsome walk to Camden Place.' It's a grand address, but one that implies the use of a carriage at all times, a privilege that Anne Elliot does not enjoy.

There's an even better reason why elevated Camden Crescent is an inspired choice of residence for vain Sir Walter. The crescent, begun around 1788, was actually supposed to form part of a much larger development, but a series of serious landslips, common at the time in that part of the city, brought work to a permanent halt with only part of the crescent completed. One result was that the grand 'central' pediment we have already mentioned never did lie in the middle of the crescent, as originally intended, because four houses due to have been added at the far end to complete the semi-circle were never built. Jane Austen, quite intentionally it seems, placed Sir Walter on shaky ground.

Camden Place is not the only address in *Persuasion* chosen with care by Jane Austen to signal something about the characters who live there. Built in the Palladian style, Queen Square, right in the centre of Bath, was among the first new developments in Bath to be designed by John Wood the Elder, former employee of Jane's ancestor, the Duke of Chandos, and one of the most important architects of Georgian Bath. On its completion in 1735 the square was the height of fashion, but by 1799 when Jane stayed there it had fallen out of favour. Though Jane herself was quite happy to lodge there ('I like our situation very much,' she wrote to her sister Cassandra), the 'in-crowd' had moved to the newer developments that had been built to the north and east of the city, like Camden Place. In *Persuasion* the Misses Musgrove pooh-pooh old-fashioned Queen Square, remarking: 'I hope we shall be in Bath in the winter; but remember, Papa, if we do go, we must be in a good situation – none of your Queen Squares for us!'

The Austens were also to live in a good situation in one of the newer areas of the city when they moved to Bath permanently in 1801, though whilst they were house-hunting, Jane wrote that her mother 'hankers after the Square dreadfully.' We can only speculate as to whether their house at 4 Sydney Place with its views of leafy Sydney Gardens just across the road was sufficiently well placed to placate Mrs Austen as none of the letters Jane Austen wrote during the three years the family lived in Sydney Place survives.

The Austens had already left Sydney Place and moved to a less fashionable part of Bath close to the River Avon by the time Jane wrote her next

In earnest contemplation of some print.

surviving letter, written in September 1804 from Lyme Regis in Dorset, where the Austens were on holiday for the second time in two years. It was these visits to Lyme, a coastal town on the south coast of England, which must have given Jane the idea to set a crucial part of the action in *Persuasion* in this attractive resort, formerly a sea port of considerable importance. It's rare that we get more than a brief description of real places in Jane Austen's novels, but in *Persuasion* she waxes lyrical about the charms of Lyme in a long paragraph which ends with the observation that 'a very strange stranger's eye it must be, who does not see charms in the immediate environs of Lyme, to make him wish to know it better.' Accordingly, her characters, the Musgroves, Anne Elliot and Captain Wentworth, who have embarked on a two-day excursion to visit Wentworth's naval friend, Captain Harville, and his family, are described as being 'wild to see Lyme.'

Why were they so wild to see it? Probably because Lyme Regis must have been a romantic place, even a little sinister; a place of pirates, and exotic comings and goings, as ship after ship docked and then set sail again. For centuries Lyme was a difficult place to reach by land too, which must have added to its air of mystery. No wheeled transport could get into the town at all until the turnpike road was built in 1759. In fact, due mainly to the textile boom in increasingly industrial northern England, Lyme Regis was in a state of some decline until its fortunes were revived by its development as a seaside resort in the late eighteenth century. In 1771, a retired radical philanthropist named Thomas Hollis, who lived nearby, bought land along the shoreline and created the town's first public promenade. Then, in 1772, the nascent seaside resort received its first celebrity endorsement when the Earl of Chatham brought his ailing son to Lyme for the sea air. The air proved highly efficacious, as the sickly boy, William Pitt the Younger, grew up to become British Prime Minister.

In a few short years, Lyme Regis was transformed into a busy resort with a reputation for being cheaper and less formal than nearby Weymouth, which was frequented by King George III. Lyme acquired hotels, boarding houses, indoor baths, bathing machines, a circulating library and smart new Regency villas on the surrounding hillsides. Seaside holidays were becoming a fixture in the English way of life. In early 1801, with the Austen family's decisive removal from Steventon to Bath on the horizon, Jane wrote to her sister Cassandra that she was becoming 'more and more reconciled to the idea ... there is something interesting in the bustle of going away & the prospect of spending future summers by the Sea or in Wales is very delightful.' By the time the Austens made the first of their two visits to Lyme Regis in 1803, the town was firmly established as an excellent place in which to recuperate from the Bath summer season with all its parties and late nights. Consequently, high season in Lyme was considerably later than it is today – September to November – and it was indeed in November 1803 that the Austens arrived for their first holiday in the town.

The young people in *Persuasion* also choose November for their visit to Lyme Regis. On arrival, they walk directly down to the beach, and 'lingering only, as all must linger and gaze on a first return to the sea, proceeded towards the Cobb.' The Cobb is Lyme's most renowned feature, famous not only from the incident in which Louisa Musgrove falls and sustains a 'severe contusion' to her head, but also as the setting for the memorable scene in John Fowles' novel, *The French Lieutenant's Woman*, and Karel Reisz's film version of 1981, when a heavily cloaked Sarah Woodruff stands at the end of the Cobb, staring out at the stormy sea.

Though no one seems quite sure where the word 'Cobb' comes from, Lyme's distinctive curving harbour has existed in some form since the thirteenth century. There are no natural harbours along this broad sweep of Dorset coast, so as soon as Lyme started to become a trading port of some importance it became necessary to create one. The original Cobb was made of huge rounded boulders piled within walls made of oak pillars, and for centuries it was actually detached from the land at high tide. It not only provided a safe harbour, but also helped to protect the crumbling shore from the fury of the sea. About 50 years before Jane Austen's first visit to the town in 1803, the Cobb was joined to the land and then rebuilt in the local Portland stone in the early nineteenth century.

Lady Dalrymple & Miss Carteret escorted by Mr Elliot & Colonel Wallis

We know from her 1804 letter from Lyme that Jane herself went for a stroll on the Cobb in the company of a Miss Armstrong, whose acquaintance she had made during the holiday. Exposed to the English Channel wind and spray on both sides, a walk along the top of the Cobb is just as bracing an experience today as it was in *Persuasion*. 'There was too much wind to make the high part of the new Cobb pleasant for the ladies, and they agreed to get down the steps to the lower, and all were contented to pass quietly and carefully down the steep flight, excepting Louisa; she must be jumped down them by Captain Wentworth.' We know the rest – Louisa insists on being jumped down the steps a second time, misses the safe arms of the Captain, falls to the ground and is 'taken up, lifeless!'

After Louisa Musgrove's fall, Captain Wentworth carries her in her 'lifeless' state to the Harvilles' house, to await the arrival of a surgeon. Plenty of local speculation has taken place over the years as to the house Jane Austen might have had in mind for the Harvilles' lodgings: even today, there is a Jane's Café in one of the buildings along the sea front which seems to fit the bill. Eventually, of course, Louisa fully recovers from her fall, and during her period of recuperation gains the heart of grieving Captain Benwick. The action of the novel quickly moves away from Lyme Regis, back to Uppercross and then very soon to Bath when Anne reluctantly joins her father and sister in Camden Place.

Later, when the Musgroves arrive in Bath, they take rooms at the White Hart Inn in Stall Street overlooking the entrance to the Pump Room where eighteenth-century visitors flocked to take the waters and parade in one of Bath's most fashionable venues. When Mary Musgrove looks out of the window of the White Hart, she is startled to see Mrs Clay standing 'deep in talk' with the villainous Mr Elliot under the colonnade, close to the entrance to the Pump Room. Later we learn that Mrs Clay is 'established under his protection' in London, after Mr Elliot's true character has been revealed to Anne by her friend, Mrs Smith.

It is also at the White Hart in the very centre of Bath, the city we now associate with Jane Austen above any other, that the miraculous denouement of the novel takes place, when Captain Wentworth hands Anne a letter confessing his enduring love for her. 'You pierce my soul. I am half agony, half hope. Tell me not that I am too late, that such precious feelings are gone for ever.' He is of course not too late. Shortly afterwards, Captain Wentworth and Anne are walking along a secluded gravel-walk towards Bath's famous Royal Crescent, their engagement renewed and their future happiness assured.

A Modern Perspective
Josephine Ross

'She began to reason with herself, and try to be feeling less'
Anne Elliot, Persuasion, Chapter 7

When Jane Austen began work on her last completed novel, *Persuasion*, in the summer of 1815, she was a writer at the height of her powers. When she finished it, in August, 1816, she was a dying woman, and would not live to see her manuscript through the printers. It is little wonder, with hindsight, that this exquisite, autumnal novel is filled, from the outset, with a sense of yearning and regret, as the heroine, Anne Elliot, resigns herself to an apparently empty future, while looking back at chances lost in her past. For Jane Austen herself, there would be no happy ending: she died, aged only 41, on 18 July, 1817, some five months before *Persuasion* came out. Yet it is tempting for her readers today to imagine that in writing this last masterpiece she was conscious of fulfilling her own extraordinary genius; and in touching on so many themes which had been dear to her throughout her life, and literary career, she was conscious of bringing her own story to a worthy close.

Persuasion opens with a charming private joke, which those in the know would have appreciated: the name given to the heroine, Anne Elliot, is that of the beloved wife of her publisher, John Murray, who in 1807 was married 'In Edinburgh … to Miss Anne Elliot, daughter of the late Charles Elliot, Esq, bookseller.' The intelligent, sensitive, fictional Anne Elliot is perhaps the most sympathetic heroine Jane Austen ever portrayed. Unlike her namesake, Mrs Murray, she is beleaguered on all sides by people and circumstances; but like her creator, she faces life with a gentle resignation, and even rueful humour, accepting that it is her destiny to promote others' well-being, rather than her own. Certainly, as a mature woman of 27, approaching 'the years of danger,' who has been separated in youth from the man she loved and must now see him court, and be courted by, others, she does not expect ever to marry and find happiness herself.

Whatever chances of marriage Jane Austen might have had in earlier years were long gone by the time *Persuasion* came to be written. The famous flirtation with her 'Irish friend', Tom Lefroy, which she had written of with pleasure almost twenty years before, was now history. How serious the relationship was, it is now impossible to establish. In letters written at the time, to her sister Cassandra, she had joked at one minute about 'Tom Lefroy, for whom I do not care sixpence', and at another, claimed (perhaps tongue-in-cheek) to be expecting an imminent proposal of marriage from him. ('I shall refuse him however,' she announced cheerfully.) What is surely in no doubt is that there was a decided attraction between the two lively young people, which seemed likely to cause neighbourhood gossip, as they danced together, 'sat down' together, and talked eagerly together of books, including – daringly – Fielding's bawdy classic, *Tom Jones*. Certainly their behaviour caused enough local talk for Tom to be 'so excessively laughed at' about her (she reported gleefully) that 'he ran away' when she and her sister called at the house of his aunt, with whom he was staying. Perhaps significantly, a surviving music book belonging to Jane Austen, dating from about this period, includes – copied out in her own hand – a popular song entitled 'Nobody Loves Like an Irishman.'

A subsequent brief romance with a young clergyman named Samuel Blackall also came to nothing, despite his apparent hints of hoping for 'a nearer interest' with the Austen family. On hearing in 1813 of his marriage to another, Jane Austen recalled him fondly as 'a piece of Perfection, noisy Perfection,' and speculated (typically) about his wife's possible character, habits and taste in food and furnishings.

The story of the author's later emotional attachments becomes more obscure and tantalising. It was said, on good authority, that in the early 1800s she actually accepted a highly-eligible proposal of marriage from the younger brother of her and Cassandra's friends, the Bigg sisters, only to change her mind overnight and flee their house, where she had been staying. Most mysteriously, a persistent tradition concerns a love-affair which apparently developed between her and an unidentified man whom she met at a seaside resort, which was expected to result in marriage, but ended tragically, with his unexpected death. 'I believe that if Jane ever loved, it was this unnamed gentleman,' her nephew and first biographer concluded, in his 1870 *Memoir* of his much-loved aunt. There can be little doubt that when Jane Austen came to write *Persuasion* she had every reason to feel empathy with a woman facing middle age with tantalising memories of the past, rather than any realistic romantic hopes for the future, uppermost in her mind, and heart.

The cause of Anne Elliot's grief – her decision, eight years earlier, to reject a marriage proposal from the man she loved – was the result of emotional pressure brought to bear on her by a woman who, since her own mother's death, she had come to look on as her closest friend and quasi-maternal mentor – Lady Russell. Such respectful, yet fond, relationships between an older woman and a younger female character, who looks up to her for

'We had a funny set-to at rat-hunting'

guidance and advice, is another recurrent theme in Jane Austen's novels which might evoke echoes of her own early life. In *Pride and Prejudice*, Lizzy Bennet – unable to turn to her own tiresome and vulgar mother for wise counsel – relies greatly on the judgement of her favourite aunt, the 'amiable, intelligent, elegant' Mrs Gardiner, for whom she feels 'a particular regard.' In *Emma*, the heroine seeks to play such a role for her trusting young protegée, Harriet Smith, with far less fortunate results. Jane Austen's relationship with her own mother, as she grew up, had become increasingly strained. Though intelligent and fond of her children, Mrs Austen was evidently a hypochondriac, obsessed with the state of her health and nerves; for all the patience and restraint of their tone, Jane Austen's letters are strewn with weary references to her mother's latest symptoms, from headaches, colds and insomnia, to – on one dramatic occasion – 'An Asthma, a Dropsy, Water in her Chest and a Liver Disorder.' (Mrs Austen would bear her sufferings with fortitude, until her death at the advanced age of 88.)

It was small wonder that, in the 1790s, while living at Steventon, Jane Austen had developed a semi-daughterly bond with a very different sort of woman – the Austens' 'elegant' and charming neighbour, Mrs Lefroy, aunt of her admirer Tom. After Mrs Lefroy was tragically killed in a riding accident in 1804, Jane Austen expressed her grief in a poem, which is the more moving for its uncharacteristically poor literary quality. It was as though, in an intensity of sorrow, her normal creative powers deserted her – resulting in such saccharine sentiments as

> 'Angelic woman! Past my power to praise'

and

> 'She speaks! 'Tis eloquence, that grace of tongue
> So rare, so lovely, never misapplied'

Mrs Lefroy's untimely death meant that Jane Austen never had the chance to develop a more mature and balanced attitude towards her older friend's perfections – unlike Anne Elliot in *Persuasion*, to whom experience brings increasing clarity of vision, and self-knowledge. While retaining her regard for Lady Russell, whose advice – though well intentioned – has proved so mistaken, she learns to rely more on her own judgement, and recognise that even the most worthy role-models may have flaws.

Lady Russell's advice that Anne should refuse to marry the man she loved, handsome, gallant young naval officer, Frederick Wentworth, was in fact somewhat deviously given. Appealing to Anne's best instincts, and concern for others' interests, she made out, forcefully, that it would be wrong for her to tie a young man to marriage and domestic responsibilities at so early a stage in an uncertain career. On this selfless motive alone, out of duty, Anne had yielded – to his lasting bitterness, and her lasting regret. In fact (as she comes to recognise), her friend's reasoning was not so honourable as her own, having more to do with snobbery than altruism. Privately, Lady Russell believed that her dear Anne – young, lovely and the daughter of a baronet – could do better than marry a penniless young sailor. Snobbery is a key theme in *Persuasion*; and no one feels its effects more keenly than the heroine herself.

Though the word did not enter the language until some twenty years after Jane Austen's death, snobbery, and the assessment of others on the basis of birth and rank, rather than individual merit, is another of the recurrent themes of Jane Austen's earlier fiction which comes to the fore in this final novel. In *Sense and Sensibility*, vulgar but kind-hearted Mrs Jennings is shown as infinitely preferable to the icily-correct, but mean-spirited Lady Middleton and Mrs John Dashwood; in *Emma*, the heroine has to learn through hard experience to prize the honest decency of yeoman farmer Robert Martin over the glib, shallow charms of pseudo-gentleman Mr Elton. In *Persuasion*, the follies and false values of snobbery are explored and exposed with a still harsher emphasis.

Persuasion opens with a reference to one of the famous guides to British genealogy, *The Peerage* and *The Baronetage*, first published by Debrett in the early 1800s, as separate volumes, and still (updated, and in combined form) a leading authority today. *The Baronetcy* is the favourite reading of Anne Elliot's vain, self-important father, who never tires of looking up his own family details, and congratulating himself on 'the blessing of a baronetcy' – even though his is the lowest form of hereditary title, carrying with it no seat in the House of Lords.

Placed it before Anne.

Jane Austen was never impressed by titles of any sort, and in this novel she is openly scathing in her criticisms of those who are. The comic touch with which, in *Pride and Prejudice*, she pokes fun at the risibly class-conscious *grande dame* Lady Catherine de Bourgh is replaced in *Persuasion* by open contempt, as she exposes the folly of Sir Walter Elliot's pride, and shows how embarrassing he and his like-minded eldest daughter, Elizabeth, are as they try to ingratiate themselves with their aristocratic cousins, the Dowager Countess Dalrymple and her daughter, the Honourable Miss Carteret. 'They were nothing,' Jane Austen writes coldly. 'There was no superiority of manner, accomplishment or understanding.' Anne, she states, 'was ashamed,' and the best efforts of even her old friend Lady Russell, and her seductive new admirer, her father's heir Mr William Elliot, to persuade her of these women's 'value,' as 'a connexion worth having,' are unsuccessful. Gently, modestly, Anne concludes, 'I suppose I have more pride than any of you.'

And so she does, but hers is proper pride – a pride in achievement, honour, dignity, duty and service to others, which Anne finds gloriously exemplified in the officers and men of the Royal Navy. Jane Austen's own beloved brothers served in the Royal Navy with distinction, in the great age of Nelson, and after. A love of the Navy is another major theme of Jane Austen's life and writings, which flowers in *Persuasion* into some of the most memorable scenes and characters she ever created, as Anne finds herself, increasingly in the company of her now-estranged admirer Captain Wentworth and his fellow-officer friends. The empty pretensions of her own circle are thrown into still sharper relief when contrasted with the genuine hospitality, friendship and family affection displayed by all the naval characters – from weatherbeaten old Admiral Croft and his devoted, doughty wife, who has sailed the world with him, to the cheerful Captain Harville, who, with 'a mind of usefulness and ingenuity,' has created 'a picture of repose and domestic happiness' in his cramped married lodgings.

The contrast between the Harvilles' seaside cottage at Lyme, with its home-made bookshelves and travel souvenirs, and the stuffy formality of Bath interiors, where Anne is forced, against her taste and wishes, to reside, could scarcely be more marked. In another of *Persuasion's* affectionate in-jokes, it is clear that domesticated Captain Harville, with his love of all things practical, from mending fishing-nets to whittling children's toys, represents a private tribute to Jane Austen's brother Frank, whose craft skills ranged from woodwork to knotting 'very nice fringe for the drawing-room curtains' as the author reported with amusement in a letter of 1807.

It is often said that, had Jane Austen been a man, she would have joined the Royal Navy. It is also surely true that, had she had the opportunity, she would have loved to marry a sailor, and share his life on board ship, as does Mrs Croft. At the happy conclusion of *Persuasion*, the narrator says fondly of Anne Elliot, 'She gloried in being a sailor's wife.' The novel is imbued throughout with a sense of the author's, as well as the heroine's, longing for 'fresh-feeling breezes,' wide horizons, active, intelligent company, and freedom from petty social conventions, such as the stifling code of giving and receiving dinner invitations, or paying ritual 'morning visits,' in strict rotation. The lifestyle of Captain Wentworth and his friends underlines the vapidity of the effete, decadent existence of Sir Walter Elliot and his circle at Bath – a place which Jane Austen (again like Anne Elliot) had come to detest. On her first visits, in the 1790s, the city still offered enough pleasures to entertain a young lady in pursuit of amusement, such as the author herself and young Catherine Morland, heroine of *Northanger Abbey*, but by 1815, when *Persuasion* was begun, Bath was long past its fashionable heyday, and had become staid and over-crowded, a place of 'vapour, shadow, smoke and confusion', which Jane Austen left – like Anne – 'with what happy feelings of escape!'

One means of escape from life's pressures on which Jane Austen could always rely, wherever she was, was reading. Her passion for literature of every kind – perhaps the strongest theme of all, in her life and writings – is, naturally, another major strand of *Persuasion*, highlighted in the discussions of 'taste in reading' which take place between Anne Elliot and young Captain Benwick. Recently bereaved of his fiancée, he has sought solace in books, 'principally in poetry.' Like the similarly-minded Marianne Dashwood in *Sense and Sensibility*, he indulges his feelings by focusing almost exclusively on the works of the Romantics, dwelling on 'the various lines which imaged a broken heart,' and 'impassioned descriptions of hopeless agony.' While sharing Benwick's pleasure in 'the first rate poets' – Scott and Byron in particular – Anne gently seeks to persuade him to temper feeling with reason. The familiar debate between the Romantic and the rational impulses, in both literature and life, is revived once more, as Anne recommends 'a larger allowance of prose in his daily study,' to include 'such works of our best moralists, such collections of the finest letters, such memoirs of characters of worth and suffering' as will 'rouse and fortify the mind' rather than exacerbate grief (and by implication, self-pity). Unlike in the author's first Bath novel, *Northanger Abbey*, there is no mention here of the pleasures of 'a good novel'; the emphasis, in these last months of her life, is on the redemptive powers of reading. The sense that, beneath her ever-positive attitude to life, Jane Austen was preparing for death, is inescapable.

Anne Elliot's struggle, throughout *Persuasion*, to control her inner feelings, and devote herself to supporting others, mirrors Jane Austen's own courageous refusal to give way to increasing physical weakness and depression while writing the novel, as the debilitating illness now generally believed, with hindsight, to have been Addison's Disease took its toll of her health and spirits. Partly (it may be assumed) in reaction to her mother's constant claims of ill health, she had never shown much sympathy in her fiction with those who were preoccupied with illness and doctors. While Fanny Price, heroine of *Mansfield Park* – a stressed and genuinely somewhat frail young woman – suffers uncomplainingly from constant headaches, selfish Mrs Bennet in *Pride and Prejudice* demands copious sympathy for her nerves and malaises. In *Emma*, a good deal of comedy is extracted from kindly, fussy, hypochondriacal old Mr Woodhouse and his elder daughter, who takes after him, as they compare symptoms, and discuss remedies, physicians, health hazards and food fads. In *Persuasion*, health issues once again come to the fore, as Anne Elliot ministers to her fretful, demanding sister, in her imaginary or exaggerated ailments. Self-centred Mary, constantly claiming to be unwell, can easily be diverted and cajoled by Anne into a rapid recovery, even when she has a sore throat. ('And my sore throats, you know, are always worse than anyone's,' she complains, in one of the most celebrated, and oft-quoted lines from *Persuasion*.)

By the time Jane Austen had completed her painstaking revisions to this final, full-length novel, which included cancelling a chapter and rewriting the end, she was deteriorating fast. Work on another, never-to-be-finished manuscript, *Sanditon*, had to be laid aside. In May 1817 she left her 'Chawton Home,' where her six extraordinary novels had been brought into being, to seek the skills of medical specialists in Winchester, where, on 18 July, pillowed on the lap of her sister Cassandra, she died.

One of her earliest admirers was the era's most famous, best-selling novelist and poet, Sir Walter Scott – whose works Anne Elliot and Captain Benwick discuss in *Persuasion*. 'What a pity such a gifted creature died so early' Scott would write in 1826. In 1821, *Persuasion* was remaindered by her, and Scott's, renowned publisher, John Murray, as having no further sales appeal for the reading public.

Her tombstone – a plain, black marble slab in Winchester Cathedral – made no mention of her literary genius. It described Jane Austen only as a former local Rector's daughter who had died 'aged 41, after a long illness,' before proceeding to praise 'The benevolence of her heart, the sweetness of her temper and the extraordinary endowments of her mind.' For those who know, and love, *Persuasion*, it is hard not to see Anne Elliot – her last heroine, and perhaps the one who most shared her own qualities of fortitude in adversity, gentleness towards others, humour, intelligence and a benevolent heart – evoked in that most moving epitaph.

Principal Characters

Sir Walter Elliot, of Kellynch Hall, Somerset, is the father of Elizabeth, Anne and Mary. 'Vanity was the beginning and end of all Sir Walter Elliot's character – vanity of person and situation. He had been remarkably handsome in his youth, and, at fifty-four, was still a very fine man. … A man who, for his own amusement, never took up any book but the Baronetage.' Sir Walter's profligacy since the death of his prudent wife 13 years before has put his family in financial straits. These are severe enough to force him to lease his estate, Kellynch Hall, to Admiral Croft and take a more economical residence in Bath.

Elizabeth Elliot, the eldest daughter of Sir Walter, 'had succeeded, at sixteen, to all that was possible of her mother's rights and consequence; and being very handsome, and very like himself, her influence had always been great.' She and her father routinely put their interests ahead of Anne's, regarding her as inconsequential.

Anne Elliot, the second daughter of Sir Walter, is 27. She possesses 'an elegance of mind and sweetness of character, which must have placed her high with any people of real understanding, was nobody with either her father or sister'. Eight years previously she had fallen in love with Captain Wentworth, but was persuaded (the *persuasion* of the title) by Lady Russell to reject his proposal, because of his poverty and uncertain future.

Charles Musgrove is husband of Mary and heir to the Musgrove estate. He had wanted to marry Anne and settled for Mary (much to the disappointment of the Musgrove family) when Anne refused him due to her continued love for Wentworth. He was 'civil and agreeable; in sense and temper he was undoubtedly superior to his wife'.

Mary Musgrove, the youngest daughter of Sir Walter, 'had acquired a little artificial importance by becoming Mrs Charles Musgrove.' She is inferior to both her sisters, but is not as repulsive and unsisterly as Elizabeth. She manages her children badly and never forgets her rank as a baronet's daughter.

Captain Frederick Wentworth is a naval officer, 'a remarkably fine young man, with a great deal of intelligence, spirit and brilliancy.' He proposed to Anne eight years before the start of *Persuasion*. At the time, he had no fortune and uncertain prospects and, under the influence of Lady Russell, Anne turned down his proposal. However, his genius and ardour combine to bring fame and fortune, and he returns to Kellynch when his sister, Mrs Croft, and her husband rent the house that the Elliots can no longer afford.

Admiral Croft is the good-natured, plain-spoken tenant at Kellynch Hall and brother-in-law of Captain Wentworth.

Sophia Croft is the sister of Captain Wentworth and wife of Admiral Croft. She offers Anne an example of a strong-minded woman who wed for love instead of money.

Captain James Benwick is a friend of Captain Harville and had been engaged to marry Captain Harville's sister Fanny, who died while Benwick was at sea. Benwick's loss has left him melancholic. His enjoyment of reading and poetry makes him one of the few characters in the story to find an intellectual connection with Anne. He ultimately becomes engaged to Louisa Musgrove.

Louisa Musgrove is the second sister of Charles Musgrove, aged about 19. She is high-spirited and has recently returned with her sister from school. Captain Wentworth admires her for her resolve and determination, especially in contrast to Anne's prudence and what he sees as Anne's lack of conviction. She is ultimately engaged to Captain Benwick.

Henrietta Musgrove is the eldest sister of Charles Musgrove, aged about 20. She is informally engaged to her cousin, Charles Hayter, but is tempted by the more dashing Captain Wentworth.

Captain Harville is a friend of Captain Wentworth. Severely wounded two years previously and discharged on half-pay, he and his family have settled in nearby Lyme for the winter.

Mrs Clay is a poor widow, daughter of Sir Walter's agent, and intimate 'friend' of Elizabeth Elliot. She tries to flatter Sir Walter into marriage, while her oblivious friend looks on, but is foiled by William Elliot who takes her as his mistress.

Lady Dalrymple is Sir Walter's cousin. She occupies an exalted position in society by virtue of wealth and rank, and Sir Walter and Elizabeth are eager to be seen at Bath in her company. There was no superiority of manner, accomplishment or understanding. Lady Dalrymple had acquired her name of "a charming woman" because she had a smile and a civil answer for everybody.'

Lady Russell is a widowed friend of the Elliots, and Anne's godmother 'of steady age and character, and extremely well provided for'. She is instrumental in Sir Walter's decision to let Kellynch Hall to avoid financial crisis. Shocked by Captain Wentworth's wit and boldness, she had persuaded Anne to turn down his proposal of marriage. While far more sensible than Sir Walter Elliot, she shares his great concern with rank and did not think Wentworth good enough for Anne because of his inferior birth and financial status. She wishes Anne to marry William Elliot, but later admits her mistakes as regards both men and that she is 'unfairly influenced by appearance in each'.

Mr William Elliot is the nephew and presumed heir of Sir Walter, who became estranged from the family when he rejected marriage to Elizabeth to wed a plebeian woman of fortune. He is now a widower and, wanting to inherit the title, he mends the net in order to keep an eye on the ambitious Mrs Clay. If Sir Walter married her, his inheritance could be endangered. When he meets Anne by accident, his interest is piqued.

Mrs Smith is an old school friend of Anne Elliot who lives in Bath. 'She was a widow and poor … she had difficulties of every sort to contend with, and in addition … had been afflicted with severe rheumatic fever.' She gets news of Bath society from her nurse, Nurse Rooke, who also works for a friend of William Elliot's. Elliot, her husband's former friend, would not exert himself to ease her financial problems, leaving her much impoverished until Captain Wentworth assists her.

Index

Bibliography

Other books about Jane Austen by the contributors to this volume

Lane, Maggie. *A Charming Place: Bath in the Life and Times of Jane Austen* (with Bridget Sudworth) (Millstream, 1988); *Jane Austen's England* (Robert Hale, 1989); *Jane Austen's Family: Through Five Generations* (Robert Hale, 1992); *Jane Austen and Food* (Hambledon Continuum, 1995); *Jane Austen's World: The Life and Times of England's Most Popular Author* (Carlton, 1996).

Ross, Josephine. *Jane Austen's Guide to Good Manners: Compliments, Charades and Horrible Blunders* (with Henrietta Webb) (Bloomsbury, 2006).

Sanderson, Caroline. *A Rambling Fancy: In the Footsteps of Jane Austen* (Cadogan Guides, 2006).

Wiltshire, John. *Jane Austen and the Body: 'The Picture of Health'* (CUP, 1992); *Recreating Jane Austen* (CUP, 2001); *Jane Austen: Introductions and Interventions* (Palgrave Macmillan, 2006).

Other useful books about Jane Austen

Armstrong, Nancy. *Desire and Domestic Fiction: A Political History of the Novel.* New York City: Oxford University Press, 1987.

Austen, Jane. *The Works of Jane Austen.* Volumes I–VI edited by R W Chapman. London: Oxford University Press, 1923–1954.

Austen-Leigh, James Edward. *Memoir of Jane Austen.* London: Oxford University Press, 1926, first published 1870.

Austen-Leigh, William and Richard Arthur Austen-Leigh. *Jane Austen: Her Life and Letters – A Family Record.* New York City: Russell & Russell, 1965.

Butler, Marilyn. *Jane Austen and the War of Ideas.* London: Oxford University Press, 1975.

Butler, Marilyn. *Romantics, Rebels, and Reactionaries: English Literature and its Background 1760–1830.* New York City: Oxford University Press, 1981.

Copeland, Edward and Juliet McMaster, eds. *The Cambridge Companion to Jane Austen.* New York City: Cambridge University Press, 1997.

Duckworth, Alistair. *The Improvement of the Estate: A Study of Jane Austen's Novels.* Baltimore: John Hopkins University Press, 1971.

Honan, Park. *Jane Austen: Her Life.* London: Weidenfeld & Nicolson, 1987.

Kaplan, Deborah. *Jane Austen Among Women.* Baltimore: John Hopkins University Press, 1992.

Kirkham, Margaret. *Jane Austen, Feminism, and Fiction.* Totowa, NY: Barnes & Noble, 1983

Le Faye, Deirdre, *Jane Austen's Letters.* New York City: Oxford University Press, 1995.

MacDonagh, Oliver. 'Receiving and Spending: Sense and Sensibility', from *Jane Austen: An Anthology of Recent Criticism.* Delhi: Pencraft International, 1996, pp.112–38.

Said, Edward. 'Jane Austen and Empire: Mansfield Park' from *Jane Austen: An Anthology of Recent Criticism.* Delhi: Pancraft International, 1996, pp.150–69.

Spense, Jon. *Becoming Jane Austen.* New York City: Hambledon Continuum, 2003.

Stovel, Bruce and Lynn Weinlos Gregg. *The Talk in Jane Austen.* Edmonton, Alberta: University of Alberta Press, 2002.

Todd, Janet. *The Cambridge Introduction to Jane Austen.* New York City: Cambridge University Press, 2006.

Tomalin, Claire. *Jane Austen: A Life.* New York City: Alfred A. Knopf, 1997.

Tyler, Natalie. *The Friendly Jane Austen.* New York City: Penguin, 1999.

Acknowledgements

The author would like to thank Dr Greg Garrard of Bath Spa University; the Jane Austen House Museum, Chawton; Anita Robson of the Godmersham Park Heritage Centre; Donna Lodge, Jackie Herring, Holly Newton and Clare Hutton and the staff of The Jane Austen Centre, Bath; Professor William Hughes of Bath Spa University; and Jay Dale.

The publisher wishes to thank Donna Lodge of The Jane Austen Centre, Lynn Webb for her editorial assistance, and all the contributors: Josephine Ross, Maggie Lane, John Wiltshire and Caroline Sanderson.

For permission to reproduce copyright images, thanks to the BBC for stills from *Pride and Prejudice* and *Mansfield Park*; to ITV/Granada for the image from *Northanger Abbey*; and to Miramax Inc for the still from *Emma*.

This edition published in 2011 by Worth Press Ltd   Copyright © Worth Press Ltd
Designed, arranged and produced by Bookcraft Ltd   www.bookcraft.co.uk

ISBN 978-1-84931-024-6

Printed in China